MARCUS AURELIUS
AND HIS TIMES

MARCUS AURELIUS AND HIS TIMES

The Transition from Paganism to Christianity

Comprising

MARCUS AURELIUS: MEDITATIONS

LUCIAN: HERMOTIMUS ⁓ ICAROMENIPPUS

JUSTIN MARTYR: DIALOGUE WITH TRYPHO ⁓ FIRST APOLOGY

WALTER PATER: MARIUS THE EPICUREAN (SELECTIONS)

With an Introduction by Irwin Edman

Published for the Classics Club by

WALTER J. BLACK · ROSLYN, NEW YORK

PRINTED IN THE UNITED STATES OF AMERICA

CONTENTS

CONTENTS

PREFACE

THE reign of Marcus Aurelius (161-180 A.D.) marked the close of the good period of the Antonine emperors, under whom Rome reached the height of her imperial dominion and administrative efficiency. He died fighting the restive barbarians on the Danube frontier and was buried not far from the camp on the site of what we now call Vienna. Under his son, the dissolute Commodus, the political decline set in that eventually ended in the collapse of the centuries-old imperial structure in the West and its replacement by the raw, unstable, barbaric kingdoms of Italy, Spain, France, and England.

Already, in the lifetime of Marcus Aurelius, the intellectual atmosphere in the magnificent capital of his empire was confused and clouded. The old confident assurance that prosperity and happiness lay in keeping faithful to the gods and the traditions of the ancestors was noticeably wavering. The stately ceremonies and customs handed down from the past were still punctiliously and lavishly performed in public, as signs of gratitude to whatever had formerly made Rome great and as a means of impressing the multitude. But few educated or thinking men now took them seriously. Their minds had been trained from youth in the schools of Greek philosophy, and Plato, Aristotle, Epicurus, and the Stoic Zeno, each had his following. But not even the illustrious philosophers received the unquestioning veneration that once they had had. They spoke, after all, with too discordant voices and out of a past too long departed. The Skeptics, who doubted that any philosopher ever had or ever could fathom the world's mystery, attracted many who scornfully refused to imagine certainties where none existed.

Other men were fatalistically accepting the astrological lore brought from the ancient East. If the eternal, all-seeing stars were the causes of everything that happened in this transitory scene below, what could anyone do but resign himself and submit? Others still were turning for comfort to a new type of religion, also brought from the East, the cults of Isis, of Mithras, and of Christ. These all in their several ways taught faith in a god of pity, repentance from sin, and hope of a heavenly immortality. Outwardly Rome still stood, more resplendent and apparently more unshakeable than ever. Inwardly she was in a state of mental and spiritual flux. The old order was losing its hold on men's minds and the new order was yet far off.

This book contains the writings of three men of the period, each eminent in his own circle at Rome, which illustrate for us the conflict of beliefs that is a characteristic feature of the age. The *Meditations* of the emperor show how latter-day Stoicism could still inspire a high-minded ruler to do his duty with fortitude and patience. The dialogues of Lucian, the rhetorician, are a Skeptic's devastating exposure of the weakness of all the old philosophies and beliefs. The works of Justin Martyr, the Christian, are full of the fervor and excitement of a convert from paganism, convinced he has a new and uniquely divine message to proclaim to mankind. With these selections we include three chapters from Walter Pater's famous book, *Marius the Epicurean*, for their vivid descriptions, first, of Marcus Aurelius and his environment, and, secondly, of a eucharistic service in a Christian house as the author fancies they may have appeared to a sensitive and cultured Roman gentleman.

PART I

Marcus Aurelius, Stoic

INTRODUCTION

Historians of philosophy have repeatedly pointed out the dramatic fact that the two leading Roman Stoics were Epictetus, a slave, and Marcus Aurelius, an emperor, and that the emperor was in his youth a pupil to the slave. Their themes and their doctrines were in large measure identical, though neither of them being a system maker can be said to have had a systematic doctrine at all. The tone, too, is to some extent the same. There is the same aspiration to serenity, though Epictetus seems more nearly to have achieved it. There is the same counsel to live independent of the pleasures and pains of life, though Marcus Aurelius seems to have been more sensitive to both. There is the same adjuration of indifference to fame and friends, though Epictetus seems naturally more remote from both. There is in both writers an identical urging to conformity with the nature of things, assumed in each instance to be reasonable and good. But in Epictetus the conformity is that of obedience to a ruler. In Marcus, though there is still the language of obedience to Nature, the tone is that of a ruler who feels the burden and the obligation of duty to be done, the carrying on of administration for and among inferiors.

The difference between the two may almost be said to be the difference in tone of a professional teacher of philosophy, rather prosy and sententious, and that of a man deeply involved in the affairs of the world, trying to fortify his own spirit in the concerns both public and private which without the buttress of philosophic serenity might lead him to melancholy or despair. "Even in a palace," Marcus Aurelius wrote, "it is possible to live well." Marcus is not a freed slave, he is not a popular professional teacher of philosophy giving in-

3

tellectual sermons to youth. The writer of these "reflections" is an emperor, a general, a man who has known the great world and seen through it, who has had power and felt the obligations and the futilities that come with it. The meditations are the writings of a conscientious public man who would have preferred, it is clear, the life of philosopher in his study or a hermit in the desert to that of the purple and the scepter. They are the reflections of a hard-working ruler in a crumbling world, persuading himself that all is for the best and that one must do one's duty as fate has ordained it, play one's part, be it that of an emperor or that of a slave.

For the *Meditations* of Marcus Aurelius, there is every reason to believe, *were* meditations, written by the emperor to comfort himself while he was a general conducting an ultimately victorious but difficult campaign in a long discouraging war. It is a book we overhear rather than read. It is the voice of an eminently placed, lonely man talking to himself to keep up his courage, trying to persuade himself that if all goes wrong, it cannot be too disastrous to a free spirit, nor if all goes well, can success be distracting to an independent mind. Part of the suasion of this book over the centuries, one suspects, is the sense that readers in later ages have had of almost eavesdropping on the solitary reflections of an honest and dedicated spirit fighting its way—and warfare is also one of Marcus' favorite metaphors—to an inward security and peace. The *Meditations* have been the bedside reading of other great administrators and men of affairs, cardinals and premiers and kings, of those who in the midst of great commitments and great events have felt it necessary to make a treaty of understanding with themselves and with the universe. Matthew Arnold read them when he was a harassed school official.

The reader needs to bear in mind who was the author of these reflections designed to guard one's integrity and inner peace in both prosperity and misfortune, in what sort of world he was writing. Why the tone of resolution rather than content, of resignation rather than joyous acceptance? Marcus Aurelius was born and bred to the purple.

He was born in Rome in 121 A.D. His uncle and adoptive father, Antoninus Pius, was a good emperor, and Marcus Aurelius had the careful education of one intended to be a future good emperor also. One of the touching things in the early part of the *Meditations* is the obviously sincere gratitude with which this high-bred Stoic thanks Providence for his good grandfather, good parents, good sister, associates, relatives and friends, and his sense of the shining example of his emperor uncle. He had good teachers, too, and in rhetoric an especially talented one, Cornelius Fronto. At the age of eleven, he dedicated himself to religion, for philosophy all his life was with him a kind of religion, the true inward religion that lay behind the rites and ceremonies of the imperial religion which he was careful and content to observe. He studied law and he studied arms. He had the education of an imperial Roman gentleman, but of a gentleman who felt something missing in the outward show and in the outer world, and felt ultimately that peace, if not happiness (which was impossible) lay in oneself. He was doubtless confirmed in this by his teacher of philosophy, later his advisor, Q. Junius Rusticus. About 146 he married his cousin, Faustina, the daughter of the emperor, and in 147 he had a daughter by her. If scandalmongering historians are to be believed, his wife did not give him great cause to believe in goodness in women, but he apparently would not know or did not know of infidelities in her that were notorious to others.

Marcus ruled as a partner emperor with the other adopted son of his uncle, one commonly known as Verus. Verus was by no means the conscientious ruler that Marcus was; he was an Epicurean by nature and no philosopher at all. There were wars and pestilences during the reign, first, a Parthian revolt in the East, then a pestilence. Then the Germans came across the Alps into Italy and a good part of the remainder of his life Marcus was engaged in directing or leading resistance to the invaders. From 169, after Verus' sudden death, Marcus ruled alone.

In 179, during a campaign against the still invading barbarians, Marcus died. The emperor was deified and became a kind of saint. There is no evidence that Marcus was a great ruler, or a great, though he was a dogged, general. There is some evidence that he assented to, if he did not approve, the persecution of the Christians, of whose doctrines he does not seem to have known very much. The distinction of Marcus lies chiefly in his book and personality. It is a small book, but heroic in character and a classic of a certain recurrent human mood and philosophic temper. It is also, like most classics, however universal its appeal across the centuries, expressive in its accent of the special lineaments and issues of its own era.

It was an age that without forcing parallels may be compared to our own. The old pattern of Roman civilization was showing signs of disintegration, the empire itself had its internal corruptions, especially in the reigns preceding those of Marcus' guardians. The empire, moreover, was besieged by external enemies, as was shown by the constant wars threatening it at its frontiers. The old state religion, to which Marcus showed scrupulous respect, was threatened, too, by mere lip service on the part of the educated, and by the rise, so seriously and severely frowned upon by officialdom, of the new strangely epidemic Christian faith. To the educated man who no longer believed in the official religion, there was another recourse, philosophy, but here there were many winds of doctrine. The educated Romans turned to the Greek tradition, but the moral and political philosophy both of Plato and Aristotle were a tradition arising out of a pattern of a Greek city state long dead. The Epicureans offered nothing but a sense of the moderate and even then precarious pleasures to be derived in a world where all was the chance collocations of atoms. It was a philosophy that might appeal to a few aesthetes; it could not persuade those burdened with a sense of responsibility and a feeling for empire. Nor could the older Greek Stoics suffice. Their concept of the absolute wise man, and his unbending conception of detachment from affairs could not appeal to men who were above all men of affairs, men of public affairs. Nor could the older Stoic concern with the fine distinctions of logic and physics offer a solace for men troubled by the entanglements and commitments of a vast, complex, uneasy empire.

It was the later Stoics to whom many educated Romans turned, Stoics of the description of Marcus Aurelius' teachers, of Epictetus and Rusticus. In the light of the Stoic conception of the ultimate and primary reasonableness of the universe, they could face the disorder about them. In the light of a philosophy that held that all ultimately made sense, that all added up to a rational good, they could play their part and overcome what would otherwise be the sense of futility that must come from the mere observable surface, or the mere surface pleasures of life—with all their insecurity and evanescence. Life was retrieved by a sense of the duty commanded by the voice of reason in each man, which was the voice of the universal reason speaking in the reason of each man. In the light of this felt obligation, Juvenal could castigate the corruptions and follies of his time. And even Christians like St. Paul could feel in the sense of the divine reason present in each man, of which the Stoics spoke, something akin to the divinity present in each man, which Paul meant when he spoke of Christ.

Marcus was speaking what was in the air, in Stoic doctrines, like those of his master Epictetus and of Epictetus' master, Usonius, and in Christian thought and feeling, of which he knew little, and in the Greek mysteries, to which he became an initiate. He was writing for himself, not for his contemporaries. He was writing a private journal, but the public of his day would have understood him. He was speaking in a period of failure of nerve, as Gilbert Murray well describes the temper of the Graeco-Roman world at this time. He was talking of the divinity that shapes our ends, and is the substance of all things. He was saying, he says it almost *ad nauseam*, that "there is no evil, nothing can hurt anything," for in the long run everything is an expression of universal good, and of omnipresent reason. Marcus tells us that in each of us is a spark of reason, in living in accordance with which, we live in accordance with the rationale of all things. Each man's reason is the spark of the universal fire of reason in the universe. The logic of oneself is a microcosm of the logos of the cosmos. When we live in accordance with our own nature, fulfilling our own characteristic function, we live also in accordance with the nature of the universe. So to live is what the Stoics nearly all called living with "good will." That will to live in accordance with our own nature and in accordance with the nature of things cannot be taken from us. While one is still alive one can live according to reason; one can do one's duty. Even death cannot destroy the reasonable man's sense of obligation—while he is still alive.

Marcus therefore counsels at once detachment and social participation in active duties. The detachment is from distraction, from the illusions and becloudings of pleasure, from the pains and evils that are largely a consequence of our failure to understand the triviality of and purely apparent character of evil, our provincialism in not seeing that what looks like an evil is good in the context of universal good. There is, Marcus holds, a Providence, a Fate, a divine necessity in which nothing happens that is not part of providential reason. In such a perspective, he believes, the illusions of pleasure to which men cling are clearly seen to be shadows. Fame is a breath; the pleasures of the senses are precarious and deceptive; wealth and friends are transient and are not in our control. In the same way, the little and the larger burdens of life are transient, too, and likewise are not of our making or within our competence. For both reasons we should learn indifference to the vulgar general inventory of miseries and joys. We should learn to live in the citadel of ourselves.

The Cynics, the predecessors of the Stoics, had counseled such a course of retreat also. But Marcus felt that the nature of man which his reason showed him was part of the civic order of nature; he was a member of the society of all reasonable men, united in their participation in reason. Each in that commonwealth, of which the Roman Empire, large as it was, was merely a provincial illustration, had his own fixed station, nature, and duties. If one was an emperor, even over foolish men, it was one's duty to do one's job, to fulfill the function for which Fate had ordained one, not for honor, for honor was an illusion, not for pleasure, for doing one's job was not always agreeable, not even in the hope that one could accomplish what one intended to accomplish for even the best-ruled empires had ended. The important thing was the virtue of exercising one's virtue, of living in accordance with reason, as reason revealed itself in one's own mind, unsuborned by the briberies of transient miseries and illusory goods. All that counted was "the good will," the pertinacious sense of doing one's duty, which is part of the universal obligation which reason sets upon all men.

There is a strain in Marcus of genuine melancholy. He could find nothing secure, permanent, or even reasonable among *human* affairs. One meets, as he says, bores, stupid men, hypocrites, and liars. But in the midst of corruption and vanity one could act oneself like a reasonable man, and one was fortified by the conviction that, whatever appearances might suggest, all in the universe was reasonable in the end. Things change, persons die, but the universe remains. Men are corrupt and nations pass away, but the reason in the universe is eternal, and in one's own life reason may remain incorruptible. "Willingly give yourself up to Clotho, [one of the Fates], allowing her to spin your thread into what thing she pleases." (IV, 34.)

Marcus' code of conduct is not one of cheer; it is one of whistling in the dark, or rather of one who so whistles because he insists that reason proves there is a clear brightness and order which the darkness veils. Fortitude is necessary, and patience and courtesy and modesty and decorum, and a will, in what may for the *moment* seem the worst of worlds, to *do* one's best. For, at least so Marcus tells himself, fundamentally in this universe, properly understood, all *is* for the best. Like Boethius, a Roman who centuries later, condemned to death unjustly for political reasons, wrote a *Consolation of Philosophy*, Marcus, too, sought in philosophy a consolation. In his modest resigned way he has provided it for generations of readers, and in our own age of chaos, he comes again with his touching faith that despite the unreasonableness of men and events, there is a deeper reason in things, a reason which is good, a reason which is God.

IRWIN EDMAN

Editor's Note: The translation of Marcus Aurelius' *Meditations* which follows is that which was made from the Greek by George Long. It has been revised and clarified by the Classics Club editors.

THE MEDITATIONS OF
MARCUS AURELIUS

I

1. From my grandfather Verus I learned good morals and the government of my temper.

2. From the reputation and remembrance of my father, modesty and a manly character.

3. From my mother, piety and generosity, and abstinence, not only from evil deeds, but even from evil thoughts; and further, simplicity in my way of living, far removed from the habits of the rich.

4. From my great-grandfather, not to go to the public schools, but to have good teachers at home, and to know that on such things a man should spend liberally.

5. From my tutor, to be neither of the Green nor of the Blue party at the games in the Circus, nor a partisan either of the Parmularius or the Scutarius at the gladiators' fights; from him too I learned endurance of hardship, and to want little, and to work with my own hands, and not to meddle with other people's affairs, and not to be ready to listen to slander.

6. From Diognetus, not to busy myself about trifling things, and not to give credit to what miracle-workers and jugglers say about incantations and the driving away of demons and such things; and not to breed quails [1] or to give myself up passionately to such things; and to tolerate free-

---

[1] Quail-fighting was a popular sport of the day.

dom of speech; and to become intimate with philosophy; and to be a hearer, first of Bacchius, then of Tandasis and Marcianus; and to write dialogues in my youth; and to like a plank bed and skin, and whatever else of the kind belongs to the Grecian discipline.

7. From Rusticus [2] I got the idea that my character needed improvement and discipline; and from him I learned not to be led astray to sophistic vanity, or to write on speculative matters, or to deliver little moral harangues, or to show myself off as a man who practices much discipline or does benevolent acts in order to make a display; and to refrain from rhetoric and poetry and fine writing; and not to walk about in the house in my outdoor robe, or to do other things of the kind; and to write my letters with simplicity, like the letter which he wrote from Sinuessa to my mother; and with regard to persons who have offended me by words, or done me wrong, to be easily pacified and reconciled, as soon as they have shown a desire to be reconciled; and to read carefully, and not to be satisfied with a superficial understanding of a book; nor hastily to give my assent to those who talk overmuch; and I am indebted to him for my acquaintance with the discourses of Epictetus, which he gave me out of his own collection.

8. From Apollonius [3] I learned freedom of will and undeviating steadiness of purpose; and to look at nothing else, not even for a moment, but reason; and to be always the same, even in sharp pains, in the loss of a child, and in long illness; and to see clearly from his living example that the same man can be both most resolute and lenient, and not peevish in giving his instruction. I had before my eyes a man who clearly considered his experience and his skill in ex-

---

[2] Q. Junius Rusticus was a Stoic philosopher whom Aurelius valued highly.

[3] Apollonius of Chalcis came to Rome in the time of Pius to be Aurelius' preceptor. He was a rigid Stoic.

pounding philosophical principles as the smallest of his merits; and from him I learned how to receive from friends what are considered favors, without being either humbled by them or letting them pass without notice.

9. From Sextus,[4] good humor and the example of a family governed in a fatherly manner, and the idea of living in accord with nature; and gravity without affectation, and to look carefully after the interests of friends, and to tolerate ignorant persons, and those friends who form opinions without consideration. He had the power of readily adapting himself to all, so that conversation with him was more delightful than any flattery. At the same time he was most highly venerated by those who associated with him; and he had the faculty both of discovering and stating, in an intelligent and methodical way, the principles necessary for living; and he never showed anger or any other passion, but was entirely free from passion, and also most affectionate; and he could express approbation without noisy display, and he possessed great knowledge without ostentation.

10. From Alexander, the grammarian,[5] to refrain from faultfinding, and not in a reproachful way to chide those who uttered any barbarous or incorrect or strange-sounding expression; but tactfully to introduce the very expression which they ought to have used, in the course of an answer or assent or inquiry about the thing, not about the word; or by some other suitable suggestion.

11. From Fronto [6] I learned to observe what envy and duplicity and hypocrisy are in a tyrant; and that generally those among us who are called Patricians are rather deficient in paternal affection.

---

[4] Sextus of Chaeronea was probably a grandson of Plutarch.

[5] Alexander, a native of Phrygia, wrote a commentary on Homer.

[6] Cornelius Fronto was a rhetorician, and a teacher of Aurelius' children. He is presented as a character in Pater's *Marius the Epicurean*. See p. 157 ff. of this volume.

12. From Alexander the Platonist, not frequently nor without necessity to say to anyone, or to write in a letter, "I have no time"; nor continually to excuse the neglect of duties required by our relation to those we live with, by alleging urgent business.

13. From Catullus,[7] not to be deaf when a friend finds fault, even if he should find fault without reason, but to try to restore him to his usual humor; and always to speak well of my teachers, as Domitius and Athenodotus are said to have done; and to love my children truly.

14. From my brother [8] Severus, to love my kin, and to love truth, and to love justice; and through him I learned to know Thrasea, Helvidius, Cato, Dion, Brutus; [9] and from him I received the idea of a state in which there is the same law for all, a state administered with regard to equal rights and equal freedom of speech, and the idea of a kingly government which respects most of all the freedom of the governed. I learned from him also consistency and undeviating steadiness in my regard for philosophy, and a disposition to do good, and to give to others readily, and to cherish good hopes, and to believe that I am loved by my friends; and in him I observed no concealment of his opinion of those whom he condemned, and that his friends had no need to conjecture what he wished or did not wish, but it was quite plain.

15. From Maximus [10] I learned self-government, and not to be led aside by anything; and cheerfulness in all circumstances, as well as in illness; and a just admixture in the moral char-

---

[7] Cinna Catullus, a Stoic philosopher.

[8] Aurelius had no brother. It has been supposed that he may mean some cousin.

[9] We know, from Tacitus (*Annal*, xiii, xvi, 21; and other passages), who Thrasea and Helvidius were. Plutarch has written the lives of the two Catos, and of Dion and Brutus. Aurelius probably alludes to Cato of Utica, who was a Stoic.

[10] Claudius Maximus was a Stoic philosopher, who was highly esteemed also by Antoninus Pius, Aurelius' predecessor. The character of Maximus is that of a perfect man. (See viii, 25.)

acter of sweetness and dignity, and to do what was set before me without complaining. I observed that everybody believed that he thought as he spoke, and that in all that he did he never had any bad intention; and he never showed amazement and surprise, and was never in a hurry, and never put off doing a thing; nor was he perplexed nor dejected, nor did he ever laugh to disguise his vexation, nor, on the other hand, was he ever passionate or suspicious. He was accustomed to do acts of kindness and was ready to forgive, and was free from all falsehood; and he presented the appearance of a man who could not be diverted from right rather than of a man who had been improved. I observed, too, that no man could ever think that he was despised by Maximus, or ever venture to think himself a better man. He had also the art of being humorous in an agreeable way.

16. In my father [11] I observed mildness of temper, and unchangeable resolution in the things which he had determined on after due deliberation; and no vainglory in those things which men call honors; and a love of labor and perseverance; and a readiness to listen to whoever had anything to propose for the common weal; and undeviating firmness in giving to every man his deserts; and a knowledge derived from experience of the right times for vigorous action and for relaxation. And I observed that he had overcome any passion for boys; and he considered himself no more than any other citizen; and he released his friends from all obligation to dine with him or compulsion to attend him when he went abroad, and those who had failed to accompany him, by reason of any urgent circumstance, always found him the same.

I observed too his habit of careful inquiry into all matters of deliberation, and his persistency; and that he never stopped an investigation as though satisfied with first appearances; and that his disposition was to keep his friends, and not to be soon

---

[11] He means his adoptive father, his predecessor, the Emperor Antoninus Pius.

tired of them, nor yet to be extravagant in his affection; and to be satisfied on all occasions, and cheerful; and to foresee things a long way off, and to provide for the smallest details without display; and to check immediately popular applause and all flattery; and to be ever watchful over the things which were necessary for the administration of the empire, and to be a good manager of the expenditure, and patiently to endure the blame which he got for such conduct. And he was neither superstitious with respect to the gods, nor did he court men by gifts or by trying to please them, or by flattering the populace; but he showed sobriety in all things and firmness, and never any mean thoughts or action, or love of novelty. And the things which conduce in any way to the comfort of life, and of which fortune gives an abundant supply, he used without arrogance and without excusing himself; so that when he had them, he enjoyed them without affectation, and when he had them not, he did not want them. No one could ever say of him that he was either a sophist or a flippant slave or pedant; but everyone acknowledged him to be a man ripe, perfect, above flattery, able to manage his own and other men's affairs. Besides this, he honored those who were true philosophers, and he did not reproach those who pretended to be philosophers, nor yet was he easily led by them. He was also easy in conversation, and made himself agreeable without any offensive affectation.

He took a reasonable care of his body's health, not as one who was greatly attached to life, nor out of regard to personal appearance, nor yet in a careless way, but so that, through his own attention, he very seldom stood in need of the physician's art or of medicine or external applications. He was ready to make way without envy to those who possessed any particular faculty, such as that of eloquence, or knowledge of the law, or morals, or anything else; and he gave them his help, that each might enjoy reputation according to his deserts; and he always conformed to the institutions of his

country, without making any show of doing so. Further, he
was not fond of change nor unsteady, but loved to stay in
the same places, and to employ himself about the same things;
and after his paroxysms of headache he came back immediately fresh and vigorous to his usual occupations. His secrets
were not many, but very few and rare, and only about public
matters; and he showed prudence and economy in putting on
public spectacles and constructing public buildings, in dona-
tions to the people, and such things; for he was one who looked
to what ought to be done, not to the reputation which a man
gets by his acts. He did not bathe at unreasonable hours; he
was not fond of building houses, nor curious about what he
ate; he did not care about the texture and color of his clothes,
or about the beauty of his slaves. His clothing came from
Lorium, where his country house was, and was usually of
Lanuvian wool.[12] We know how he behaved to the toll-col-
lector at Tusculum who asked his pardon; and such was his
behavior always. There was in him nothing harsh, or im-
placable, or violent, or, as one may say, anything carried to
the sweating point; but he examined things one by one, as if
he had plenty of time, and without confusion, in an orderly
way, vigorously and consistently. And that might be applied
to him which is recorded of Socrates,[13] that he was able either
to leave or to take those things which many are too weak
to abstain from, and cannot enjoy in moderation. But to be
strong enough either to do the first or to be sober in the
second is the mark of a man who has a perfect and invincible
soul, such as he showed in the illness of Maximus.

17. To the gods I am indebted for having good grand-
fathers, good parents, a good sister, good teachers, good associates, good kinsmen and friends, nearly everything good.
Further, I owe it to the gods that I was not pushed into any

---

[12] Lorium was a villa on the coast north of Rome where Aurelius was
brought up.

[13] Xenophon, *Memorabilia*, 3, 15.

offense against any of them, though I had a disposition which, if opportunity had offered, might have led me into something of this kind; but, through their favor, there never was such a concurrence of circumstances as put me to the trial.

Further, I am thankful to the gods that I was not longer brought up with my grandfather's mistress, and that I preserved the flower of my youth, and that I did not make proof of my virility before the proper season, but even deferred the time; that I was subjected to a ruler and a father who was able to take away all pride from me, and to bring me the knowledge that it is possible for a man to live in a palace without wanting either guards or embroidered robes, or torches and statues, and suchlike show; but that it is in such a man's power to bring himself very near the fashion of a private person, without becoming thereby either meaner in thought, or less forceful in action, when things must be done for the public interest in a manner that befits a ruler.

I thank the gods for giving me a brother [14] who was able by his moral character to rouse me to vigilance over myself, and who, at the same time, pleased me by his respect and affection; that my children have not been stupid or deformed in body; that I was not more proficient in rhetoric, poetry, and the other studies, in which I should perhaps have been completely engaged, if I had seen that I was making progress in them; that I promptly placed those who brought me up in the stations of honor they seemed to desire, without putting them off with promises of doing it some time after, because they were then still young; that I received clear and frequent impressions of what is meant about living in accordance with nature; so that, so far as depended on the gods, and their gifts, and help, and inspiration, nothing hindered me from living according to nature, though I still fall short of it through my own fault, and through not observing the admonitions of the gods, and, I may almost say, their dictates; that my body has held

---

[14] His brother by adoption, Lucius Verus.

out so long in such a kind of life; that I never touched either Benedicta or Theodotus, and that, after having fallen into some fits of love, I was cured; and, though I was often out of humor with Rusticus, I never did anything of which I had occasion to repent; that, though it was my mother's fate to die young, she spent the last years of her life with me; that, whenever I wished to help any man in his need, or on any other occasion, I was never told that I had not the means of doing it; and that to myself the necessity never arrived of receiving anything from another; that I have such a wife, so obedient, and so affectionate, and so simple; that I had abundance of good masters for my children; and that remedies have been shown to me by dreams, among other things, against blood-spitting and dizziness. And that, when I had an inclination to philosophy, I did not fall into the hands of any sophist, and that I did not waste my time on the ordinary philosophers or in solving syllogisms, or investigating appearances in the heavens; for all these things require the help of the gods and fortune.

Among the Quadi, by the Granua.[15]

II

1. Begin the morning by saying to yourself, I shall meet with the busybody, the ungrateful, arrogant, deceitful, envious, unsocial. All these things happen to them by reason of their ignorance of what is good and evil. But I who have seen the nature of the good that it is beautiful, and of the bad that is ugly, and the nature of him who does wrong, that it is akin to mine, not only of the same blood or seed, but

---

15 The Quadi lived in the southern part of Bohemia and Moravia. Aurelius made a campaign against them. Granua is probably the river Graan, which flows into the Danube.

that it participates in the same intelligence and the same portion of divinity, I can neither be harmed by any of them, for no one can fix on me what is ugly, nor can I be angry with my brother, nor hate him. For we are made for co-operation, like feet, like hands, like eyelids, like the rows of the upper and lower teeth. To act against one another then is contrary to nature; and it is acting against one another to be vexed and to turn away.

2. Whatever this is that I am, it is a little flesh, breath, and the ruling part. Throw away your books; no longer distract yourself; it is not allowed. But as if you were now dying, despise the flesh; it is blood and bones and a network, a tissue of nerves, veins, and arteries. See the breath also, what kind of a thing it is, air, and not always the same, but every moment sent out and again sucked in. The third is the ruling part. Consider thus: You are an old man; no longer let this part be a slave, no longer be pulled by the strings like a puppet by self-seeking impulse, no longer be either dissatisfied with your present lot, or shrink from the future.

3. All that is from the gods is full of providence. The workings of chance are not separated from nature or without an interweaving and dependence on the dispositions of providence. From providence all things flow. And side by side with it is necessity, and that which works to the advantage of the whole universe, of which you are a part. But that is good for every part of nature which the nature of the whole brings to pass, and which serves to maintain this nature. Now the universe is preserved, both by the changes of the elements and by the changes of the things compounded. Let these principles be enough for you; let them always be fixed opinions. But cast away the thirst after books, that you may not die murmuring, but cheerfully, and thankful from your heart to the gods.

4. Remember how long you have been putting off these things, and how often you have received an opportunity from

the gods and yet have not used it. You must now at last perceive of what kind of a universe you are a part, and the true nature of the lord of the universe of which your being is a part, and how a limit of time is fixed for you, which if you do not use for clearing away the clouds from your mind, it will go and you will go, and it will never return.

5. Every moment think steadily as a Roman and as a man to do what you have in hand with perfect and simple dignity, and kindliness, and freedom, and justice; and to give yourself relief from all other thoughts. And you will give yourself relief, if you do every act of your life as if it were the last, renouncing all carelessness and passionate resistance to the commands of reason, and all hypocrisy, and self-love, and discontent with the portion which has been given to you. You see how few the things are which a man needs to lay hold of in order to live a life which flows in quiet, and is like the life of the gods; for the gods on their part will require nothing more from him who observes these things.

6. Is violence done you? Do no violence to yourself, my soul! Soon the opportunity of honoring yourself will be at an end. Every man's life is enough; but yours is nearly finished, though your soul honors not yourself, but places your felicity in the souls of others.

7. Do things external which happen to you distract you? Give yourself time to learn something new and good, and cease to be whirled around. But then you must also avoid going astray the other way. For those too are triflers who have worn themselves out by activity, and yet have no goal to which they direct their movements or their thoughts.

8. Through not observing the thoughts of another a man is seldom unhappy; but he who does not observe the movements of his own mind must of necessity be unhappy.

9. This you must always bear in mind: what is the nature of the whole, and what is my nature, and how this is related to that, and what kind of part it is of what kind of whole; and

there is no one who can hinder you from always doing and saying the things which are in accord with the nature of which you are a part.

10. Theophrastus, in his comparison of wrong acts—such a comparison as one might make to fit the common notions of mankind—says, like a true philosopher, that offenses committed through desire are more blameworthy than those committed through anger. For a man excited by anger seems to abandon his reason with pain and unconscious shrinking; but he who sins through desire, overpowered by pleasure, seems more intemperate and more unmanly in his offenses. Rightly then, and like a philosopher, he said that a sin committed with pleasure is more blameworthy than one committed with pain. The first is more like a person who has been wronged and through pain compelled to be angry; but the second is moved by his own impulse to do wrong, and carried on to sin by desire.

11. Since it is possible that you may be quitting life this very moment, govern every act and thought accordingly. But to go away from mankind, if there are gods, is no thing to be afraid of, for the gods will do you no evil; and if they do not exist, or if they have no concern for human affairs, why should I live in a universe devoid of gods or devoid of providence? But in truth they do exist, and they do care for human things, and they have put it entirely in man's power not to fall into real evils. As to other troubles, if they were really evil, they would have provided for them also, and given man the power not to fall into them. Now that which does not make a man worse, how can it make his life worse? But neither because it was ignorant, nor because with the knowledge it had not the power to guard against or correct these things, could the nature of that universe have overlooked them; nor could it have made so great a mistake, either through want of power or want of skill, that the real good and evil should happen indiscriminately to good men and bad. But death certainly, and life, honor, and dishonor, pain and pleasure, all these things do happen alike to good men and bad, for they are things which make us neither better nor worse. Therefore they are really neither good nor evil.

12. How quickly all things disappear, bodies into the universe, memories of them in time. What is the nature of sense objects, and particularly of those which attract with the bait of pleasure or terrify by pain, or are known everywhere for their vapory fame; how worthless, and contemptible, and sordid, and perishable, and dead they are—all this it is the part of the intellect to observe. To observe too what people they are whose opinions and voices create a reputation; what death is, and how, if a man looks at it in itself, and by the abstract power of reflection analyzes the features of it which strike the imagination, he will discover it is nothing else than an operation of nature; and he who fears the course of nature is a child. Death, however, is not only a work of nature, but it is also a thing that fulfills the purposes of nature. Observe, too, how man comes near to the Deity, and by what part of him, and when this part of him is so disposed.

13. Nothing is more wretched than the man who travels about everywhere, and pries into things beneath the earth, as the poet says, and strives to conjecture the thoughts of his neighbors, without perceiving that it is sufficient to attend to the divinity within him, and to reverence it sincerely. And to revere the divinity means keeping it pure from passion and frivolity, and content with gods and men. For the government of the gods merits veneration for its excellence; and the deeds of men should be dear to us by reason of our kinship with them. Sometimes they even move our pity by reason of their ignorance of good and evil; this defect is as great as the blindness which cannot tell white from black.

14. Though you were to live three thousand years, or three million, still remember that no man loses any other life than this which he now lives, or lives any other than this which he now loses. The longest and the shortest thus come to the same. For the present is the same to everyone, though the past is not the same, and what is lost appears to be a mere moment. For a man cannot lose either his past or his future: for what a man has not, how can anyone take from him? These two things then you must bear in mind: the first, that all things from eternity repeat the same forms and come round in a circle, and that it makes no difference whether a man gazes at the same things for a hundred years or two hundred, or an infinite time; and the second, that the longest liver and he who dies soonest lose just the same. For the present is the only thing a man can lose, if it is true that it is the only thing he has, and that a man cannot lose a thing which he has not.

15. Remember that all is but opinion. For what the Cynic Monimus said is obvious: and obvious too is the use of what he said, if a man accepts what may be got out of it only as far as it is true.

16. The soul of man does violence to itself, first of all, when it becomes an abscess and, as it were, a tumor on the universe, as far as it can. For to be vexed at anything that happens is a separation of ourselves from nature, in some part of which the natures of all other things are contained. Secondly, the soul does violence to itself when it turns away from any man, or moves against him with the intention of harming him, as do the souls of the angry. In the third place, the soul does violence to itself when it succumbs to pleasure or pain. Fourthly, when it plays a part, and acts or speaks insincerely or untruly. Fifthly, when it performs any act or any movement aimlessly, and does anything thoughtlessly and without considering what it is, whereas even the smallest things ought to be designed for an end; and the end of rational beings is to follow the reason and the law of the most ancient city and commonwealth.

17. The time of human life is but a point, and the substance is a flux, and its perceptions dull, and the composition of the body corruptible, and the soul a whirl, and fortune inscrutable, and fame a senseless thing. In a word, everything which belongs to the body is a flowing stream, and what belongs to the soul a dream and a vapor, and life is a warfare and a stranger's sojourn, and future fame is oblivion. What then is there which can guide a man? One thing and only one, philosophy. Now this consists in keeping the divinity within us free from violence and unharmed, superior to pain and pleasure, doing nothing without a purpose, nor yet falsely and with hypocrisy, not feeling the need of another man's doing or not doing something; and, furthermore, accepting all that happens and all that is allotted us, as coming from the source, wherever it is, whence it itself came; and, finally, waiting for death with a cheerful mind, since it is nothing but a dissolving of the elements of which each living being is composed. If the elements themselves are not harmed by each continually changing into another, why should a man feel any dread of the change and dissolution of all his elements? For it is as nature wills it, and nothing is evil which nature wills.

At Caruntum.[1]

III

1. We ought to remember not only that our life is daily wasting away and a smaller part of it is left, but also that if a man should live longer, it is quite uncertain whether his mind will stay strong enough to understand things, and retain the power of contemplation to strive after knowledge of the divine and the human. For if he begins to sink into dotage,

---

[1] Caruntum was a town of Pannonia, on the south bank of the Danube, about thirty miles east of Vienna, then known as Vindobona. Historians say that Aurelius stayed at Caruntum for three years during his war with the Marcomanni.

he still may perspire and take food and keep his imagination and appetite, and other powers of the kind; but the power of making himself useful, and filling up the measure of his duty, and clearly distinguishing appearances, knowing whether he should retire from life, and whatever else of the kind requires a disciplined reason, all this is already dead in him. We must make haste then, not only because we are daily nearer to death, but also because our perception of things and understanding of them cease first.

2. We ought to observe also that even the small characteristics of things produced according to nature have something in them pleasing and attractive. For instance, when a loaf of bread is baked there are cracks in the surface, and these breaks, which are contrary to the purpose of the baker, are beautiful in their way, and stimulate the appetite. Again, figs when they are quite ripe gape open; and ripe olives when they are near to rotting are particularly good to look at. And ears of corn bending down, and a lion's eyebrows, and the foam which flows from the mouth of a wild boar, and many other things— though they are far from beautiful, if one examines them separately—still, because they are characteristics of things formed by nature, help to adorn them, and please the eye. Thus if a man has a feeling for and deep insight into the things produced in the universe, there is hardly one of their characteristics that will not seem to him of a sort to give him pleasure. So he will look on the gaping jaws of living wild beasts with as much pleasure as on those which painters and sculptors depict in imitation; and in an old woman and an old man he will perceive a certain ripeness and comeliness; and will look on the attractive loveliness of young persons with chaste eyes. Many such beauties will show themselves, not pleasing to every man, but to him who has become truly at home with nature and her works.

3. Hippocrates, who cured many diseases, himself fell sick and died. The Chaldeans foretold the deaths of people, and

then fate caught them too. Alexander, Pompey, and Julius Caesar, who had destroyed so many whole cities, and in battle cut to pieces so many thousands of horsemen and foot soldiers, themselves too at last departed this life. Heraclitus, who speculated so much on the conflagration of the universe, was swollen with dropsy and died in a plaster of dung. Vermin destroyed Democritus and another kind of vermin killed Socrates.[1] What does all this mean? You have taken ship, you have made the voyage, you have come to port; disembark. If you come to another life, there are gods enough even there; but if to a state without sensation, you will no more be gripped by pains and pleasures, or be slave to the vessel, which is as much inferior as that which serves it is superior; for the latter is all intelligence and deity; the former earth and corruption.

4. Waste not the remainder of your life in thoughts about others, except when you are concerned with some unselfish purpose. For you are losing an opportunity to do something else, when you have such thoughts as: "What is such a person doing, and why, and what is he saying, and what is he thinking, and what is he contriving?"—and whatever else of the kind makes us forget to observe our own ruling principle. We ought to check in the course of our thoughts everything that is without a purpose and useless, but most of all meddling and maliciousness. A man should train himself to think only of those things about which if you were suddenly asked, "What have you now in your thoughts?"—with perfect openness you might immediately answer, This or That; so that from your words it should be plain that everything in you is sincere and kindly, and befitting a social animal, and one that cares not for thoughts of pleasure or sensual enjoyments or any rivalry or

---

[1] Heraclitus, Democritus, and Socrates were three of the best-known Greek philosophers. Heraclitus, who taught that the world was made of fire, was looked on as a forerunner of the Stoics. From Democritus the Epicureans took their theory that the world was a product of invisible atoms whirling blindly through space. Socrates was the ethical teacher to whom Plato paid homage in his dialogues.

envy or suspicion, or anything else for which you would blush if you were to say it was in your mind. For such a man, who delays not to enter among the best, is like a priest and minister of the gods and uses the divinity which is within him, which keeps him uncontaminated by pleasure, unharmed by pain, untouched by insult, feeling no wrong, a fighter in the noblest fight, one who cannot be overpowered by passion, steeped in justice, accepting with all his soul everything that happens and is assigned to him as his portion. Not often, nor without some great necessity and for the general interest, does he conjecture what another says, or does, or thinks. For it is only what belongs to himself that he is concerned about; he thinks constantly of what is assigned to him out of the sum total of things, and makes his own acts fair, and is persuaded that his own lot is good. For the lot assigned to each man moves along with him and carries him along with it. He remembers also that every rational being is his kinsman, and that to care for all men is natural to man; and that a man should not care for the opinion of everybody but of those only who live according to nature. As for those who live not so, he bears always in mind what kind of men they are both at home and abroad, both by night and by day, and what they are, and with what companions they live their evil life. Accordingly, he values not at all the praise which comes from such men, since they are not satisfied even with themselves.

5. Labor not unwillingly, nor without regard to the common interest, nor without due consideration, nor with distraction; nor express your thoughts with studied eloquence. Be not either a man of many words, or busy about too many things. Make the divinity within you guardian of a living being, manly, of ripe age, a statesman, a Roman, and an emperor, who keeps his post like a man waiting for the signal to summon him from life, ready to go, needing neither the oath nor any man's testimony. Be cheerful also, and depend not on

external help or on the tranquillity which others give. A man must stand erect, not be held erect by others.

6. If you find in human life anything better than justice, truth, temperance, fortitude, in a word, anything better than your own mind's self-satisfaction in the things it enables you to do according to right reason, and in the fate that is assigned you without your own choice; if, I say, you see anything better than this, turn to it with all your soul, and enjoy that which you have found to be best. But if nothing appears to you better than the divinity planted in you, which has subjected all your appetites and carefully examines all impressions, and, as Socrates said, has detached itself from the persuasions of sense, and has submitted itself to the gods, and cares for mankind; if all things else are trifles compared with this, give way to nothing else. For if you once diverge and incline to that, you will no longer without distraction be able to give preference to the good thing which is your own proper possession; for it is not right that anything of another kind, such as popular praise, or power, or enjoyment of pleasure, should compete for a place with that which is rationally and socially good. Such things, even though they may seem for a moment to be harmonious, all at once get the mastery and carry us away. But do you, I say, simply and freely choose the better part and hold to it. "But that which is useful is the better." Well then, if it is useful to you as a rational being, keep to it; but if it is only useful to you as an animal, say so. Maintain your judgment without arrogance; only take care that you make the inquiry by a sure method.

7. Think nothing profitable to you which compels you to break a promise, to lose your self-respect, to hate any man, to suspect, to curse, to act the hypocrite, to desire anything that needs walls and curtains about it. For he who values his own intelligence and the divinity within him and the worship of its excellence before all else, plays no tragic part, does not groan, does not need either solitude or much company. And,

what is more than all, he lives without either pursuing or flying from life; but whether for a longer or a shorter time his
soul shall stay enclosed in his body, he cares not at all. Even
if he must depart immediately, he will go as readily as if he
were doing anything else which can be done decently and
with order. All through life he takes care of this only, that his
thoughts turn not away from what should concern an intelligent being and a member of a civil community.

8. In the mind of one disciplined and purified you will find
no corrupt matter, or impurity, or any sore skinned over. Nor
when fate overtakes him is his life incomplete, as one may say
of an actor who leaves the stage before quite finishing the
play. Besides, there is in him nothing servile, or affected, or
too closely bound, or yet detached; nothing worthy of blame,
nothing that seeks a hiding-place.

9. Honor the faculty which produces opinion. On this
faculty it entirely depends whether there exists in your ruling
part any opinion inconsistent with nature and the constitution
of a rational being. And this faculty urges freedom from hasty
judgment, friendship towards men, and obedience to the gods.

10. Cast away then all other things, hold only to these few
truths; bear in mind also that every man lives only in the
present, which is an indivisible point, and that all the rest of
his life is either past or uncertain. Short then is the time which
any man lives; and short too the longest posthumous fame,
and even this is handed on by a succession of poor human beings, who will very soon die, and who know not even themselves, much less one who died long ago.

11. To the aids already mentioned add this one also: Make
for yourself a definition or description of every object presented to you, so as to see distinctly what it is in its own naked
substance, complete and entire, and tell yourself its proper
name, and the names of the things of which it is compounded
and into which it will be dissolved. For nothing so elevates
the mind as to be able to examine methodically and truly every

object which comes before you in life, and always to look at things so as to see at once what kind of universe this is, and what kind of service each performs in it, and what value each has in relation to the whole, and what it has for man, who is a citizen of that loftiest city, to which all other cities are as families. What is this thing, and of what is it composed, and how long will it naturally last, this thing which now makes an impression on me? What virtue does it demand of me; is it gentleness, courage, truth, fidelity, simplicity, contentment, and the rest? Thus, on every occasion, a man should say: "This comes from God"; or, "This is from the decree and spinning of the thread of destiny, or some such coincidence and chance"; or, "This is from one of the same stock as myself, a kinsman and partner, but who knows not his true relation to nature. I do know, and for this reason I act towards him in accordance with the natural law of fellowship, benevolently and justly. At the same time, in things indifferent I attempt to judge the value of each."

12. If you work at that which is before you, following right reason seriously, vigorously, calmly, without allowing anything else to distract you, but keeping your divine part pure, as if you were bound to give it back immediately; if you hold to this, expecting nothing, but satisfied to live now according to nature, speaking heroic truth in every word which you utter, you will live happy. And there is no man able to prevent this.

13. As surgeons always have their instruments and knives ready for cases which suddenly need their skill, so do you have principles ready for the understanding of things divine and human, and for every act, even the smallest, remembering the bond which unites the divine and human to one another. For neither will you do any human thing well without at the same time having regard to things divine, nor vice versa.

14. No longer wander at random. You shall not live to read your own memoirs, or the acts of the ancient Romans and

Greeks, or the selections from books which you were reserving for your old age. Hasten then to the goal which you have before you. Throw away vain hopes and come to your own aid, while yet you may, if you care at all for yourself.

15. Men know not how many things are signified by the words stealing, sowing, buying, keeping the peace, seeing what ought to be done; for this cannot be done by the eyes, but by another kind of vision.

16. Body, soul, mind: to the body belong sensations, to the soul impulses, to the mind principles. To receive the impressions of forms by means of sense belongs to all animals; to be pulled by the strings of desire belongs both to wild beasts and to womanish men, to a Phalaris and a Nero; to have a mind that selects what it thinks suitable belongs also to men who do not believe in the gods, who betray their country, and do impure deeds when they have shut the doors. If then all these qualities are common to the creatures I have mentioned, there is still what is peculiar to the good man, to be pleased and content with what happens, and with the thread which is spun for him; and not to defile the divinity which is planted in his breast, or disturb it by a crowd of impressions, but to preserve it tranquil, following it obediently as a god, neither saying anything contrary to truth, nor doing anything contrary to justice. And if the world refuses to believe in his simplicity, modesty, and contentment, he is neither angry with anyone, nor does he deviate from the path which leads to the end of life, to which a man ought to come pure, calm, ready to depart, freely and perfectly reconciled to his lot.

IV

1. When the ruling mind acts according to nature, it so takes the events which happen as to always easily adapt itself to whatever is presented to it and whatever is possible. For it requires no special materials, but moves toward its purpose, imposing only certain conditions. It makes material for itself out of what opposes it, as fire lays hold of what falls into it. A small light might have been extinguished; but when the fire is strong, it soon appropriates to itself the stuff which is heaped on it, consumes it, and rises higher by means of this very material.

2. Do every act with a purpose, and according to the perfect rules of art.

3. Men seek retreats for themselves, houses in the country, seashores, and mountains; and you too are wont to desire such things very much. But this is altogether a mark of the common sort of man, for it is in your power, whenever you shall choose, to retire into yourself. For nowhere with more quiet or more freedom from trouble does a man retire than into his own soul, particularly when he has within him such thoughts that by looking into them he is at once perfectly tranquil; and this tranquillity, I am sure, is nothing but the good ordering of the mind. Constantly then grant yourself this retreat and refreshment; let your principles be brief and fundamental, which, as soon as you shall call them to mind, will be sufficient to cleanse the soul completely, and send you back free from all discontent with the stale things to which you return. For with what are you discontented? With the wickedness of mankind? Recall to your mind these ideas, that rational animals were made for one another, that forbearance is a part of justice, that men do wrong involuntarily. Consider how many already have lived in mutual enmity, suspicion, hatred, and conflict, and now lie dead, reduced to ashes; and be quiet at last. But perhaps you are dissatisfied with what is assigned you out of the universe. Recall to your thoughts this alternative: either there is a providence or only atoms; remember the arguments by which it has been proved that the world is, as it were, one city or community. But perhaps bodily ailments still distress you. Consider then that the mind, when it has once drawn apart and discovered its own power, alters not with the breath, whether that comes gently or violently; think also of all that you have heard and assented to about pain and pleasure. But perhaps a longing for the thing called fame torments you. See how soon everything is forgotten; look at the chaos of infinite time on each side of the present, and the emptiness of applause, and the fickleness and poor judgment of those who pretend to praise, and the narrowness of the space within which it is confined. For the whole earth is but a point, and in that how small a nook is this your dwelling, and how few are there within it, and what kind of people are they who will praise you?

Remember then to retire into this little realm of your own; above all, do not distract or strain yourself, but be free and look at things as a man, as a human being, as a citizen, as a mortal. Among the maxims readiest to your hand to which you shall return, let there be these two: one, that things cannot touch the soul, for they are external and remain motionless, and our perturbations spring from the opinion that is within; the other, that all these things, which you see, are changing now and soon will no longer be; bear constantly in mind how many of these changes you have already witnessed. The universe is transformation: life is a succession of views.

4. If the faculty of understanding is common to us all, the reason also, through which we are rational beings, is common. If this is so, common also is that reason which tells us what to do, and what not to do. If this is so, there is a law common to all men also. If this is so, we are fellow citizens and members of some political community, and thus the world is in a way one commonwealth. Of what other common political community will anyone say that the whole human race are members? And from thence, from this share in a common community, comes also our intellectual faculty and reasoning faculty and our capacity for law; from where else do they come? For as my earthly part is my portion of certain earth,

and my watery part from another element, and what is hot and fiery in me comes from some other distinct source (for nothing comes out of nothing, just as nothing returns to non-existence), so also my intellectual part has its own origin.

5. Death, like generation, is a mystery of nature, a combining of certain elements, and a dissolving into the same; in no wise a thing of which a man should be ashamed, for it is appropriate to the nature of a rational animal, and not contrary to the design of our constitution.

6. Some things are naturally done by some kinds of persons; it is a matter of necessity; and if a man will not have it so, he will not allow a fig tree to have juice. But bear this firmly in mind, that within a very short time both you and he will be dead; and soon not even your names will be left behind.

7. Take away your opinion, and there is taken away the complaint, "I have been hurt." Take away the complaint, "I have been hurt," and the hurt is gone.

8. Whatever does not make a man worse does not make his life worse, nor does it harm him either without or within.

9. It was expedient in nature that it should be so, and therefore necessary.

10. Consider that everything which happens, happens justly, and if you observe carefully, you will find it to be so. I do not say this only as regards the continuity of the sequence of things, but as regards what is just, as if it were ordered by one who assigns to everything its value. Observe then, as you have begun; and whatever you do, do it as befits that character of goodness in the sense in which a man is rightfully supposed to be good. Hold to this rule in every act.

11. Do not have the opinion of things that he has who does you wrong, or that he wishes you to have, but look at them as they are in truth.

12. A man should always have these two rules in readiness: first, to do only what the reason of your ruling and legislating faculty suggests for the service of men; second, to change your opinion, whenever anyone at hand sets you right and un-settles you in an opinion. But this change of opinion should come only because you are persuaded that something is just or to the public advantage, and the like, not because it appears pleasant or increases your reputation.

13. Have you reason? "I have." Why, then, do you not use it? For if it does its own proper work what else do you wish?

14. You have lived as a part. You shall disappear in that which produced you; rather, you shall be received back into the creative principle by a transformation.

15. Many grains of frankincense on the same altar; one falls first, another after; but it makes no difference.

16. If you will return to your principles and the worship of reason, within ten days you will seem a god to those to whom you are now a beast and an ape.

17. Do not act as if you would live ten thousand years. Death hangs over you. While you live, while it is in your power, be good.

18. How much trouble he avoids who does not look to see what his neighbor says or does or thinks, but only what he does himself, that it may be just and pure. As Agathon says, "Look not around at the depraved morals of others, but run straight along your course without straying from it."

19. He who feels an overwhelming desire for posthumous fame does not consider that all those who remember him will themselves also die very soon; then they also who succeed them, until the whole remembrance of him is extinguished, for it is transmitted by men who foolishly admire and perish. Even suppose that those who remember you are immortal, and that the remembrance will be immortal, what then is it to you? Not only what is it to the dead, but what is it to the living? What is praise, except indeed so far as it has some utility? And you are now ignoring unseasonably the present gift of nature, clinging to what someone says hereafter.

20. Whatever is in any way beautiful is beautiful in itself, and has its end in itself, and praise is no part of it. Neither worse then nor better is a thing made by being praised. I say this too of things called beautiful by the vulgar, for example, material things and works of art. That which is really beautiful has no need of anything; no more than law, no more than truth, no more than generosity or modesty. Which of these things is made beautiful by being praised, or spoiled by being blamed? Is a jewel like an emerald damaged if it is not praised? Or gold, ivory, purple, a lyre, a dagger, a flower, a shrub?

21. If souls go on living, how does the air hold them all from eternity? But how, we reply, does the earth have room for the bodies of those who have been buried from times so remote? Just as here the changing of these bodies after lasting a certain time, and their dissolution, make room for other dead bodies, so the souls which are released into the air, after subsisting for a while, are transmuted and diffused, and turned into fire and absorbed into the creative intelligence of the universe, and in this way make room for the fresh souls which come to dwell there. This is the answer which a man might give, supposing that souls continue to exist. And we must think not only of the number of bodies which are thus buried, but also of the number that are daily eaten by us and the other animals. What a number is consumed, and thus in a manner buried in the bodies of those who feed on them! Nevertheless, the earth receives them too through the changing of these bodies into blood, and their transformation into air or fire.

How can we find the truth in this case? Divide it into what is matter and what is cause (VII, 29).

22. Do not be tossed about, but in every act have respect for justice, and at every impression preserve the faculty of understanding.

23. Everything is right for me, which is right for you, O Universe. Nothing for me is too early or too late, which comes in due time for you. Everything is fruit to me which your seasons bring, O Nature. From you are all things, in you are all things, to you all things return. The poet says, "Dear city of Cecrops"; [1] and will you not say, "Dear city of Zeus"?

24. "Busy yourself with but few things," says the philosopher, "if you would be tranquil." But consider if it would not be better to say, "Do what is necessary, and whatever the reason of an animal naturally social requires, and as it requires"? For this brings not only the tranquillity which comes from doing well, but also that which comes from doing few things. For most of what we say and do is unnecessary, and if a man leaves them out, he will have more leisure and less trouble. So on every occasion a man should ask himself, "Is this one of the unnecessary things?" Further, a man should leave off not only unnecessary acts, but also unnecessary thoughts, for thus superfluous acts will not follow after.

25. Try how the life of the good man suits you, the life of one content with his portion of the whole, and with his own just acts and kindly disposition.

26. Have you seen this side? Look also at the other. Do not be disturbed. Make yourself all simplicity. Does anyone do wrong? It is himself that he wrongs. Has anything happened to you? Well, within the universe from the beginning every event was apportioned and allotted to you. In a word, your life is short. You must make the most of the present with the aid of reason and justice. Be sober even in your relaxation.

27. Either it is a well-ordered universe or a chaos huddled together, though still a universe. But can order subsist in you, and disorder in the All? And this too when all things are so separate and diffused and yet sympathetic?

28. A black character—a womanish character, a stubborn

---

[1] Cecrops was a fabled king of Attica, who, according to the legend, built the first citadel at Athens. The "city of Cecrops" then was at Athens.

character, bestial, childish, animal, stupid, false, scurrilous, fraudulent, tyrannical.

29. If the man is a stranger to the universe who does not know what is in it, no less is he a stranger who does not know what is going on in it. He is a runaway, who flies from the concerns of society; he is blind, who shuts the eyes of his understanding; he is poor, who has need of another, and finds not in himself all things helpful for life. He is a sore on the universe who withdraws and separates himself from the reason of our common nature and is displeased with the things that happen; for the same nature that produces them has produced you too. He is a social outcast, who cuts his own soul off from the one common soul of all reasonable beings.

30. This is a philosopher without a tunic, the other is without a book. Here is another half naked: "Bread I have not," he says, "but I abide by reason." And I get no livelihood out of my learning, but I abide by reason.

31. Love the art, poor as it may be, which you have learned, and be content with it; and pass through the rest of life like one who has with his whole soul entrusted to the gods all that he has; be neither the tyrant nor the slave of any man.

32. Consider, for an example, the times of Vespasian.[2] You will see all the same things, people marrying, bringing up children, sick, dying, fighting, feasting, trafficking, farming, flattering, pushing, suspecting, plotting, wishing for someone to die, grumbling about the present, loving, heaping up treasure, coveting the consulship and kingly power. Well, the life of those people is all over. Come on next to the time of Trajan. Again, all is the same. Their life too is gone. In like manner survey other epochs of time and other nations, and see how many after mighty efforts fell and were resolved into the elements. But chiefly recall those whom you yourself have known, distracting themselves about vanities, neglecting to do

---

[2] The emperor Vespasian (68-79 A.D.) reigned a century before Marcus Aurelius, the emperor Trajan (98-117 A.D.), a generation later.

what was in accord with their proper nature, and to hold firmly to it and be content with it. And here you must remember to give attention to everything in its proper value and proportion. For then you will not be dissatisfied, if you give to trifles no more care than is fit.

33. The words that once were in current use are now antiquated; so also the names of men famed of old are now growing antiquated—Camillus, Caeso, Volesus, Leonatus, and soon it will be so of Scipio and Cato, then Augustus, then also Hadrian and Antoninus. For all things quickly pass away and become a mere tale, and oblivion buries them. And this I say of men who shone in a wondrous way. As for the rest, as soon as they have breathed out their breath, they are gone, and no one speaks of them. In conclusion, what is even eternal fame? A mere nothing. What then is there for which we ought to take serious pains? Only this: to have thoughts just, acts social, words which never lie, and a disposition which gladly accepts whatever happens, as necessary, as usual, as flowing from a principle and source of a familiar kind.

34. Willingly give yourself up to Clotho,[3] allowing her to spin your thread into whatever she pleases.

35. Everything lasts only for a day, both that which remembers and that which is remembered.

36. Observe constantly that all things come about by change; accustom yourself to reflect that the nature of the universe loves nothing so much as changing things that are and making new things like them. For everything that exists is in a way the seed of what will be. But you are thinking only of the seeds which are cast into the earth or into a womb; this is a very dull notion.

37. You soon will die, and you are not yet simple, nor free from perturbations, and the dread of being hurt by external things, nor are you kindly disposed toward all; nor do you yet see that wisdom consists only in acting justly.

[3] One of the Fates.

38. Examine men's ruling principles, especially those of the wise, what kind of things they avoid, and what kind they pursue.

39. Your evil lies not in another man's mind; nor yet in any change and mutation of your bodily covering. Where is it then? It is in that part of you that has the power of forming opinions about evil. Let this power then not form opinions, and all is well. If that which is nearest to it, the poor body, is cut, burnt, filled with matter and rottenness, nevertheless let the part which forms opinions about such things be quiet; that is, let it judge that nothing is either bad or good that can happen equally to the bad man and the good. For that which happens equally to one who lives contrary to nature and to one who lives according to nature, is neither according to nature nor contrary to nature.

40. Regard the universe often as one living being, having one substance and one soul; and observe how all things act with one movement; and how all things co-operate as the causes of all that exists; observe too the continuous spinning of the thread and the single texture of the web.

41. You are a little soul bearing about a corpse, as Epictetus used to say.

42. It is not evil for things to undergo change, nor good for things to arise in consequence of change.

43. Time is like a river made up of events that happen, and a violent stream; for as soon as a thing has appeared it is carried away, and another comes in its place; and this will be carried away too.

44. Everything that happens is as familiar and well known as a rose in spring and fruit in summer; such is disease, and death, and calumny, and treachery, and whatever else delights fools or vexes them.

45. In the sequence of things those which follow are always aptly fitted to those which have gone before; for the sequence is not like a mere string of disjointed things, which has only an enforced order, but it is a rational connection; and as all existing things are arranged harmoniously together, so the things that come into existence keep not merely a succession, but a certain wonderful relationship (VI, 38; VII, 9).

46. Always remember the saying of Heraclitus, that earth dies to become water, and water dies to become air, and air dies to become fire, and conversely. And think too of him who forgets whither the way leads, and the men who quarrel with what they most intimately commune with, the reason that governs the universe; and think the things they daily meet with are strange. Consider that we ought not to act and speak as if we were asleep, for in sleep we seem to be acting and speaking; and that we ought not, like children who learn only from their parents, simply act and speak as we have been taught.

47. If any god told you that you should die tomorrow, or certainly the day after tomorrow, you would not care much whether it was the third day or the morrow, unless you were completely mean-spirited—for the difference is too small to consider. So think it no great matter to die after as many years as you can name rather than tomorrow.

48. Constantly remember how many physicians are dead after contracting their eyebrows over the sick so many times; and how many astrologers, after predicting with great to-do the deaths of others; and how many philosophers, after endless discourses on death or immortality; how many heroes, after killing thousands; how many tyrants, who used their power over other men's lives with terrible insolence as if they themselves were immortal; and how many cities are entirely dead; Helice and Pompeii and Herculaneum, and others innumerable. Add to your reckoning all whom you have known, one after another. One man after burying another is laid out dead, and another buries him; and all this in a short time. In conclusion, observe always how ephemeral and worthless human things are, and how what was yesterday a little juice,

tomorrow will be a mummy or ashes. Pass then through this moment of time in harmony with nature, and end your journey in content, as an olive falls when it is ripe, blessing nature who produced it, and thanking the tree on which it grew.

49. Be like the cliff against which the waves continually break; but it stands firm and tames the fury of the water around it.

Am I unhappy, because this has happened to me? Not so, but I am happy, though this has happened to me, because I am still free from pain, neither crushed by the present nor fearing the future. For such a thing might have happened to any man; but every man would not have remained free from pain on such an occasion. Why then is the former rather a misfortune than the latter a good fortune? And do you in any case call that a misfortune, which is not a violation of man's nature? And does a thing seem to you a violation of man's nature, when it is not contrary to the purpose of man's nature? Well, you know the purpose of nature. Will this which has happened prevent you from being just, magnanimous, temperate, prudent, secure against rash opinions and falsehood; will it keep you from having modesty, freedom, and every other quality, the presence of which gives to man's nature all that is its own? Remember, too, this maxim on every occasion that tempts you to vexation: "This is not a misfortune; and to bear it nobly is good fortune."

50. It is a simple but still a useful help towards contempt of death, to pass in review those persons who tenaciously stuck to life. What more did they gain than those who died early? Certainly they lie in their tombs somewhere at last, Cadicianus, Fabius, Julianus, Lepidus, and others like them, who carried out many to be buried, and then were carried out themselves. All in all, the interval between birth and death is small; consider with how much trouble, and in what sort of company and in what a feeble body this interval is laboriously passed.

Do not then consider life a thing of any value. For look to the immensity of time behind you, and to the time which is before you, another boundless space. In this infinity then what difference is there between one who lives three days and one who lives three generations? [4]

51. Always hasten by the short way: and the short way is the natural one. Say and do everything in conformity with sound reason. For such a rule frees a man from trouble and strife and artifice and ostentatious display.

V

1. Whenever in the morning you rise unwillingly, let this thought be with you: "I am rising to the work of a human being. Why then am I dissatisfied if I am about to do the things for which I was brought into the world? Or was I made to lie under the bedclothes and keep myself warm?" "But that is more pleasant," you say. Do you live then to take your pleasure, and not at all for action and exertion? Do you not see the little plants, the little birds, the ants, the spiders, the bees, working together to set in order their several parts of the universe? And are you unwilling to do the work of a human being, not eager to do what belongs to your nature? "But I must have rest also." You must; nature, however, has fixed bounds to this. She has fixed bounds too to both eating and drinking, yet you go beyond these bounds, beyond what is enough; yet in your work it is not so, and you stop short of what you can do. So you love not yourself, for if you did, you would love your nature and her will. Those who love their own trades exhaust themselves in working at them, un-

---

[4] An allusion to Homer's Nestor, who was living at the war of Troy among the third generation.

washed and without food; but you value your own nature less than the carpenter values his craft, or the dancer his dancing art, or the lover of money his money, or the vainglorious man his little glory. Such men, when they have a strong love for a thing, choose neither to eat nor to sleep until they perfect the thing they care for. But is service to society less valuable in your eyes and less worthy of your labor?

2. How easy it is to obliterate and wipe away every impression which is troublesome or unsuitable, and immediately to be in complete tranquillity.

3. Think no word and deed beneath you which is in accordance with nature; and be not diverted by some people's faultfinding, nor by their words, but if a thing is good to do or say, do not consider it unworthy of you. For these other persons have their own guiding principle and follow their own impulses. Do not regard such things, but go straight on, following your nature and the common nature; and the way of both is one.

4. I pass through the things which happen according to nature until I fall and rest, breathing out my breath into that element from which I daily draw it in, and falling upon that earth out of which my father collected his seed, and my mother her blood, and my nurse her milk; out of which for so many years I have been supplied with food and drink; which bears me when I tread on it and abuse it for my many purposes.

5. You say that you have no keenness of wit. Be it so; but there are many other things of which you cannot say that nature has not endowed you. Show those qualities then which are perfectly in your power—sincerity, gravity, patience in labor, aversion to pleasure, contentment with your lot and with little, frankness, dislike of superfluity, freedom from pettiness. Do you not see how many qualities you are immediately able to exhibit, as to which you have no excuse of natural incapacity and unfitness, and yet you still remain voluntarily below what you might be? Or are you compelled

because nature furnished you poorly to murmur, and be stingy, and to flatter, and to find fault with your poor body, and to try to please other men, and to make a great display, and to be so restless in your mind? No, by the gods; you might have been delivered from these things long ago. But if in truth you can be accused of being rather slow and dull of comprehension, you must exert yourself about this also, not neglecting it nor yet finding pleasure in your dullness.

6. One man, when he has done a service to another, is ready to set it down on his account as a favor conferred. Another is not apt to do this, but still in his own mind he thinks of the other man as his debtor, and knows what he has done. A third hardly knows what he has done, but is like a vine which has produced grapes, and asks nothing more once it has produced its proper fruit. As a horse when it has run its race, a dog when it has tracked its game, a bee when it has made its honey, so a man when he has done a good act does not call out for others to come and see, but goes on to another act, as a vine goes on to produce again the grapes in season. "Should a man then be one of these, who act thus without being conscious of it?" Yes. "But a man must observe what he is doing; for it is characteristic of the social animal to perceive that he is working in a social manner, and, then, to want his companion also to perceive it." It is true what you say, but you do not rightly understand what I have now said; for this reason you will become one of those I first mentioned, for they are misled by a certain show of reason. But if you will choose to understand the meaning of what I said, do not fear that on that account you will omit any social act.

7. A prayer of the Athenians: "Rain, rain, O dear Zeus, down on the plowed fields of the Athenians and on the plains." In truth we either ought not to pray at all, or we ought to pray in this simple and noble fashion.

8. Just as we understand when we are told that Aescu-

lapius [1] prescribed for this man horseback exercise or bathing in cold water or going without shoes; so we must understand it when we are told that nature prescribed for this man sickness or mutilation or loss or something else of the kind. For in the first case, prescribed means something like this: he prescribed this treatment for this man as a thing adapted to restore health; in the second case it means that which happens to each man is fixed for him in a manner suitable to his destiny. For this is what we mean when we say that things are suitable to us, as workmen say of squared stones in walls or pyramids, that they are suitable when they fit together into a given whole. For in everything there is one fitness. And as the universe is made up of all bodies to be the body it is, so out of all existing causes fate is made up to be the cause it is. Even ignorant people understand what I mean, for they say, "This thing befell So-and-So. This then was sent and this was appointed to him." Let us then accept our destiny, as well as the prescriptions of Aesculapius. Many, as a matter of fact, even among his prescriptions are disagreeable, but we accept them in the hope of health. Take the performing and accomplishment of the things which common nature judges to be good, as you take your health. So accept everything which happens, even though it seems disagreeable, because it leads to the health of the universe and to the prosperity and felicity of Zeus. For he would not have brought on any man what he has brought, if it were not useful for the whole. Neither does the nature of anything, whatever it may be, cause anything which is not suitable to that which is under its direction. For two reasons then you should be content with whatever happens to you; first, because it was done for you and prescribed for you, and had some reference to you from the beginning, and the most ancient causes spun it with your destiny; sec-

---

[1] Aesculapius was the god of healing. A physician or priest of the healing art might also be called an Aesculapius.

ondly, because even that which happens separately to each individual is to the power which administers the universe a cause of felicity and perfection, nay even of its own continuance. For the perfection of the whole is mutilated, if you cut off anything whatever from the network and continuity of either the parts or the causes. And you do cut something off, as far as it is in your power, when you are displeased and try to put it out of your way.

9. Be not unhappy, or discouraged, or dissatisfied, if you do not succeed in acting always by the right principles; but when you have failed, try again, and be content if most of your acts are consistent with man's nature. Love that to which you return; do not return to philosophy as if she were a schoolmaster, but behave like those who have sore eyes and apply a bit of sponge or an egg, or like another who applies a plaster or a water lotion. For thus you will not fail to obey reason, and will find rest in it. And remember that philosophy requires only the things which your nature requires. But you would have something else which is not according to nature. You may object: "Why, what is more agreeable than this I am doing?" But is not this just how pleasure deceives us? And consider whether magnanimity, freedom, simplicity, equanimity, piety, are not more agreeable. And what is more agreeable than wisdom itself, when you think of the security and the happy course of all things which result from the faculty of understanding and knowledge?

10. The world is so enveloped in veils that it has seemed to many distinguished philosophers altogether unintelligible. Nay even to the Stoics themselves it is difficult to understand. And all our views are changeable; for where is the man who never changes? Carry your thoughts then on to the objects themselves, and consider how short-lived they are and worthless, and how they may be the possession of a filthy wretch or a whore or a robber. Then turn to the morals of those who

lived with you; hardly is it possible to endure even the best of them, to say nothing of being hardly able to endure oneself. In such darkness and dirt, in so constant a flux of substance and time and motion and things moved, what there is worth being highly prized or even seriously pursued, I cannot imagine. On the other hand, it is a man's duty to comfort himself, and wait for his natural dissolution and not be vexed at the delay, but rest in these two ideas: first, that nothing will happen to me which is not in harmony with the nature of the universe; and second, that it is in my power never to act contrary to my god and divinity, for there is no man who can compel me to this.

11. About what am I now employing my soul? Frequently I must ask myself this question, and inquire, what have I now in that part of me they call the ruling principle? And whose soul have I now—that of a child, of a young man, of a feeble woman, of a tyrant, of a domestic animal, or of a wild beast?

12. What kind of things they are that the crowd thinks good, we may learn from this. If man should decide on certain things as being really good, such as prudence, temperance, justice, fortitude, he would not, after having decided on them, consent to listen to anything not in harmony with the really good. But if a man has accepted as good the things which appear good to the crowd, he will yet listen and enjoy as very appropriate the jibes of the comic writers. Thus even the crowd perceives the difference. For were it not so, a jibe against real good would not offend and would not be rejected, while, when applied to wealth, and methods for getting luxury or fame, we accept it as fitting and witty. Go on then and ask if we should value and believe those things to be good to which, when we think of them, we know the jest of the comic writer might be aptly applied—that he who has them, through pure excess of luxury has not a spot to be comfortable in.

13. I am composed of form and matter; neither of them will perish into nothingness, as neither of them came into being out of nothingness.[2] Every part of me then will be reduced by change into some other part of the universe, that again will change into another part of the universe, and so on forever. And as a result of such a change, I too now exist, and those who begot me existed, and so on forever in the other direction. For nothing prevents us from saying this, even if the universe works by definite periods of revolution.

14. Reason and the reasoning art—philosophy—are powers sufficient to themselves and for their own work. They start from a first principle which is their own, and make their way to the end which they set before them; and this is why reasonable acts are called right acts, for they proceed by the right road.

15. None of the things ought to be called a man's which do not belong to him, as man. Such things are not required of a man, nor does man's nature promise them, nor are they a means by which man's nature attains its end. Neither then does the end of man lie in such things, nor that which consummates this end, that is, the good. Besides, if any such things did belong to man, it would not be right for him to despise them and set himself against them; nor would a man deserve praise who showed that he did not want these things, nor would he who stinted himself of them be good, if indeed these things were good. But now the more of these things a man deprives himself of, or of other things like them, or, when he is deprived of any of them, the more patiently he endures the loss, to that same degree he is a better man.

16. Such as are your constant thoughts, such will be the character of your mind; for the soul is colored by the thoughts. Color it then with a continuous line of thoughts

---

[2] This is Aristotelian theory.

such as these: that wherever a man can live, there he can also live well. "But he has to live in a palace." Well then, he can live well even in a palace. Again, consider that for whatever purpose a thing has been designed, for this it has been designed, and towards this it is carried; and where the end is, there also is the advantage and the good of the thing. Now the good for a reasonable animal is society; that we are made for society I have shown already. Is it not plain that lower things exist for the sake of the higher? And the things which have life are superior to the things which have not; and of living beings the higher are those which have reason.

17. To look for the impossible is folly: and it is impossible that bad men should not do bad deeds.

18. Nothing happens to any man which he is not framed by nature to bear. The same misfortunes may happen to another, who either because he does not see what has happened or because he wants to show a great spirit, is firm and comes out unharmed. It is a shame to let ignorance and complacency be stronger than wisdom.

19. Outward things cannot touch the soul, not in the least degree; nor have they admission to the soul, nor can they turn or move the soul; but the soul turns and moves itself alone. Whatever judgments it may think proper to make, it makes for itself of the things which present themselves to it.

20. Man is the nearest thing to me, in just so far as I must do good to men and bear with them. But when men act as obstacles to my proper work, man becomes to me one of the things that are indifferent, as much so as the sun or wind or a wild beast. These, it is true, may impede my work, but they are no hindrance to my intentions and disposition, which have the power of changing and adapting themselves to conditions. For the mind converts and changes every obstacle to its activity into an aid; so that obstacles to action actually further it and help us along the road.

21. Honor what is best in the universe; this is what controls all things and directs all things. In like manner, honor also what is best in yourself; and this is akin to the other. For in yourself also, it is that which controls everything else, and your life is directed by it.

22. That which does no harm to the state does no harm to the citizen. In the case of any appearance of harm, apply this rule: "If the state is not harmed by this, neither am I hurt." But if the state is harmed, you must not be angry with him who injures the state; show him where his error is.

23. Think often of the speed with which things pass and disappear, both the things which are and the things which are being produced. For matter is like a river in a continual flow, and the activities of things are constantly shifting, and the causes work in infinite varieties; there is hardly anything which stands still. And consider this which stands near you, this boundless abyss of the past and the future in which all things disappear. Why then is he not a fool who is puffed up over such things or plagued about them, making himself miserable? For they vex him only for a time, and a very short time.

24. Think of universal substance, of which you have a very small portion; and of universal time, of which a short and indivisible moment has been assigned to you; and of the fate which is fixed by destiny, and how small a part of it you are.

25. Does another do me wrong? Let him look to it. The disposition was his and the activity was his. I have what universal nature wills me to have; and I do what my own nature wills me to do.

26. Let that part of your soul which leads and governs be undisturbed by motions of the flesh, whether of pleasure or of pain; let it not mingle with them, but let it set a wall around itself and keep those emotions in their place. But when the emotions rise up to the mind by virtue of the sympathy that naturally exists in a body which is all one, then you must not strive to resist the feeling, for it is natural: but let not your ruling part add to the feeling the opinion that it is either good or bad.

27. Live with the gods. And he does live with the gods who constantly shows them that his soul is satisfied with what is assigned to him, and that it obeys all the divinity wills—that divinity which Zeus has given every man as his guardian and guide, a portion of himself, his understanding and reason.

28. Are you irritated with one whose arm-pits smell? Are you angry with one whose mouth has a foul odor? What good will your anger do you? He has this mouth, he has these arm-pits. Such emanations must come from such things. "But the man has reason," you will say, "and he could, if he took pains, discover wherein he offends." I wish you well of your discovery. Now you too have reason; by your rational faculty, stir up his rational faculty; show him his fault, admonish him. For if he listens, you will cure him, and have no need of anger —you are not a ranter or a whore.

29. As you intend to live hereafter, it is in your power to live here. But if men do not permit you, then slip away out of life, yet as if you felt it no harm. The house is smoky, and I leave it. Why do you call this trouble? But as long as nothing of the kind drives me out, I stay, I am free, and no man shall hinder me from doing what I choose; and I choose to do what befits the nature of a rational and social animal.

30. The mind of the universe is social. Accordingly it has made inferior things for the sake of superior, and has tied the superior to one another. You see how it has subordinated, co-ordinated, and assigned to each its proper lot, and brought together into concord with one another the things which are best.

31. How have you behaved hitherto towards the gods, your parents, brothers, children, teachers, towards those who looked after your infancy, your friends, kinsfolk, slaves?

Consider if you have hitherto behaved to them all in such a way that it may be said of you:

 Never has he wronged a man in deed or word.[3]

And call to recollection how many things you have experienced, and how many things you have endured; and how the history of your life is now complete and your service ended; and how many beautiful things you have seen: and how many pleasures and pains you have despised; and how many things called honors you have spurned; and to how many ill-minded folks you have shown a kind disposition.

 32. Why do unskilled and ignorant souls confound those who have skill and wisdom? But what soul has skill and wisdom? The soul which knows beginning and end, and knows the reason which pervades all substance and which through all eternity in periodic cycles administers the universe.

 33. Soon, very soon, you will be ashes or a skeleton, a name or not even a name; and what is name but sound and echo? And the things much valued in life are empty and rotten and trifling, like little dogs biting one another, and like children quarreling, laughing, and then straightway weeping. But fidelity and modesty and justice and truth are fled

 Up to Olympus from the wide-spread earth.[4]

What then is there now to detain you here, if the objects of sense are changeable and never stand still, and our organs of perception are dull and easily receive false impressions, and the poor soul itself is an exhalation from the blood. But wide repute amidst such a world as this is an empty thing. Why then do you not wait in tranquillity for your end, whether that is extinction or removal to another state? And until that time comes, what is your duty? Why, what else but to venerate the gods and bless them, and do good to men,

---

[3] Homer, *Odyssey*. See Classics Club edition, p. 54.

[4] Hesiod, *Works and Days*, V, 197.

and practice tolerance and self-restraint; but as to whatever lies beyond the confines of your poor flesh and breath, to remember that it is neither yours nor in your power.

34. You can pass your life in a calm flow of happiness, if you can take the right way, and think and act in the right way. The two things common both to the soul of God and to the soul of man, and to the soul of every rational being, are not to be hindered in their purpose by another; and to hold as good the disposition to justice and the practice of it, and in this to let your desire find its satisfaction.

35. If the fault is neither my own nor the result of my own badness, and the common weal is not hurt, why trouble about it? What hurt is it to the common weal?

36. Do not be carried away rashly by the appearance of things. Help everyone according to your ability and their fitness. If they have suffered a loss in matters indifferent, do not imagine it to be a calamity, for that is a bad habit; but as the old man, when he went away, asked for his foster-child's top, remembering that it was a top, so do you in this case also.

When you are declaiming on the rostra, have you forgotten, man, what these things really are? "Yes, but they are matters of great importance to the people." Will you too then be made a fool for these things? Wheresoever stranded, I can at any time become a man of fortune, for fortune means that a man has found for himself a happy lot; and a happy lot is a good disposition of the soul, good impulses, good actions.

VI

1. The substance of the universe is obedient and pliable, and the reason which governs it has itself no cause for doing evil, for it has no malice, nor does it do evil to anything, nor

is anything harmed by it. But all things are made and perfected through this reason.

2. Care not whether you are cold or warm, if you are doing
your duty; or whether you are weary or satisfied with sleep;
or whether ill-spoken of or praised, or whether dying or
doing anything else; for dying is one of the acts of life; it is
enough in this act also to do well what there is to do (VI, 28).

3. Look beneath the surface. Let neither the peculiar quality of anything nor its value escape you.

4. All existing things change quickly; and they will either
be reduced to vapor, if indeed all substance is one, or they
will be dispersed.

5. The reason which governs knows what its own nature
is, and what it does, and on what material it works.

6. The best way of avenging yourself is not to become
like the wrongdoer.

7. Take pleasure and comfort in one thing, in passing from
one social act to another social act, thinking of God.

8. The ruling mind rouses and turns itself, and while it
makes itself what it is and what it wills to be, it also makes
everything that happens appear to be what it wills it shall be.

9. In accord with the nature of the universe every single
thing takes place; certainly it is not according to any other
nature that they are brought to pass, whether a nature that
outwardly envelopes this, or a nature that is included within
this nature, or a nature outside and independent of this (XI, 1;
VI, 40; VIII, 5).

10. The universe is either a confusion, an intermingling of
atoms, and a scattering; or it is unity and order and providence. If it is the former, why do I wish to tarry amid such
a haphazard confusion and disorder? Why do I care about
anything but how I may at last become earth? And why do
I trouble myself, for my elements will be scattered, whatever
I do. But if the other supposition is true, I revere, I stand firm,
and I trust in him who governs (IV, 27).

11. When circumstances have compelled you to be a little disturbed, return to yourself quickly, and do not continue out of tune longer than the compulsion lasts; for you will be more the master of the harmony by continually returning to it.

12. Suppose you had a stepmother and a mother at the same time, you would be dutiful to your stepmother, but still you would constantly return to your mother. Let the court and philosophy now be to you as stepmother and mother; return to philosophy frequently and repose in her, for through her your life in the court becomes tolerable, and you are tolerable to the court.

13. When we have meat before us and other viands, we still have the impression that this is but the dead body of a fish, and this but the dead body of a bird or of a pig; and again, that this Falernian wine is only a little grape juice, and this purple robe some sheep's wool dyed with the blood of a shellfish. Such then are our impressions, and they reach to the things themselves and penetrate them; so we see what kind of things they are. In just the same way ought we to act all through life, and where things appear most worthy of our liking, we should lay them bare and look at their worthlessness and strip them of all the words by which they were exalted. For outward show is a wonderful perverter of reason, and when you are most sure that the things you are busy about are worth your pains, it is then that it cheats you most. Consider what Crates says even of Xenocrates.

14. Most things which the multitude admire are connected with objects of the most general kind, things formed by bare cohesion, or natural organisms, such as stones, wood, fig trees, vines, olives. But men, who are a little more rational, admire things united by some living principle, such as flocks and herds. Men who are still more instructed admire things inspired by a universal soul, but rational, such as a soul skilled in some art, or expert in some other way, or rational simply as possessing a number of slaves.[1] But he who values a rational soul, that is, universal and framed for political life, regards nothing but this. Above all else he keeps his own soul in a condition and in an activity right for reason and social life, and he co-operates to this end with men of the same kind as himself.

15. Some things are pressing into existence and others are hurrying out of it; and of that which is coming into existence a part is already extinguished. Motion and change are continually renewing the world, just as the uninterrupted course of time is always renewing the infinite duration of ages. In this flowing stream, on which there is no abiding, what is there of the things that hasten by on which a man would set a high price? It would be as if a man should fall in love with a sparrow flying by, that has already passed out of sight. Every man's life is but an exhalation of the blood and a little breathing of the air. For like drawing in the air and giving it back, which we do every moment, the whole quickening power, received at birth, is now given back to the element whence it came.

16. Neither is transpiration, as in plants, a thing to be valued, nor respiration, as in tame animals and wild beasts, nor impressions from the appearance of things, nor subjection to desire, like a puppet on strings, nor crowding in herds, nor getting nourishment from food; this last is merely an act of separating and parting with the useless part of our food. What then is worth your esteem? To be greeted with clapping of hands? No. Neither should we value the clapping of tongues, for the praise of the multitude is a clapping of tongues. Suppose then that you have dispensed with the worthless thing called fame, what remains that is worth having? This, in my opinion, to move yourself and govern your-

---

[1] The Roman aristocrat gratified his tastes by "collecting" and maintaining an establishment of highly gifted slaves—scribes, philosophers, and skilled craftsmen.

self in harmony with your proper nature, which is the end of all occupations and all arts. For the aim of every art is right adaptation of the product to the end for which it is produced. The vine-planter who looks after his vines and the trainer of horses and dogs labor for this end. The education and teaching of youth aim also at something. In this is the value of the education and the teaching. And if this is achieved, you will not seek anything else. Will you go on desiring many other things too? Then you will be neither free, nor sufficient for your own happiness, nor clear of passion. For of necessity you must be envious, jealous, and suspicious of those who can take away the things valued by you and plot against those who have them. Of necessity a man must be always in a state of perturbation who wants any of these things; besides, he must often find fault with the gods. But to reverence and honor your own mind will make you content with yourself, and serviceable to society, and at peace with the gods, praising all they give and have ordained.

17. Above, below, all around are the movements of the elements. But the motion of virtue is not theirs: it is something more divine; advancing by a way hardly observed, it goes happily on its road.

18. How strangely men act! They will not praise those who are living at the same time with themselves; but to be themselves praised by posterity, by persons they have never seen and never will see, this they set a high value on. But it is much the same as if you should grieve because those who lived before you did not praise you.

19. Because a thing is difficult for you to do do not think it is impossible for any man; but whatever is possible for any man to do and right for his nature, think that you can achieve it too.

20. Suppose a man scratches you with his nails in gymnastic exercises and hits your head and wounds it. We show no signs of vexation, nor are we offended, nor do we suspect him afterwards as a treacherous fellow; we are on our guard against him, but not as an enemy, nor yet with suspicion, but we quietly get out of his way. Let your behavior be like this in all spheres of life; let us overlook many things in those who are only like antagonists in the gymnasium. For it is in our power, as I said, to get out of their way, and to feel no suspicion or hatred.

21. If any man can convince and show me that I do not think or act right, I will gladly change; for I seek truth, by which no man was ever injured. But he is injured who abides in his error and ignorance.

22. I do my duty. Other things do not trouble me, for they are either things without life, or things without reason, or things that have wandered and know not the way.

23. As for the animals which have no reason and, generally, all things and objects, since you have reason and they have none, use them in a generous and considerate spirit. Treat human beings, since they have reason, in a social spirit. And on all occasions call on the gods, and do not worry yourself over the length of time you shall spend doing this; even three hours so spent are well-spent.

24. Alexander the Macedonian and his groom were brought by death to the same state; for either they were received back into the same creative principles of the universe, or they were alike dispersed among the atoms.

25. Consider how many things in the same indivisible time take place in each of us, things affecting the body and things affecting the soul; then you will not wonder that many more things, or rather all things which come into existence in the one and the all which we call the Cosmos exist in it at the same time.

26. If any man should ask you how to spell the name Antoninus, would you shout each letter angrily? What then, if he grows angry, will you be angry too? Or will you quietly tell him the letters? So in this life also remember that each duty is made up of certain parts. These it is your duty to ob-serve and, without showing impatience or anger toward those who are angry with you, go on your way and finish that which is set before you.

27. How cruel it is not to allow men to strive for the things which seem to them suitable to their natures and profitable! Yet in a way you are not allowing them to do this, when you are vexed because they do wrong. For they are certainly moved to do things they suppose to be suitable to their na-tures and profitable to them. "But it is not so." Teach them then, and show them without being angry.

28. Death is a cessation of impressions through the senses, and of pulling of the strings which move our appetites, and of discursive movements of our thoughts, and of service to the flesh.

29. It is a shame when the soul is first to give way in this life, and the body does not give way.

30. Take care that you turn not into a Caesar, that you are not dyed with that dye; for such things happen. Keep your-self simple, good, pure, serious, free from affectation, a friend of justice, a worshiper of the gods, kind, affectionate, strenu-ous in all right acts. Strive to advance toward what philosophy tried to make you. Reverence the gods, and help men. Life is short. There is only one fruit of this earthly life, a pious disposition and social acts. Do everything as a disciple of Antoninus. Remember his constancy in rational behavior, his even temper in all things, his piety, and the serenity of his countenance, his sweetness, his disregard of empty fame, and his effort to understand things; how he would never let any-thing pass without having first carefully examined it and clearly understood it; how he bore with those who blamed him unjustly without blaming them in return; how he did nothing in a hurry; how he refused to listen to calumnies; how exact an examiner of manners and actions he was, not given to reproach people, nor timid, nor suspicious, nor

pedantic; with how little he was satisfied in the way of lodg-
ing, bed, dress, food, servants; how laborious and patient;
how he was able because of his sparing diet to hold out to
evening, not even requiring to relieve himself by evacuations
except at the usual hour; his firmness and steadiness in friendship; how he tolerated freedom of speech in those who opposed his opinions; the pleasure he had when any man showed
him anything better; and how religious he was without super-
stition. Imitate all this and you may have as good a conscience
as he had when your last hour comes.

31. Return to your sober senses and recall yourself. When
you have roused yourself from sleep and perceived that they
were only dreams which troubled you, then in your waking
hours look at the things about you as you looked at the
dreams.

32. I consist of a little body and a soul. Now to this little
body all things are morally indifferent, for it is not able to
perceive differences. But to the understanding all things are
indifferent, except its own activities; and these are all in its
power; of these, however, only its present acts matter; for
both the future and the past activities of the mind are for
the present indifferent.

33. Neither the labor of the hand nor of the foot is contrary to nature, so long as the foot does a foot's work and
the hand a hand's. Then neither for man as man is labor
contrary to nature, so long as he does the things of a man.
And if the labor is not contrary to his nature, neither is it an
evil to him.

34. How many pleasures have been enjoyed by robbers,
patricides, tyrants!

35. Do you not see how craftsmen accommodate themselves up to a certain point to those who are novices in their
craft, yet hold fast to the principles of their art and refuse to
depart from them? Is it not strange that an architect or a
physician should have more respect for the principles of his

art than man for his own reason, which he shares with the gods?

36. Asia and Europe are but corners of the universe; all the sea a drop in the universe; Athos a little clod of the universe; the present time a point in eternity. All things are small, changeable, perishable. All things come from that universal ruling power either directly or as indirect consequence. Accordingly the lion's gaping jaws, and all harmful things like thorns or mud, are the outcome of the grand and beautiful. Do not imagine they are different in kind from that which you revere, but form a just opinion of the source of all.

37. He who has seen the present age has seen all, both all that has taken place from eternity and all that will be through time without end; for all things are of one kind and of one form.

38. Consider frequently the connection of all things in the universe and their relation to one another. For things are somehow implicated with one another, and all in a way friendly to one another; for one thing follows in order after another, and this is by virtue of their active movement and mutual agreement and the unity of their substance.

39. Adapt yourself to the things among which your lot has been cast and to the men among whom you have your portion; love them, and do it truly, sincerely.

40. Every instrument, tool, vessel that does what it is made for is good, though he who made it is not there. But when things are formed by nature, there is within them and abides in them the power which made them; wherefore the more should you reverence this power, and think that, if you live and act according to its will, everything in you is in accord with intelligence. Thus also in the universe the things which belong to it are in accord with intelligence.

41. If of the things not within your power you suppose some to be good for you and others evil, it must be that, when one of the bad things befalls you or the loss of one of the

good things, you still blame the gods, and hate men too, whoever are the cause of the misfortune or the loss, or are sus-
pected of being probably the cause; and we do much injustice,
because we do not regard these things as indifferent. But if
we think that only the things which are in our power are
good or bad, we have no reason either for finding fault with
God or taking a hostile attitude to man.

42. We are all working together to one end, some with
knowledge and design, others without knowing what they
do; like men asleep, of whom Heraclitus I think it is says that
they too are laborers and co-operators in what goes on in the
universe. But men co-operate after different fashions; even
those who find fault with what happens are co-operating
abundantly; for the universe has need even of such men as
these. It remains for you to understand among what kind of
workmen you station yourself; for he who rules all things
will certainly make a right use of you, and receive you among
some group of co-operators and those whose labors conduce
to the one end. But do not play such a part as the mean and
ridiculous verse in the play, which Chrysippus speaks of.

43. Does the sun attempt to do the work of the rain, or
Aesculapius the work of Ceres? And how is it with the stars,
are they not different and yet they work together to the
same end?

44. If the gods have decreed about me and about the things
which must happen to me, they have decreed well, for it is
absurd to imagine a deity without forethought; and as for
doing me harm, why should they desire that? What advantage would result from it to them or to the whole, which
is the special object of their providence? But if they have
issued no decree about me individually, they have certainly
ordained things for the whole at least, and the things which
happen by way of result in the general arrangement I ought to
accept with pleasure and be content with them. But if the
gods decide nothing—which is wicked to believe—let us

neither sacrifice nor pray nor swear by them nor do anything else we did when we believed the gods were present and lived with us. If then the gods have no care of the things which concern us, I can take care of myself, and I can inquire into what is useful; and to every man that is useful which is in harmony with his constitution and nature. My nature is rational and social; and my city and country, so far as I am Antoninus, is Rome, and so far as I am a man, is the world. Whatever then is of use to these societies is of use to me.

45. Whatever happens to the individual is for the interest of the universal; this should be sufficient. But further, you will observe this general truth, that whatever is profitable to any man is profitable also to other men. Take the word profitable here in the common sense as applying to things of the middle sort (neither good nor bad).

46. Even as it happens to you in the theater and such places that the continual sight of the same things or the monotony makes the show wearisome, so it is all through life; for everything above and below is the same and comes from the same. How long then to the end?

47. Think continually that all kinds of men of all kinds of professions and of all nations are dead, and let your thoughts come down even to Philistion and Phoebus and Origanion. Now turn your thoughts to other generations. We too must remove to that place where so many great orators, so many noble philosophers, Heraclitus, Pythagoras, Socrates, so many heroes of former days, and so many generals after them, and tyrants, have gone; and in their train, Eudoxus, Hipparchus, Archimedes,[2] and other men of keen natural talents, great minds, great lovers of labor, versatile, confident, mockers, even of the perishable and ephemeral life of man, such as

---

[2] Eudoxus, Hipparchus, and Archimedes were mathematicians, astronomers, and physicists who carried further the development of Greek science from the fourth to the second century before Christ.

Menippus and others like him. Consider of all these that they have long been dust. What harm is this to them, or what to those whose names are quite unknown? Only one thing here is worth much, to pass your life in truth and justice, and show benevolence even to liars and unjust men.

48. When you wish to enjoy yourself, think of the virtues of those who live with you; the activity, for instance, of one, the modesty of another, the liberality of a third, and some other good quality of a fourth. For nothing is so cheering as examples of the virtues exhibited in the characters of those who live with us, when they appear in all possible abundance. Wherefore we must keep them before us.

49. Are you rebellious because you weigh so many pounds less than three hundred? Be not rebellious then that you must live only so many years and not more; for as you are satisfied with the amount of substance which has been assigned you, so be content with the time.

50. Let us try to persuade men to behave reasonably. But for yourself, act even against their will, when the law of justice directs you that way. If, however, anyone forcibly obstructs you, resign yourself to contentment and tranquillity; at the same time, make use of his obstruction to exercise some other virtue. Remember that you made your attempt conditionally, that you did not expect to do the impossible. What then did you expect? To make the attempt as you have done. And you have attained your object, even if the things which you were striving to reach are not accomplished.

51. The lover of fame relies on other men's activities for his own good; the lover of pleasure on his sensations; but the man of understanding knows that his own acts are his good.

52. It is in our power to refrain from any opinion about things and not to be disturbed in our souls; for things in themselves have no natural power to force our judgments.

53. Accustom yourself to listen carefully to another man's words, and as much as possible be in the speaker's mind.

54. That which is not good for the swarm, is not good for the single bee.

55. If the sailors abused the helmsman or the sick the doctor, would they listen to anybody else and how then could the helmsman ensure the safety of those in the ship or the doctor the health of his patients?

56. How many of the people who came into the world with me are already gone out of it!

57. Honey tastes bitter to the jaundiced and water is horrible to a person with rabies; and a ball is a fine thing to little children. Why then am I angry with anyone? Do you think that a false opinion has less power than bile in the jaundiced or poison in one who is bitten by a mad dog?

58. No man can hinder you from living according to the reason of your own nature; nothing will happen to you contrary to the reason of universal nature.

59. What kind of people are those whom men strive to please, and for what objects, and by what kind of acts? How soon will time cover all things, and how many has it covered already!

VII

1. What is evil? It is something you have often seen. And whatever happens, keep this in mind, that it is something you have seen again and again. Everywhere up and down you will find the same things with which histories are filled, in the olden times, in medieval times, and today, repeating themselves in our cities and homes. There is nothing new; all things are familiar and quickly over.

2. How can our opinions cool down unless the impressions on which they rest are obliterated? But it is in your power continuously to fan your thoughts into a flame. I can have the opinion about anything which I ought to have. If I can, why then am I disturbed? The things which lie outside my mind need have no relation at all to my mind. Be sure of this and you stand erect. It is in your power to restore yourself to life. Look at things again as you once looked at them, for this will bring you new life.

3. A piece of pageantry, a stage play, flocking sheep and herding cows, exercise with spears, bones cast to puppies, crusts tossed into fishponds, the laboring of ants over their burdens, the running about of frightened little mice, puppets dancing on strings—all are the same. Your duty in the midst of such things is to show good humor and not a proud air; and to understand that a man is worth just as much as the things about which he busies himself.

4. In conversation you should attend to what is being said, and in action you should observe what is happening. In the first, you should see immediately the end intended, and in the second, watch carefully for the meaning.

5. Is my understanding sufficient for this work or not? If sufficient, I use it for the work as an instrument given me by universal nature. If it is not sufficient, then either I retire from the work and give place to one who can do it better, unless there is some reason why I ought not to do so; or else I do it as well as I can, allying myself with a man who with the aid of my intelligence can do what it wanted and what is useful for the general good. For whatsoever I can do either alone or with another ought to be directed only toward that which is useful and advantageous to society.

6. How many who were once celebrated by fame have now been lost in oblivion, and how many who once celebrated the fame of others have long been dead!

7. Be not ashamed to take help; your business is to do your duty as a soldier does in an assault on a town. Suppose you are

lame and cannot mount the battlements alone: with the help of another you can reach them.

8. Let not the future disturb you. You will face it with the same reason which you now use for present things.

9. All parts of the universe are interwoven with one another, and the bond is sacred. Nothing is unconnected with some other thing. For all things have been co-ordinated and combined to form the same universe. There is one universe made up of everything, and one God who pervades everything, and one substance, one law, one common reason in all intelligent animals, and one truth; perchance indeed there is one perfection for all beings of the same stock, who participate in the same reason.

10. Everything material soon disappears into the sum of being; and every form is soon taken back into the universal reason; and the memory of everything is soon overwhelmed in time.

11. To a rational being the act that is according to nature is according to reason.

12. Stand erect, or be helped to stand erect (III, 5).

13. As it is with members of unified bodies, so it is with rational beings that exist separate, but are designed for co-operation. You will realize this more if you say often to yourself: "I am a member of a system of rational beings." But if you say only you are a part, you do not yet love mankind from your heart; doing good does not yet delight you for its own sake; you still do it merely as an act of politeness, not yet as doing good to yourself.

14. Let accidents happen as they will on the parts that feel the injury. And parts that have felt may complain, if they choose. But I, unless I think that the accident is an evil, am not injured. And it is in my power not to think so.

15. Whatever anyone else does or says, my duty is to be good; just as gold, or an emerald, or purple always says:

"Whatever anyone else does or says, I must be an emerald and keep my color."

16. The ruling mind does not disturb itself; I mean, does not frighten itself or cause itself pain. If anyone else can frighten or pain it, let him do so. The mind itself of its own judgment will not turn to such ways. Let the body take care, if it can, that it suffers nothing, but let it speak, if it suffers. But the soul, the seat of fear and pain, has full power to form an opinion about these things and need suffer nothing, unless at times it deviates into such an opinion. The mind in itself wants nothing, unless it creates a want for itself; therefore it is both free from perturbation and unimpeded, if it does not perturb and impede itself.

17. Happiness is a good divinity, or a good thing. What then are you doing here, O imagination? Go away, I intreat you by the gods, as you did come, for I want you not. But you are come as you have been used to do. I am not angry with you; only go away.

18. Is anyone afraid of change? Why, what can be done without change? What is more pleasing or more suitable to universal nature? Can you take a bath unless the wood undergoes a change? Can you be nourished, unless your food undergoes a change? Can anything else useful be accomplished without change? Do you not then see that for yourself also change is the same, and equally necessary for the universal nature?

19. Through the universal substance as through a furious torrent all bodies are carried, while by their nature united with and co-operating with the whole, as the parts of your body do with one another. How many a Chrysippus, how many a Socrates, how many an Epictetus has time already swallowed up? Apply this same thought to every man and thing (v, 23; vi, 15).

20. One thing only troubles me, that I may do something

which the nature of man forbids, or in the way it forbids, or at a forbidden time.

21. Soon you will have forgotten all things; and soon all things will have forgotten you.

22. It is peculiar to man to love even those who do him wrong. This happens, if when they do wrong you remember they are kinsmen, and wrong you through ignorance and unintentionally, and soon both of you will die; above all, that the wrongdoer has done you no harm, for he has not made your mind worse than it was before.

23. The universal nature out of the universal substance, as if it were wax, now molds a horse; when it has broken this up, it uses the material for a tree, then for a man, then for something else; and each of these things lasts for a very short time. But it is no hardship for the vessel to be broken up, as there was none for it to be fastened together (VIII, 50).

24. A scowling look is quite unnatural. When one often assumes it, the result is that all one's comeliness fades and at last is so completely extinguished that it cannot again be lighted up at all. Look to conclude from this that scowls are contrary to reason. For if all knowledge of doing wrong is lost, what reason is there for living any longer?

25. Nature, that governs the whole, will soon change all things which you see, and out of their substance will make other things, and again other things from the substance of them, in order that the world may be ever new (XII, 23).

26. When a man has done you any wrong, immediately consider with what notions of good and evil he acted in doing wrong. When you have seen this, you will pity him and will neither wonder nor be angry. For either you think the same thing to be good that he does or something of the same kind; it is your duty then to pardon him; but if you do not hold the same notions of good or evil, you will more readily be charitable to him who is in error.

27. Think less of what you have not than of what you have;

of the things you have select the best; then reflect how eagerly you would have labored for them, if you had them not. At the same time, however, take care you do not through being so pleased with them accustom yourself to so overvalue them as to be distressed if ever you should lose them.

28. Retire into yourself. The nature of the rational principle that rules us is to be content with itself when it does what is just, and so secures tranquillity.

29. Subdue the imagination. Check the drives of impulse. Confine your care to the present. Understand well what happens to you and to others. Divide and distribute every object between its causal and its material elements. Think of your last hour. Let the harm done by another man stay where the harm was done (VIII, 29).

30. Pay attention to what is being said. Let your understanding keep pace with what is being done and the causes of it (VII, 4).

31. Adorn yourself with simplicity and modesty and with indifference towards the things which are neither good nor bad. Love mankind. Follow God. The poet says that law rules all. It is enough to remember that law rules all.

32. As for death, whether it is a dispersion, or a dissolution into atoms, or annihilation, it is either extinction or change.

33. As for pain, a pain that is intolerable carries us off; but that which lasts a long time is bearable; the mind maintains its own tranquillity by retiring into itself and the ruling faculty is not injured. As for the parts which are hurt by the pain, let them, if they can, give their opinion of it.

34. As for fame, look at the minds of those who seek fame, observe what they are, and what kind of things they avoid, and what kind of things they pursue. And consider that as one heap of sand piled on another hides the sand of the first, so in life an earlier exploit is soon covered by those which come after.

35. A saying of Plato: [1] " 'A man with a lofty mind, who takes a view of all time and all substance, can he, do you suppose, regard human life as anything great?' 'Not possibly.' 'Such a man will think, too, that death is no evil.' 'Certainly not.' "

36. From Antisthenes: "It is a royal thing to do good and to be abused."

37. "To have a countenance obedient, regulated and composed as the mind commands, and a mind not regulated and composed by itself is a base thing."

38. It is not right to vex ourselves at things,
    For they care nought about us.[2]

39. To the immortal gods and us give joy.

40. Life must be reaped like the ripe ears of corn:
    One man is born; another dies.[3]

41. If gods care not for me and for my children,
    There is a reason for it.

42. For the good is with me, and the just.[4]

43. "No joining with others in their wailing, no violent emotion."

44. From Plato: [5] "But I would make this man a sufficient answer, which is this: 'You are wrong if you think a man who is good for anything at all should count over the hazards of life or death, and should not rather look to this only in all he does, whether what he is doing is just or unjust, and the work of a good or a bad man.'

45. "For this, men of Athens, is the truth; wherever a man has taken his stand, thinking it the best place for him, or has

---

[1] Plato, *Republic*, VI. See Classics Club edition, p. 371. There follows a collection of sayings, maxims, and bits of verse (not in every case correctly quoted or complete) which Marcus Aurelius thought the wise man should frequently call to mind.

[2] From the *Bellerophon* of Euripides.

[3] From *Hypsipyle* of Euripides.

[4] From the *Acharnians* of Aristophanes.

[5] From the *Apology*. See Classics Club edition, pp. 51, 53.

been stationed by his commander, there in my opinion he ought to stay and abide the hazard, reckoning nothing, either death or anything else, worse than the baseness of deserting his post." [6]

46. "But my good friend, consider whether nobility and goodness are not something different from saving and being saved; for we must not allow that they consist of living such or such a time, at least for one who is really a man; nor should he be fond of life, but entrusting it to God, believing what the women say, that no man can escape his destiny; and he should next inquire how best he may live the time he has to live." [7]

47. Follow the courses of the stars, as if you were going along with them; and consider constantly the changes of the elements into one another; for such thoughts purge away the filth of this earthly life.

48. This is a fine saying of Plato: [8] That he who discourses of men should look at earthly things as if he viewed them from some higher place; should look at them in their assemblies, armies, labors on the soil, their marriages, treaties, births and deaths, the noise of the courts of justice, the desert places, the various nations of barbarians, the feasts, lamentations, markets, the mixture of all things and orderly combination of contraries.

49. Consider the past; the great shifts in political supremacy. You may foresee also the things which will be. For they will certainly keep the same form; they cannot possibly deviate from the order in which they take place now. Accordingly, to have contemplated human life for forty years is the same as to have contemplated it for ten thousand years. For what more will you see?

50. What has grown from the earth goes back to the earth,

---

[6] From the *Apology*. See Classics Club edition, pp. 51, 53.

[7] From the *Gorgias* of Plato.

[8] It is not in the extant writings of Plato.

> But what has sprung from heavenly seed,
> Back to the heavenly realms returns.[9]

This means either a dissolution of intertwining atoms, or a similar dispersion of unfeeling elements.

51. With food and drinks and cunning magic arts
Turning the channel's course to 'scape from death.[10]
The breeze which heaven has sent
We must endure, and toil without complaining.

52. Another may be more expert in thwarting his opponent; but he is not more social, nor more modest, nor better disciplined to meet all that happens, nor more considerate to the faults of his neighbors.

53. Where every act must be performed in accord with the reason which is common to gods and men, we have nothing to fear; when we can profit by activity which is successful and in harmony with our nature, we need suspect no harm.

54. Everywhere and at all times it is in your power to accept reverently your present condition, to behave justly to those about you, and to exert your skill to control your thoughts, that nothing shall steal into them without being well examined.

55. Look not around to discover other men's motives, but look straight to what nature leads you, both universal nature, through the things that befall you, and your own nature, through the acts you are compelled to do. Every being must do what its constitution requires, and all other things have been constituted to serve rational beings, just as among irrational things the inferior exists for the sake of the superior, and things with reason exist for the sake of one another.

The primary principle then in man's constitution is the social. The second is not to yield to the temptations of the body; for it is the peculiar mark of the rational and intelli-

---

[9] From the *Chrysippus* of Euripides.
[10] The first two lines are from the *Suppliants* of Euripides.

gent agent to set its own bounds and never to be overpowered by the activity either of the senses or the appetites, for both are animal. But the intelligent agent claims superiority and does not permit itself to be overpowered by the others. With good reason, for it is formed by nature to make use of all the rest. The third mark of a rational constitution is freedom from error and deception. Let your mind hold fast to these things and go straight on, and it has what is its own.

56. Consider yourself to be dead, and to have completed your life up to the present time; then live out according to nature the remainder which is allowed you.

57. Love only that which happens to you and is woven with the thread of your destiny. For what is more suited to your needs?

58. Whatever happens, keep before your eyes those who have borne the same things, how they were vexed and grieved and full of complaining. And now where are they? Nowhere. Then why do you choose to act in the same way? Why do you not leave these agitations, which are foreign to your nature, to those who cause them or are moved by them? Why are you not wholly intent on making the right use of your misfortunes? For if you will use them well, they will be a material for you to work on. Only attend to yourself, and resolve to be a good man in every act, remembering that that on which the act is based is in itself indifferent.

59. Dig within. Within is the fountain of good, and it will ever bubble up, if you will ever dig.

60. The body ought to be controlled and to avoid contortion in motion or attitude. For what the mind shows in the face by maintaining the expression of intelligence and propriety, that ought to be required in the whole body also. But all these things should be observed without affectation.

61. Life is more like wrestling than dancing, in that it should stand ready and firm to meet onsets, however unexpected.

62. Always be sure whose approbation it is you wish to secure, and what ruling principles they have. Then you will neither blame those who offend involuntarily, nor will you want their approbation, if you look to the sources of their opinions and appetites.

63. No soul, says the philosopher, voluntarily deprives itself of truth, or of justice, temperance, benevolence, or of any other good thing. It is most necessary to bear this constantly in mind, for thus you will be more gentle towards all.

64. In every pain remind yourself that there is no dishonor in it, nor does it impair your governing intelligence; it does not damage it either in its rational or social aspects. Indeed in the case of most pains let this remark of Epicurus aid you, that pain is neither intolerable nor everlasting, if you bear in mind that it has its limits, and if you add nothing to it in imagination; and remember this too, that we do not perceive that many things which are disagreeable to us are the same as pain, such as excessive drowsiness, and being feverish, and having no appetite. When you are discontented about any of these things, say to yourself that you are yielding to pain.

65. Take care not to feel toward the inhuman, as human beings too often feel toward each other.

66. How do we know that Telauges was not superior in character to Socrates? For it is not enough that Socrates died a more noble death, and disputed more skillfully with the sophists, and spent the night in the cold with more endurance, and that when he was bid to arrest Leon of Salamis, he considered it more noble to refuse, and that he walked in a swaggering way in the streets—though as to this one fact, one doubts if it was true. But we ought to inquire what kind of a soul it was that Socrates possessed, and if he was able to be content with being just towards men and reverent towards the gods, neither idly vexed on account of men's villainy, nor yet making himself a slave to any man's ignorance, nor re-

ceiving as strange anything that fell to his share, nor enduring it as intolerable, nor allowing his understanding to be affected by the ills of the miserable flesh.

67. Nature has so mingled the intelligence with the composition of the body, as to have allowed you the power of self-determination and of bringing under subjection all that is your own. It is very possible to be godlike and to be recognized as such by no one. Always bear this in mind; and also that very little indeed is necessary for a happy life. And because you have despaired of becoming a dialectician and skilled in the knowledge of nature, do not for this reason renounce the hope of being both free and modest and social and obedient to God.

68. It is in your power to live free from all compulsion and in the greatest tranquillity of mind, even if all the world cry out against you as much as they choose, and even if wild beasts tear you limb from limb. For what hinders the mind, in the midst of all this, from being tranquil and truly judging all surrounding things, and readily using the material presented to it, so that the judgment may say to the thing which falls under its observation: This you are in reality, though in the opinion of men you may appear to be of a different kind; and use may say to opportunity: You are the thing I was seeking; for whatever presents itself is material for virtue, both rational and political, and in a word, for the exercise of art, which belongs to man or God. Everything which happens has a relationship either to God or man, and is neither new nor difficult to handle, but familiar and fit matter to work on.

69. The perfection of moral character consists in this, in passing every day as the last, and in being neither violently excited nor torpid nor hypocritical.

70. The immortal gods are not vexed because they must tolerate men as they are and so many of them bad; still they take care of them in all ways. But you, who are destined to

end so soon, are you weary of enduring the bad, and this too when you are one of them?

71. It is a ridiculous thing for a man not to fly from his own wickedness, which is indeed possible, but to fly from other men's wickedness, which is impossible.

72. Whatever the rational and social faculty finds to be neither reasonable nor social, it correctly judges to be inferior to itself.

73. When you have done a good act and another has received it, why do you still want something more, as fools do, either to have the credit for a good act or the recompense?

74. No one tires of receiving what is useful. But it is useful to act according to nature. Do not then tire of receiving what is useful by doing what is useful to others.

75. The nature of the All moved to make a world of order. Either everything that takes place follows by way of consequence or the movements are governed by no rational principle. If you remember this, it will make you more tranquil in many things (ix, 21; vi, 44).

VIII

1. This may help to keep you from vainglory: that you cannot claim to have lived the whole of your life, or even from your youth upward, as a philosopher; but both to others and to yourself it is plain that you are far from philosophy. You have fallen into confusion then, so that it is no longer easy for you to get the reputation of a philosopher. If then you have truly seen what the facts are, never mind what others think of you, and be content to live the rest of your life as nature wills. Observe then what it wills, and let nothing else distract you; for you have experienced many wanderings without having found happiness anywhere. Where is happiness then? In doing what man's nature requires. How then shall a man do this? By having principles from which come his affections and his acts. What principles? Those which relate to good and bad: the belief that there is nothing good for man which does not make him just, temperate, manly, free; and that there is nothing bad which does not produce opposite results.

2. Of every action ask yourself, "What does this mean to me? Shall I repent it?" A little time and I am dead, and all is gone. What more do I seek, if what I am now doing is the work of an intelligent and social being, and one who is under the same law with God?

3. Alexander and Caesar and Pompey, what are they in comparison with Diogenes and Heraclitus and Socrates? For the latter were acquainted with things, and their causes, and their matter, and the ruling principles of these men were the same; but as to the former, how much foresight did they have, and to how many things were they slaves?

4. Remember that men will go on doing the same things even if you should burst in protest.

5. This is the chief thing: Do not be perturbed, for all things are according to the law of nature; and in a little time you will be nobody and nowhere, like Hadrian and Augustus. In the next place, keep your eyes fixed steadily on your business, remembering it is your duty to be a good man, and do what a man's nature demands without turning aside; and speak as it seems to you most just, only let it be with a good temper and with modesty and without hypocrisy.

6. Nature has this work to do: to shift and to change, to remove from here and to carry there. All things are change, yet we need not fear anything new. All things are familiar and even the distribution of them also remains the same.

7. Every nature is contented with itself when it goes on its way well; and a rational nature goes on its way well when in its thoughts it assents to nothing false or uncertain; when it

directs its movements to social acts only; when it confines its desires and aversions to the things which are in its power; and when it is satisfied with everything that is assigned to it by the common nature. For of this common nature every particular nature is a part, as the nature of the leaf is a part of the nature of the plant; except that in the plant the nature of the leaf is part of a nature which has not perception or reason, and is subject to impediments; but the nature of man is part of a nature which is not subject to impediment, and is intelligent and just, since it gives to everything in equal portions and according to its worth, times, substance, cause, activity, and incident. Only do not look for exact equality between individual and individual; but take all the parts of one thing together and compare them with all parts taken together of another.

8. You have no time or opportunity to read and to know everything; but you do have time and opportunity to check arrogance, to be superior to pleasure and pain and love of fame, and not to be vexed at stupid and ungrateful people, and even to care for them.

9. Let no man hear you finding fault with court life or with your own (v, 16).

10. Repentance is a kind of self-reproof for having neglected something useful; for that which is good must be something useful, and the good man's object in life. But no good man would ever repent of having refused any sensual pleasure. Pleasure therefore is neither good nor useful.

11. Of each particular thing, ask: "What is it in itself, in its own constitution? What is its substance and material? And what is its causal nature? And what is it doing in the world? And how long will it abide?"

12. When you rise from sleep with reluctance, remember that it is in accord with your constitution and with human nature to perform social acts, but sleeping is common also to irrational animals. And that which belongs to the individual nature is more proper and pleasing to it (v, 1).

13. Constantly, if possible, as every impression presents itself, consider its real nature and proper qualities, and reason with yourself about it.

14. Whatever man you meet with, immediately say to yourself, "What are his principles of good and bad?" For if with respect to pleasure and pain and the causes of each, and with respect to fame and dishonor, death and life, he has such and such opinions, it will seem nothing wonderful or strange to me, if he does such and such things; and I shall bear in mind that he is compelled to do so.

15. Imagine being surprised that a fig tree produces figs, or if the world produces such and such things; and shame to the physician who is surprised that a man has a fever and to the helmsman if the wind is unfavorable.

16. Remember that to change your opinion and to follow him who corrects your error is not a surrender of freedom. Your action follows your own judgment and understanding and keeps the course your mind has set.

17. If a fault is in your own power to correct, why do you persist in it? But if in the power of another, whom do you blame—the atoms or the gods? Both are foolish. You must blame nobody. For if you can, correct the cause; but if you cannot do this, correct at least the thing itself; if you cannot even do this, what purpose is served by finding fault? For nothing should be done without a purpose.

18. That which has died does not drop out of the universe. If it stays here, it also changes here, and is dissolved into its proper parts, which are elements of the universe and of yourself. And these too change, and murmur not.

19. Everything exists for some end, a horse, a vine. Why do you wonder? Even the sun will say, I am for some purpose, and the rest of the gods will say the same. For what purpose then are you? To enjoy pleasure? Does reason allow this?

20. Nature has regard in everything no less to the end than to the beginning and the continuance, just like the man who throws up a ball. What good is it then for the ball to be thrown up, or harm for it to come down, or even to lie fallen? And what good is it to the bubble while it holds together, or what harm when it is burst? The same may be said of a candle also.

21. Turn a thing inside out, and see what it is; and what kind of a thing it becomes when it has grown old, or is diseased, or in decay. Short-lived are both the praiser and the praised, the rememberer and the remembered; and this is but a corner of this part of the world; and not even here do all agree, no, not anyone with himself; and the whole world, too, is a point in the universe.

22. Attend to the matter which is before you, whether it is an opinion or an act or a word.

You get what you deserve: for you choose rather to become good tomorrow than to be good today.

23. Am I doing anything? I do it with reference to the good of mankind. Does anything happen to me? I take what comes, referring all to the gods, and the source of all things, from which all that happens is derived.

24. As bathing appears to you to be—oil, sweat, dirt, filthy water, all things disgusting—so is every part of life and every material thing.

25. Lucilla saw Verus die, and then Lucilla died. Secunda saw Maximus die, and then Secunda died. Epitynchanus saw Diotimus die, and then Epitynchanus died. Antoninus saw Faustina die, and then Antoninus died. And so on; first Hadrian, then Celer. And those sharp-witted men, either seers or men inflated with pride, where are they? For instance, Charax, Demetrius the Platonist, and Eudaemon, and anyone else like them. All ephemeral, dead long ago. Some indeed have not been remembered even for a short time, and others have become the heroes of fables, and still others have disappeared even from fables. Remember this then, that this little compound, yourself, must either be dissolved, or your poor breath must be extinguished, or be removed and placed elsewhere.

26. It is satisfaction to a man to do the proper work of a man. Now it is a proper work of a man to be benevolent to his own kind, to despise the movements of the senses, to form a just judgment of plausible appearances, and to survey the nature of the universe and of the things which happen in it.

27. Man has three relations: the one to the body which surrounds him; the second to the divine cause from which all things come to all; and the third to those who live with him.

28. Pain is either an evil to the body—and in that case, let the body say what it thinks of it—or to the soul; but it is in the power of the soul to maintain its own serenity and tranquillity, and refuse to view it as an evil. For every judgment and movement and desire and aversion is within, and no evil can penetrate there.

29. Wipe out fancies by often saying to yourself: "Now it is in my power to allow no evil in my soul, nor desire, nor perturbation; but looking at all things, I see what is their proper nature, and I use each according to its value." Remember this power which you have from nature.

30. Speak both in the Senate and to every man, whoever he may be, appropriately, not with any affectation; use plain language.

31. Augustus' court, wife, daughter, descendants, ancestors, sister, Agrippa, kinsmen, intimates, friends, Areius, Maecenas, physicians and sacrificing priests—the whole court is dead. Then turn to the rest, not considering the death of a single man, but of a whole race, like the Pompeians; and the words which are engraved upon tombs: The Last of his Race. Then consider what trouble those before them have had that they might leave a successor; and that of necessity someone must be the last, and then finally the death of a whole race.

32. It is your duty to order your life well in every single act; and if every act does its duty, as far as possible, be content; and no one can prevent that. "But some external obstacle

might stand in the way," you say. Nothing will stand in the way of your acting justly, soberly, and considerately. "But may not some form of action be prevented?" Possibly, but by acquiescing in the hindrance and by being content to adopt that alternative, another opportunity of action is immediately put before you in place of that which was prevented, and one which will fit in to the whole of which we are speaking.

33. Receive wealth or prosperity without arrogance; and be ready to let it go cheerfully.

34. If you ever saw a hand cut off, or a foot, or a head lying anywhere apart from the rest of the body—this is what a man does with himself who is not content with what happens, and separates himself from others, or does anything unsocial. Suppose that you have detached yourself from the natural unity— for you were made by nature a part, but now you have cut yourself off—yet here there is this beautiful provision, that it is in your power again to reunite with it. God has allowed this to no other part, after it has been separated and cut asunder, to come together again. But consider the benevolence by which he has distinguished man, for he has put it in his power not to be separated at all from the universal; and when he has been separated, he has allowed him to return and to be united and to resume his place as a part.

35. As the nature of the universal has given to every rational being all the other powers that it has, so we have received from it this power also. For as the universal nature converts and fixes in its predestined place everything which stands in the way and opposes it, and makes such things a part of itself, so also the rational animal is able to make every hindrance into his own instrument and to use it to further his endeavor.

36. Do not disturb yourself by thinking of the whole of your life. Let not your thoughts at once embrace all the various troubles which you may expect to befall you. But on every occasion ask yourself, "What is there in this which is intolerable and past bearing?" For you will be ashamed to

confess. In the next place, remember that neither the future nor the past pains you, but only the present. But this is reduced to a very little, if you only circumscribe it, and scold yourself if you are unable to bear even this.

37. Does Panthea or Pergamus now sit by the tomb of Verus? Does Chaurias or Diotimus sit by the tomb of Hadrian? That would be ridiculous. Well, suppose they did sit there, would the dead be conscious of it? And if conscious, would they be pleased? And if pleased, would that make them immortal? Was it not in the order of destiny that these persons too should become old women and old men and then die? And when they died what would their lovers do? All comes to foul smell and corruption in the end.

38. If you are sharp-sighted, see and judge wisely, says the philosopher.

39. In the constitution of the rational animal I see no virtue which is opposed to justice; but I see a virtue which is opposed to love of pleasure, and that is temperance.

40. If you take away your opinion about what seems to give you pain, you yourself stand in perfect security. You ask, "Who is this self?" The reason. "But I am not reason." Be it so. Then let reason not trouble itself. But if any other part of you suffers, let it keep its suffering to itself (VII, 16).

41. Hindrance to the perceptions of sense is an evil to the animal nature. Hindrance to the impulses is equally an evil to the animal nature. And something else also is equally an impediment and an evil to the constitution of plants. So that which is a hindrance to the intelligence is an evil to the intelligent nature. Apply all these things then to yourself. Does pain or sensuous pleasure affect you? The senses will look to that. Has any obstacle opposed you in your efforts towards an object? If indeed you were making this effort without any reservation, certainly this obstacle is an evil to you as a rational animal. But if you accept the usual course of things, you have not yet been injured or even impeded.

The things, however, which are proper to the understanding, no one may impede, for neither fire, nor iron, nor tyrant, nor abuse, touches it in any way. When it has been made a sphere, it continues a sphere (XI, 12).

42. It is not fitting that I should give myself pain, for I have never intentionally given pain even to another.

43. Different things delight different people; it is my delight to keep the ruling faculty sound without turning away either from any man or from any of the things which happen to men, but looking at and receiving all with welcome eyes and using everything according to its value.

44. Lay hold securely upon this present time; for those who prefer to pursue posthumous fame do not consider that the men of after time will be exactly like those they cannot bear now; and both are mortal. And what does it matter to you what these men say or what opinion they hold about you?

45. Take me and cast me where you will; for there I shall keep my divine part tranquil, that is, content, if it can feel and act in harmony with its proper constitution. Is this change of place sufficient reason why my soul should be unhappy and worse than it was, by cringing or craving, cowering or flinching? What indeed is worth that?

46. Nothing can happen to any man which is not a human accident; nor to an ox which is not according to the nature of an ox; nor to a vine, nor to a stone, that is not according to the nature of each. Why should you complain, if what is usual and natural happens to each thing? Nature brings nothing that you cannot bear.

47. If you are pained by any external thing, it is not this thing which disturbs you, but your own judgment about it. And it is in your power to wipe out that judgment now. But if anything in your own disposition gives you pain, who hinders you from correcting the principle at fault? And even if you are pained because you are not doing some particular thing which seems to you to be right, why do you not rather act than complain? "Some insuperable obstacle is in the way." Do not be grieved then, for the cause of its not being done depends not on you. "But it is not worth while to live if this cannot be done." Take your departure from life contentedly then, dying just as he dies who is in full activity and well pleased with the things which are obstacles.

48. Remember that the ruling faculty is invincible, when once it rallies, if it does nothing which it does not choose to do, even if it resist from mere obstinacy. How much more then when its judgment is rational and made with deliberation! Therefore the mind which is free from passions is a citadel, for man has nothing more secure to which he can fly for refuge and be impregnable. He then who has not seen this is an ignorant man; but he who has seen it and does not fly to this refuge is unhappy.

49. Do not draw inferences in excess of what first appearances report. Suppose it has been reported to you that a certain person speaks ill of you. This has been reported; but that you have been injured, that has not been reported. I see that my child is sick; that I see, but that he is in danger I do not see. Thus always abide by the first appearances and add nothing to them from within, and then you are unaffected. Or rather add this, the recognition that everything which happens is a part of the world order.

50. A cucumber is bitter—throw it away. There are briars in the path—turn aside from them. This is enough. Do not add, "And why were such things put into the world?" For you will be ridiculed by a man who is acquainted with nature, as you would be ridiculed by a carpenter and a shoemaker if you found fault because you found shavings and cuttings in their workshop from the things which they make. And yet they have places where they can throw these shavings and cuttings, but nature has no external space; now the wondrous part of her art is that though she has circumscribed herself, everything within her which appears to decay and

grow old and be useless she changes into herself, and again makes new things from these very same, so that she requires neither substance from without, nor wants a place into which she may cast that which decays. She is content then with her own space, and her own matter and her own art.

51. Neither in your actions be sluggish nor in your conversation without method, nor wandering in thought, nor let there be in your soul either inward contention or external effusion; nor in life be so busy as to have no leisure.

Suppose men kill you, cut you in pieces, curse you. What then can these things do to prevent your mind from remaining pure, wise, sober, just? For instance, if a man should stand by a limpid pure spring, and curse it, the spring does not stop sending up pure water; and if he should cast dirt and filth into it, it will speedily disperse them and wash them out, and will not be at all polluted. How then shall you possess a perpetual fountain? By imbuing yourself hourly with freedom, benevolence, simplicity, and modesty.

52. He who does not know what the world is, does not know where he is. And he who does not know for what purpose the world exists, does not know who he is or what the world is. But he who has failed in any one of these things could not even say for what purpose he exists himself. What then do you think of him who seeks the praise of those who applaud, of men who know not where they are or who they are?

53. Do you wish to be praised by a man who curses himself thrice every hour? Would you wish to please a man who does not please himself? Does a man please himself who repents of nearly everything that he does?

54. Do not let your breathing only act in concert with the air which surrounds you, but let your intelligence also now be in harmony with the intelligence which embraces all things. For the mind power is diffused in all parts and pervades all things for him who is willing to draw it to him, just as the atmosphere is for him who is able to breathe it.

55. Generally, wickedness does no harm at all to the universe; and particularly the wickedness of one man does no harm to another. It is only harmful to him who has it in his power to be released from it as soon as he wills.

56. To my own free will, the free will of my neighbor is just as indifferent as his breath and his flesh. For though we are made especially for the sake of one another, still the ruling power of each of us has its own office, for otherwise my neighbor's wickedness would be my harm, which God has not willed in order that my happiness may not depend on another.

57. The sun appears to be poured down and diffused in all directions, and yet it is not exhausted. For this diffusion is extension. Accordingly its rays are called "extensions" because they are extended. But one may judge what kind of a thing a ray is, if he looks at the sun's light through a narrow opening in a darkened room, for it is extended in a straight line, and as it were divided when it meets with a solid body which stands in the way and intercepts the air beyond; but there the light remains fixed and does not glide or fall off. Such then ought to be the outpouring and diffusion of the understanding, and it should make no violent or impetuous collision with the obstacles in its way; nor yet fall down, but be fixed and enlighten that which receives it. For a body will deprive itself of light if it does not admit it.

58. He who fears death either fears the loss of sensation or a different kind of sensation. But if you have no sensation, neither will you feel any harm; and yet if you acquire another kind of sensation, you will be a different kind of being and you will not cease to live.

59. Men exist for the sake of one another. Teach them then or bear with them.

60. An arrow moves in one way, the mind in another.

The mind indeed, even when it moves cautiously and plays inquiringly around a subject, is nevertheless moving straight on toward its goal.

61. Enter into every man's ruling faculty; and also let every man enter into yours.

IX

1. He who acts unjustly acts irreverently. For since the universal nature has made rational animals for the sake of one another, to help one another according to their worth, but in no way to injure one another, he who transgresses her will is clearly guilty of impiety toward the highest divinity. And he too who lies is guilty of impiety to the same divinity; for the universal nature is the nature of all things that are; and all things that are have a relation to all things that come into existence. And further, this universal nature is named truth, and is the prime cause of all things that are true. He then who lies intentionally is guilty of impiety inasmuch as he acts unjustly by deceiving; and he also who lies unintentionally, inasmuch as he is at variance with the universal nature, and inasmuch as he disturbs the order by fighting against the nature of the world: for he fights against it, who is moved of himself to that which is contrary to truth, for through neglect of the powers received from nature he can no longer distinguish falsehood from truth.

And indeed he who pursues pleasure as good, and avoids pain as evil, is guilty of impiety. For of necessity such a man must often find fault with the universal nature, alleging that it assigns things to the bad and the good contrary to their deserts, because frequently the bad are in the enjoyment of pleasure and possess the things which procure pleasure, but the good have pain for their share and the things which cause pain. And further, he who is afraid of pain will sometimes also be afraid of some of the things which will happen in the world, and even this is impiety. And he who pursues pleasure will not abstain from injustice, and this is plainly a sinful act.

Now with respect to the things toward which the universal nature is equally affected—for it would not have made both unless it was equally affected towards both—towards these, they who wish to follow nature should be of the same mind, and equally affected. With respect to pain, then, and pleasure, or death and life, honor or dishonor, which the universal nature employs equally, whoever is not equally affected is manifestly guilty of sin. And I say that the universal nature employs them equally instead of saying that they happen alike to those who are produced in continuous series and to those who come after them by virtue of a certain original movement of Providence, according to which it moved from a certain beginning to this ordering of things, having conceived certain reasons of the things which were to be, and having determined the generative power of substances and changes and such like successions (VII, 75).

2. It would be a man's happiest lot to depart from mankind without having had any taste of lying and hypocrisy and luxury and pride. However, to breathe one's last when one has had enough of these is the next best thing. Have you determined to stick to vice, and has not experience yet induced you to flee this pestilence? For the destruction of the understanding is a pestilence, much more indeed than any such corruption in the air about us. For this corruption is a pestilence of animals, in so far as they are animals, but the other is a pestilence of men in so far as they are men.

3. Do not despise death, but be well content with it, since this too is one of those things which nature wills. For such

as it is to be young and to grow old, and to increase and to reach maturity, and to have teeth and beard and gray hairs, and to beget, and to be pregnant and to bring forth, such also is dissolution. This then is consistent with the character of a reflecting man, to be neither careless nor impatient nor contemptuous with respect to death, but to wait for it as one of the operations of nature. As you now wait for the time when the child shall come out of your wife's womb, so be ready for the time when your soul shall fall out of this envelope. But if you require also a vulgar kind of comfort which shall reach your heart, you will be best reconciled to death by observing the objects from which you are going to be removed, and the morals of those with whom your soul will no longer be mingled. For it is not your right to be offended with men, but it is your duty to care for them and to bear with them gently; and yet to remember that your departure will be not from men who have the same principles as yourself. For this is the only thing, if there be any, which could draw us the contrary way and attach us to life, to be permitted to live with those who have the same principles as ourselves. But now you see how great is the trouble arising from the discordance of those who live together, so that you may say, "Come quick, O death, lest perchance I, too, should forget myself."

4. He who does wrong does wrong against himself. He who acts unjustly acts unjustly to himself, because he makes himself bad.

5. Not only he who does but he who fails to do a certain thing acts wrongly.

6. Your present opinion founded on understanding and your present conduct directed to social good, and your present disposition of contentment with everything which happens—that is enough.

7. Wipe out fancy; check desire; extinguish appetite; keep your ruling faculty in control.

8. Among irrational animals one life is distributed; but among rational animals one intelligent soul is distributed: just as there is one earth for all things which are of an earthy nature, and we see by one light, and breathe one air, all of us that have the faculty of vision and all that have life.

9. All things which share a common element move towards that which is of the same kind with themselves. Everything which is earthy turns towards the earth, everything which is liquid flows together, and everything which is of an aerial kind does the same, so that they require the application of force to keep them apart. Fire indeed moves upwards on account of the elemental fire; and so ready it is to be kindled with all fire that every substance which is somewhat dry is easily ignited, because there is less mingled with it that is a hindrance to ignition. Accordingly, everything also which participates in the common intelligent nature moves in like manner towards that which is of the same kind, or moves even more. For so much as it is superior in comparison with all other things, in the same degree also is it more ready to mingle with and to be fused with its counterpart. Among animals devoid of reason we find swarms of bees and herds of cattle, and the nurture of young birds, all manifestations of love; for even in animals there are souls, and that power which brings them together is seen to exert itself in the superior degree, and in such a way as never has been observed in plants or in stones or in trees. But among rational animals there are political communities and friendships, and families and meetings of people; and in wars, treaties and armistices. But in the things which are still superior, even though they are separated from one another, unity in a manner exists, as in the stars. Thus the ascent to the higher degree is able to produce a sympathy even in things which are separated. See, then, what now takes place. For only intelligent animals have now forgotten this mutual desire and inclination, and in them alone the flowing together is not seen. But though men strive to avoid this union, they are caught and held by it, for their nature is too strong for them; and you will see what I say, if you only observe. Sooner, then, will one find anything earthy which comes in contact with no earthy thing than a man altogether separated from other men.

10. Both man and God and the universe produce fruit, at the proper season. It matters not that usage has especially affixed these terms to the vine and like things. Reason produces fruit both for all and for itself, and there are produced from it other things of the same kind as reason itself.

11. If you are able, correct by teaching those who do wrong; but if you cannot, remember that charity is given you for this purpose. And the gods too extend charity to such persons, helping them attain health, wealth, reputation —so kind they are. And it is in your power also. Who hinders you?

12. Labor not as one who is wretched, nor yet as one who would be pitied or admired: but direct your will to one thing only, to put yourself in motion and to check yourself as the social law requires.

13. Today I have got out of all trouble, or rather I have cast out all trouble, for it was not outside, but within, in my opinions.

14. All things are the same, familiar, ephemeral, worthless; everything now is just as it was in the time of those whom we have buried.

15. Things stand outside of us, just as they are, neither knowing aught of themselves, nor expressing any judgment. What is it then, which does judge for them? The ruling faculty.

16. Not in passivity but in activity lies the evil and the good of the rational social animal, just as his virtue and his vice lie not in passivity but in activity.

17. For the stone which has been thrown up it is no evil to come down, nor indeed any good to have been carried up (VIII, 20).

18. Penetrate inward into men's ruling principles, and you will see what judges you are afraid of, and how they judge themselves.

19. All things are changing: and you yourself are in continuous mutation and, in a manner, in continuous destruction, and the universe too.

20. It is your duty to leave another man's wrongful act where it is (VII, 29; IX, 38).

21. The end of activity, cessation from movement and opinion—what may be termed their death—is no evil. Now consider your life, your childhood, youth, manhood, and old age—for here also every change was a death. Is this anything to fear? Turn your thoughts now to your life under your grandfather, then under your mother, then under your father; and you find many other differences, changes, and endings. Ask yourself, "Is this anything to fear?" In like manner, then, neither are the end and surcease from life itself anything to fear.

22. Hasten to examine your own ruling faculty, that of the universe, and of your neighbor; your own, that you may make it just; that of the universe, that you may remember of what you are a part; that of your neighbor, that you may know whether he has acted ignorantly or with knowledge, and that you may also consider that his ruling faculty is akin to yours.

23. As you yourself are a component part of a social system, so let every act of yours be a component part of social life. Whatever act of yours then has no reference either immediately or remotely to a social end, this tears asunder your life.

24. Children's quarrels, their games, "poor breath carrying about a corpse," [1]—are not the representations of the "mansions of the dead" [2] more solid and real?

25. Examine into the essence of the form of an object, and detach it altogether from its material part, and then contemplate it; then determine the full span which a thing of this peculiar form is naturally made to endure.

26. You have borne infinite troubles through not being contented with your ruling faculty, when it does the things which it is constituted by nature to do. But enough!

27. When another blames or hates you, or when men say injurious things about you, approach their poor souls, penetrate within, and see what kind of men they are. You will discover that there is no reason to take trouble that these men may have a good opinion of you. However, you must be well disposed towards them, for by nature they are friends. And the gods, too, aid them in all ways, by dreams, by signs, toward the attainment of their aims.

28. The periodic movements of the universe, up and down and to and fro, continue from age to age. And either the universal intelligence imparts each separate impulse, in which case be content with the result of its activity; or it puts itself in motion once, and everything else comes by way of sequence, in a manner; or indivisible elements are the origin of all things. In a word, if there is a god, all is well; and if chance rules, be not you too governed by it.

Soon the earth will cover us all; then the earth, too, will change, and the things which result from change will continue to change forever, and these again forever. For if a man reflects on the changes and transformations which follow one another wave upon wave, he will feel contempt for everything which is perishable (XII, 21).

---

[1] Epictetus said that man was "a soul carrying about a corpse."

[2] This may mean a dramatic representation of the state of the dead, or possibly it is a reference to the underworld, as described in Book XI of the *Odyssey*.

29. The universal cause is like a winter torrent: it carries everything along with it. But how worthless are all these poor people who are engaged in matters political, and, as they suppose, are playing the philosopher! All drivelers. Well then, man, do what nature now requires. Set yourself in motion, if it is in your power, and do not look about you to see if anyone is watching; nor yet expect Plato's Republic, but be content if the smallest thing goes on well, and consider such an event to be no small matter. For who can change men's principles? And without a change of principles what else is there than the slavery of men who groan while they pretend to obey? Come now and tell me of Alexander and Philippus and Demetrius of Phalerum. They themselves shall judge whether they discovered what the common nature required, and behave themselves accordingly. But if they acted like tragedy heroes, no one has condemned me to imitate them. Simple and modest is the work of philosophy. Draw me not aside to insolence and pride.

30. Look down from above on the countless herds of men and their countless solemnities, and the infinitely varied voyagings in storms and calms, and the differences among those who are born, who live together and die. And consider, too, the life lived by others in olden time, and the life of those who will live after you, and the life now lived among barbarous nations, and how many know not even your name, and how many will soon forget it, and how they who perhaps now are praising you will very soon blame you, and that neither a posthumous name is of any value, nor reputation, nor anything else.

31. Let there be freedom from perturbation with respect to the things which come from external causes, and in actions whose cause lies in yourself, be just; that is, let impulse and action terminate in social acts, for this is according to your nature.

32. Clear from your mind the many useless things which disturb you, for they lie entirely in your opinion; and you will then gain for yourself ample space by comprehending the whole universe in your mind, and by contemplating the eternity of time, and observing the rapid change of each thing, how short is the time from its birth to its dissolution, and the illimitable time before its birth as well as the equally boundless time after its dissolution.

33. All that you see will quickly perish, and those who have been spectators of its dissolution will very soon perish too. And he who dies at the extremest old age will be brought into the same condition with him who died prematurely.

34. What are the ruling principles of these men, and about what kind of things are they busy, and for what kind of reasons do they love and honor? Imagine that you see their poor souls laid bare. When they think that they do harm by their blame or good by their praise, what an idea!

35. Loss is nothing else than change. But the universal nature delights in change, and in obedience to her all things are now done well, and from eternity have been done in like form, and will be such through endless time. What then do you say? That all things have been and all things always will be bad, and that no power has ever been found among all the gods to set them right, but the world has been condemned to be bound in never-ceasing evil? (IV, 45; VII, 18).

36. Decay is the material substance of all things—water, dust, bones, filth. What is marble but the callosities of the earth? Gold and silver are but sediments; garments, only bits of hair; purple dye, shellfish blood; and everything else is of the same kind. And even the breath is a thing of the same kind, changing from this to that.

37. Enough of this complaining and groaning and ape-like chatter. Why are you disturbed? What is there new in this? What unsettles you? Is it the form of the thing? Look at it. Or is it the matter? Look at it. Besides these, there is nothing. Towards the gods, then, now at last become simpler and better. It is the same whether we look at these things for a hundred years or three.

38. If any man has done wrong, the harm is his. But perhaps he has not done wrong.

39. Either all things proceed from one intelligent source and come together as in one body, and the part ought not to find fault with what is done for the benefit of the whole; or there are only atoms, and nothing else but mixture and dispersion. Why then are you disturbed? Say to the ruling faculty, "Are you dead, corrupted, playing the hypocrite? Are you a mere beast, chewing a cud?"

40. Either the gods have no power or they have power. If they have no power, why do you pray to them? But if they have power, why do you not pray for deliverance from the fear or the desire or the pain, which a thing causes, rather than pray that any of these things should or should not happen? For certainly if they can help at all, they can help to this end. But perhaps you will say that the gods have placed all that in my own power. Well, then, is it not better to use what is in your power like a free man than to desire in a slavish and abject way what is not in your power? And who has told you that the gods do not aid us even in the things which are in our power? Begin then to pray for such things, and you will see. One man prays to be able to lie with a certain woman; rather should he pray to be freed of desire for her. Another prays to be rid of his enemy; he should pray against wanting to be rid of him. Instead of praying that you may not lose your little one, pray for release from fear. Turn your prayers this way, and see what comes.

41. Epicurus says, "In sickness my conversation was not about my bodily sufferings, nor did I talk on such subjects to those who visited me; but I continued to discourse on the nature of things as before, keeping to the main point, how the mind, while participating in such movements as go on in the poor flesh, shall be free from disturbance and maintain its proper good. Nor did I," he adds, "give the physicians an opportunity of putting on solemn looks, as if they were doing something great, but my life went on well and happily." Do, then, the same that he did both in sickness, if you are sick, and in any other circumstances; for never to desert philosophy in any events that may befall us, and to keep from trifling talk with an ignorant man or one unacquainted with nature is a principle of all schools of philosophy. But be intent only on what you are now doing and on the instrument by which you do it.

42. When you are offended with any man's shameless conduct, immediately ask yourself, "Is it possible that there should be no shameless men in the world?" It is not possible. Do not, therefore, require what is impossible. For this man is one of those shameless men who must be in the world. Similarly, in the case of the knave, the faithless, and every man who does any kind of wrong. When once you remember that it is impossible to do away with such men, you will become more kindly disposed toward everyone. It is also useful to perceive what virtue nature has given to man to cope with every wrongful act. As an antidote against the stupid man, she has given mildness, and against some other kind of man, some other power. And in all cases it is possible for you to correct by teaching the man who has gone astray; for every man who errs misses his object and is astray. Besides, what harm has he done you? For you will find that no one among those against whom you are irritated has done anything by which your mind could be made worse; and that which is to you evil and harmful has its foundation only in the mind. And what harm is done, or what is there strange, if the man who has not been instructed acts in the manner of an uninstructed one? Consider whether you should not blame yourself, because you did not expect such a man to act in such a way. For reason has given you faculties enabling

you to foresee that he would commit this error, and yet you have forgotten and are amazed that he has done so. But most of all, when you blame a man as faithless or ungrateful, turn to yourself. For the fault is manifestly your own, if you trusted a man with such a disposition to keep his promise, or if, when conferring your kindness, you did not do it on principle, or in such a way as to have received from your very act all the profit. For what more do you want when you have done a man a service?

Are you not content when you have done something in harmony with your nature, and do you seek to be paid for it? Does the eye demand a reward for seeing, or the feet for walking? For as these members are formed for a particular purpose, and by working according to the law of their being obtain what is their own, so also, as man is formed by nature for acts of benevolence, when he has done anything benevolent or in any way conducive to the common interest, he has acted in harmony with his constitution, and he gets what is his own.

X

1. Will you then, my soul, never be good and simple, all one and naked, clearer to sight than the body which encompasses you? Will you never enjoy an affectionate and contented disposition? Will you never be full and without a want of any kind, longing for nothing more, either animate or inanimate, for the enjoyment of pleasures? Nor yet desiring time wherein you shall have longer enjoyment, or place, or pleasant climate, or society of men with whom you may live in harmony? But will you be satisfied with your present condition, and pleased with all about you, and will you convince yourself that you have everything and that it comes from the gods, that everything is well for you, and will be well whatever shall please them, and whatever they shall give you for the perfect living being, the good and just and beautiful, which generates and holds together all things, and contains and embraces all things which are dissolved for the production of other like things? Will you never be such that you shall so dwell in community with gods and men as neither to find fault with them at all, nor to be condemned by them?

2. Observe what your nature requires, so far as you are governed by nature only: then do it and accept it, if your nature shall not be made worse for it. And next you must observe what your nature requires as far as you are a living being, and this you may do, unless it involves injury to your nature as a rational being. But the rational being is consequently also a social being. Follow these rules then, and trouble yourself about nothing else.

3. Everything which happens either happens in such a way that you are formed by nature to bear it or not to bear it. If what happens to you is within your strength to bear, bear it without complaining; if it is beyond your strength, do not complain, for it will perish after it has destroyed you. Remember, however, that you are formed by nature to bear everything which your own opinion can make endurable and tolerable, by thinking that it is either your interest or your duty to do so.

4. If a man is mistaken instruct him kindly and show him his error. If you are not able to do this, blame yourself, or blame not even yourself.

5. Whatever may happen to you, it was prepared for you from all eternity; and the implication of causes was from eternity spinning the thread of your being, and of that which is incident to it (III, 11; IV, 26).

6. Whether the universe is a concourse of atoms or nature's law, let this be first established, that I am a part of the whole which is governed by nature; next, I am intimately related to the parts which are of the same kind with myself. For remembering this, inasmuch as I am a part, I shall be discontented with none of the things which are assigned to me out of the whole; for nothing is injurious to the part, if it is for the advantage of the whole. For the whole contains nothing which is not for its own good; and all natures indeed have this common principle, but the nature of the universe has this principle besides, that it cannot be compelled even by any external cause to generate anything harmful to itself. By remembering then that I am a part of such a whole, I shall be content with everything which happens. And inasmuch as I am in a manner intimately related to the parts which are the same kind with myself, I shall do nothing unsocial, but I shall rather direct myself to the things which are of the same kind with myself, and I shall turn all my efforts to the common interest, and avert them from the contrary. Now if these things are done so, life must flow on happily, just as you may observe that the life of a citizen is happy if he continues a course of action which is advantageous to his fellow citizens, and is content with whatever the state may assign to him.

7. The parts of the whole which are comprehended in the universe must of necessity perish, that is, they must undergo change. But if this is both an evil and a necessity to the parts, the whole could not escape deterioration, seeing the parts are subject to change and prone to perish in various ways. Did nature herself design to do evil to the things which are parts of herself, and to make them subject to evil and of necessity fall into evil, or have such things happened without her knowing it? Both these suppositions are indeed incredible. But if a man should even drop the term "nature" as an efficient power, and should speak of these changes as natural, even then it would be ridiculous to affirm at the same time that the parts of the whole are naturally subject to change, and at the same time to be surprised or vexed as if something were happening contrary to nature, particularly such as the dissolution of things into the original elements. For there is either a dispersion of the elements out of which everything has been compounded, or a change from the solid to the earthy and from the spiritual to the aerial, so that these parts are taken back into the universal reason, whether this at certain periods is consumed by fire or renewed by eternal changes.[1] And do not imagine that the solid and the spiritual part belong to you from the time of your begetting. For it received its increase only yesterday and the day before, so to speak, from the food you eat and the air you breathe. This then that has received changes from without is not that which your mother brought forth. But even admitting that you are intimately bound up with that, by your individuality, this does not affect the argument.

8. When you have assumed these attributes—good, modest, true, rational, equable, magnanimous—take care that you do not change them; and if you should lose them, quickly return to them. And remember that the term "rational" was intended to signify a discriminating attention to every separate thing and freedom from negligence; and that equanimity is the voluntary acceptance of the things which are assigned to you by the common nature; and that magnanimity is the elevation of the intelligent part above the pleasurable or painful sensations of the flesh, and above fame, and death, and all such trials. If then you keep true to these attributes, without desiring that others should recognize that you have them, you will be another person and will enter on another life. For to

---

[1] One of the Stoic doctrines was that the world was periodically destroyed by fire and then again renewed.

continue to be such as you had hitherto been, and to be torn in pieces and defiled in such a life, is the character of a very stupid man, one overfond of his life, and like those half-devoured fighters with wild beasts, who though covered with wounds and gore, still entreat to be kept to the following day, to be flung once more to the same claws and bites. Therefore, fix yourself firmly in the possession of these few attributes, and if you are able to stand fast, stand fast as if you were transported to the Happy Isles.[2] But if you find yourself falling, and cannot maintain your hold, go courageously into some nook where you can still hold on, or even depart at once from life, not in passion, but with simplicity and freedom and modesty, after doing this one thing, at least, bravely—to leave it thus. In order, however, to aid the remembrance of these attributes, it will greatly help you, if you remember the gods, and that they do not wish to be flattered, but wish all reasonable beings to be made like themselves, and be as the fig tree doing the work of a fig tree, the dog a dog's, the bee a bee's, and man a man's work.

9. A stage play, war, terror, torpor, slavery—all these will daily help to wipe out your sacred principles. How many things without studying nature do you overlook, and how many do you neglect! But it is your duty to look on and to do everything, that at the same time the power of dealing with circumstances is perfected, and the contemplative faculty is exercised, and the confidence which comes from the knowledge of each separate thing is maintained without being apparent nor yet concealed. Ah, when will you enjoy simplicity, gravity, and when the knowledge of every separate thing, both what it is in substance, and what place it has in the universe, and how long it is formed to exist and

---

[2] The Happy Isles or Isles of the Blessed are frequently spoken of by Greek and Roman writers. They were the abode of heroes such as Achilles and Diomed.

of what things it is compounded, and to whom it can belong, and who are able both to give it and take it away?

10. A spider is proud when it has caught a fly; so is a man when he has caught a hare, another when he has taken a fish in a net, another when he has killed wild boars or bears, another when he has captured Sarmatians. Are they not all brigands, if you look into their principles? [3]

11. Acquire the contemplative way of seeing how all things change into one another, and constantly attend to it, and exercise yourself about this part of philosophy. Nothing is so apt to produce magnanimity. Such a man has put off the body, and as he sees that at any moment he must go away from among men and leave everything here, he gives himself entirely up to just actions, and in everything else that happens he resigns himself to the universal nature. But as to what any man shall say or think about him or do against him, he never even thinks of it, being himself contented with these two things, with acting justly in what he now does, and being satisfied with what is now assigned to him; and he lays aside all distracting and busy pursuits, and desires nothing else than to run the straight course and by so doing follow God.

12. What need is there of suspicious fear, since it is in your power to inquire what ought to be done? And if all is clear, go forward content, without turning back; but if all is not clear, stop and take the best of counsel. But if any other things oppose you, go on according to your powers with due consideration, keeping to that which appears just. For it is best to aim at this, and if you fail, let your failure be in making this attempt. He who follows reason in all things is both tranquil and active at the same time, and also cheerful and collected.

13. Inquire of yourself as soon as you awaken from sleep whether it will make any difference to you if another does

---

[3] Since he warred against the Sarmatians, Aurelius is here confessing that he is no different from the rest.

what is just and right. It will make no difference (VI, 32; VIII, 55).

Have you forgotten that those who assume arrogant airs in bestowing their praise or blame on others are the same in bed and at table? Have you forgotten what it is they pursue and avoid, how they steal—not with hands and feet, but with their most valuable part, by means of which, if a man chooses, he arrives at fidelity, modesty, truth, law (VII, 17).

14. To nature who gives and takes back all, the man who is instructed and modest says, "Give what thou wilt; take back what thou wilt." And he says this not proudly, but obediently and with good will.

15. Little of life remains to you. Live as on a mountain. For it makes no difference whether a man lives there or here, if he lives everywhere as a citizen of the world. Let men see, let them know a real man who lives according to nature. If they cannot endure him, let them kill him. For that is better than to live as they do.

16. No longer talk about the kind of man a good man ought to be, but be one.

17. Constantly contemplate the whole of time and the whole of substance, and consider that all things as to substance are a seed of a fig, and as to time the turning of a screw.

18. Look at everything that exists, and observe that it is already in dissolution and in change, by putrefaction and dispersion, or by its own way of death.

19. Consider what men are like—eating, sleeping, breeding, easing themselves, and so forth. Look at their wantonness, their arrogance and rages. But a short time ago how many of them bowed the knee—and for what ends; and after a little time consider in what condition they will be.

20. What the universal nature brings to each thing, and when it brings it, is for its good.

21. "The earth loves the shower"; and "the solemn ether loves"; and the universe loves to make whatever is about to be. I say then to the universe that I love as thou lovest. And is it not also said, "this or that loves to be produced"? [4]

22. Either you live here and have already accustomed yourself to it, or you are going away, and this was your own wish; or you are dying and have discharged your duty. Besides these things there is nothing: be of good cheer then.

23. Let this always be plain to you, that this piece of land is like any other; and that what is here is the same as what is on top of a mountain, or on the seashore, or wherever you choose; as Plato says of his philosopher, whose retreat is "like a shepherd's fold on a mountain." [5]

24. What of my ruling faculty at this minute, and what am I making of it? For what purpose am I using it? Is it void of understanding? Is it loosed and rent asunder from social life? Is it melted into and mixed with the poor flesh so as to move together with it?

25. The slave who flies from his master is a runaway; the law is master and he who breaks the law is a runaway. Vexation, anger, and fear mean refusal of something, past, present, or to come, ordained by him who rules all things, Law, who allots to every man what is fit. He then who fears or is grieved or is angry is a runaway.

26. A man deposits a seed in a womb and goes away, and another cause takes up the work and makes a child. What a flower from what a seed! Again, the child swallows food, and then another cause takes it and makes perception and motion and, in short, life and strength and other things—how

---

[4] These words are from Euripides. They are cited by Aristotle, in the *Nicomachean Ethics*. It was the fashion of the Stoics to play on the meaning of words, and here Aurelius takes the verb "loves," which in Greek has also the sense of "is wont," "uses," and the like. He finds in the common language a philosophical truth.

[5] Plato, *Theaetetus*, 174.

many and how strange! Observe then the things which are produced in such a hidden way and see the power behind them—just as we perceive the power that carries things downwards and upwards, not with the eye, but still no less plainly (VII, 75).

27. Consider that the things of the present also existed in times past; and consider that they will be the same again. And place before your eyes, from your own experience or from the pages of history, these dramas and scenes: the courts of Hadrian, Antoninus, Philip, Alexander, Croesus; all the same plays, only with different actors.

28. Imagine every man who is grieved at anything or discontented to be like a sacrificial pig which kicks and squeals. Like this pig also is he who on his bed in silence laments the bonds in which we are held. And remember that it is given only to the rational animal to go along freely with all that comes; merely to submit is a necessity imposed on all.

29. Point by point, whenever we do anything, let us pause and ask ourselves if death is a dreadful thing because it deprives us of *this*.

30. When you are offended at any man's fault, turn to yourself and study your own failings; for example, in thinking that money, or reputation, or pleasure are good things. By attending to this you will quickly forget your anger, if this consideration is also added: that the man is compelled to act as he does; if you can, take away from him the compulsion.

31. When you see Satyron, Eutyches, or Hymen, think of some follower of Socrates; and let the sight of Euphrates remind you of Eutychion or Silvanus; Alciphron of Tropaeophorus; Xenophon of Crito or Severus; a look at yourself, of some Caesar of the past. And in every other case, reflect: Where are they all now? Nowhere, or nobody knows where. In this way you will come to look at human things as smoke and nothingness; especially if you reflect at the same time

that what has once changed will never again exist through all eternity. What a brief span is the period of your life! Why are you not content to pass it in an orderly way? What matter and opportunity for your activity are you avoiding? For what are such things but exercises for the reason, viewing the happenings of life in their true nature? Persevere until you have made these things your own, just as the healthy stomach assimilates its food, or a blazing fire makes flame and brightness out of everything that is thrown into it.

32. Let it not be in any man's power to say truly of you that you are not simple and good; let it be a lie if anyone shall think anything of this kind about you; this is wholly in your power. For who shall hinder you from being good and simple? You have only to decide to live no longer, if you cannot be such a man. For in that case, it does not stand with reason that you should live.

33. With this material, what can be done or said in the way most conformable to reason? For whatever this may be, it is in your power to do or say it, and do not make excuses that you are hindered. You will never cease lamenting until your mind is in such a condition that you will make use of all materials and every opportunity to fulfill the law of your being, enjoying this as luxury-lovers enjoy pleasure. For a man ought to consider as an enjoyment everything which it is in his power to do according to his own nature; and the opening is always there.

Now it is not given to a cylinder to move everywhere by its own motion, nor yet to water nor to fire, nor to anything else which is governed by nature or an irrational soul, for the things which check them are many. But intelligence and reason are able to go through everything that opposes them, and in such manner as they are formed by nature and as they choose. Recall the facility with which the reason will find a way, as a stone drops or a cylinder rolls down an inclined plane—and look no further. For all these obstacles either affect the body only which is a dead thing; or, except through opinion and the yielding of the reason itself, they do not crush or do any kind of harm; for if they did he who felt it would immediately be injured. Now in the case of things of a certain constitution, whatever harms any of them, that which is so affected becomes consequently worse; but in this case the man becomes both better, if one may say so, and more worthy of praise by making right use of these accidents. And finally remember that nothing harms the citizens which does not harm the state; nor does anything harm the state which does not harm law. But so-called misfortunes do not harm law. What then does not harm law harms neither state nor citizen.

34. To him who is imbued with true principles even the briefest and commonest precept is sufficient to remind him that he should be free from grief and fear. For example,

> Leaves, some the wind scatters on the ground—
> So is the race of men. [6]

Leaves also are your children; and leaves too are they who cry out their praises or curses, or secretly blame or sneer; and leaves, too, are those who shall receive and transmit a man's fame to the future. For all such things as these "are produced in the season of spring," as the poet says; then the wind casts them down; then the frost produces other leaves in their places. But a brief existence is common to all things, and yet you pursue and avoid things as if they would be eternal. A little time and your eyes will close; and he who attends you to your grave another will soon lament.

35. The healthy eye ought to see all visible things and not to say, "I wish for green things"; for this is the condition of a diseased eye. And the healthy hearing and smelling should be ready to perceive all that can be heard and smelled. And the healthy stomach ought to receive food as the mill receives

---

[6] Homer, *Iliad*. See Classics Club edition, p. 91.

that which it was made to grind. And, accordingly, the healthy understanding ought to be prepared for everything which happens; but that which says, "Let my dear children live, and let all men praise whatever I may do," is an eye which seeks for green things, or teeth which seek for soft things.

36. There is no man so fortunate that there shall not be by him when he is dying some who are pleased with what is going to happen. Suppose that he was a good and wise man, will there not be at the last some to say of him, "Let us at last breathe freely being relieved from this schoolmaster"? "It is true that he was harsh to none of us, but I perceived that he tacitly condemns us." This is what is said of a good man. But in our own case how many other things are there for which there are many who wish to get rid of us. You will consider this then when you are dying, and you will depart more contentedly by reflecting thus: "I am going away from such a life, in which even my associates in behalf of whom I have striven so much, prayed, and cared, themselves wish me to depart, hoping perchance to get some little advantage by it." Why then should a man cling to a longer stay here? Do not, however, for this reason go away less kindly disposed to them, but preserving your own character, and continuing friendly and benevolent and kind, and on the other hand not as if you were torn away; but as when a man dies a quiet death, the soul is easily separated from the body, such also ought your departure from men to be. Nature united the elements of which she compounded you, and now she dissolves the union. Well, I am but separated from kinsmen, unresisting and unrebellious; for this too is according to nature.

37. Whatever is being done, accustom yourself as much as possible to inquire, "Why is this man doing this thing?" But begin with yourself, and examine yourself first.

38. Remember that what pulls the strings is hidden within: this is the power of persuasion, this is life, this—if one may say so—is man. In contemplating yourself never include the

vessel which surrounds you and these organs attached to it. They are like tools, differing in this only, that they grow to the body. For indeed there is no more use in these parts without the cause that moves and checks them than in the weaver's shuttle or the writer's pen or the driver's whip.

XI

1. These are the properties of the rational soul; it sees itself, analyzes itself, and makes itself what it wills, bears and enjoys its own fruit, while in the vegetable or animal world the fruit is enjoyed by others; it obtains its own wherever the limit of life may be fixed. In a dance or in a play an interruption leaves the action incomplete; not so with the soul; at every point and wherever it may be stopped, its task is full and complete, so that it can say, "I have what is my own." And further, it traverses the whole universe and the surrounding vacuum, and surveys its form, and extends itself into the infinity of time, and embraces and comprehends the periodical regeneration of all things, and it comprehends that those who come after us will see nothing new, nor have those before us seen anything more, but he who is forty years old, if he has any understanding at all, has seen everything, by virtue of the uniformity of things past and to come. This too is a property of the rational soul, love of one's neighbor, and truth and modesty, and to value nothing more than itself, which is also the property of law. Thus right reason differs not at all from the reason of justice.

2. You will set little value on the delights of song and dance and the pancratium,[1] if you will break up the melody into its

---

[1] The Pancratium was a popular form of athletic combat, in which

several sounds, and ask yourself as to each, if this is what enchanted you? For you will be prevented by shame from confessing it. And in the matter of dancing, if at each movement and attitude you will do the same; and similarly with the pancratium. In all things, then, except virtue and virtuous acts, remember to apply yourself to their several parts, and by this division to come to value them little. Apply this rule to your whole life.

3. O for a soul that is ready at any moment to be separated from the body, either to be extinguished or dispersed or continue to exist! This readiness must come from a man's own judgment, not from mere obstinacy, as with the Christians,[2] and considerately and with dignity, in a way that will persuade others, without tragic show.

4. Have I done something for the general interest? Well, I have had my reward. Let this be always present to your mind; and never grow weary.

5. What is your art? To be good. And how is this achieved except by understanding general principles, some about the nature of the universe, and others about man's own constitution?

6. Tragedies, the first form of drama, were brought on the stage as a means of reminding men of the things which happen to them, and that it is according to nature for things to happen so, and that, if you are delighted with what is shown on the stage, you should not be troubled with what takes place on the larger stage. For you see that the play must end in such a way, and that even in such cries as "O Cithaeron," [3] there

---

the contestants were free to use any form of technique, that of a boxer as well as that of a wrestler.

[2] This is the emperor's only allusion to the Christians.

[3] Sophocles, *Oedipus Rex*. The wretched king Oedipus, having learned the extent of his doom, calls on the hill Cithaeron, where as an infant he was taken to die,—"O Cithaeron, why didst thou shelter me?"

is strength to bear. And the dramatists give us words of help, such as the following:

> *Me and my children, if the gods neglect,*
> *This has its reason too.*[4]

And again,

> *We must not chafe at that which happens;*

And

> *Life's harvest reap like the wheat's fruitful ear.*

And other things of the same kind.

After tragedy the old comedy was introduced. This had a magisterial freedom of speech, and by its very plainness of speaking was useful in reminding men to beware of insolence, somewhat in the style used by Diogenes.

But as to the middle comedy which came next, note what it was; and for what object the new comedy was introduced, which gradually sank down into a mere mimic artifice. That some good things are said even by these writers everyone knows; but what is the main purpose of this school of drama, to what end does it look?

7. It seems plain that there is not another condition of life so well suited for philosophy as this in which you now find yourself.

8. A branch cut off from the adjacent branch must of necessity be cut off from the whole tree also. So too a man when he is separated from another man has fallen off from the whole social community. Now as to a branch, another cuts it off, but a man by his own act separates himself from his neighbor when he hates him and turns away from him, and he does not know that he has at the same time cut himself off from the whole social system. Yet he has this privilege

---

[4] For this and the following quotations, see VII, 38, 40, 41.

certainly from Zeus who framed society, for it is in our power to grow again to that which is near to us, and again to become a part which helps to make up the whole. However, if this kind of separation happens often, it makes it difficult for that which detaches itself to be brought to unity and to be restored to its former condition. Finally, the branch, which from the first grew together with the tree, and has continued to have one life with it, is not like that which after being cut off is then ingrafted, but it is something like what the gardeners mean when they say that it grows with the rest of the tree, but has not the same mind with it.

9. As those who try to stand in your way when you are proceeding according to right reason will not be able to turn you aside from your proper action, so neither let them drive you from your benevolent feelings towards them, but be on your guard equally in both matters, not only in the matter of steady judgment and action, but also in the matter of gentleness towards those who try to hinder or otherwise trouble you. For it is a weakness to be vexed at them as it is to be diverted from your course of action and to give way through fear; for both are equally deserters from their post, the man who acts through fear, and the man who is alienated from his natural brother and friend.

10. Nature is never inferior to art, for the arts imitate nature. If so, nature in its most perfect and comprehensive form cannot fall short of art. Now all arts do the inferior things for the sake of the superior: therefore the universal nature does so too. And indeed here is the origin of justice, and in justice all other virtues have their foundation; for justice will not be observed if we either care for secondary things, or are easily deceived, or careless, or changeable (v, 16; vii, 55).

11. The things—which either to get or to avoid you go to so much trouble—come not to you, but you, rather, go to them. Let then your judgment about them be at rest, and they will remain quiet too, and you will not be seen either pursuing or avoiding.

12. The spherical form of the soul maintains its figure, when it is neither extended towards any object, nor contracted inwards, nor dispersed, nor sinks down, but is illuminated by light, by which it sees the truth, the truth of all things and that which is in itself (VIII, 41, 45; XII, 3).

13. Does any man despise me? Let him see to that. But I shall see to this, that I be not discovered doing or saying anything worthy of contempt. Shall any man hate me? That is his affair. But I will be mild and benevolent towards everyone, ready to show his mistake to this very man, not reproachfully, nor yet as making a display of my forbearance, but nobly and honestly, like the great Phocion,[5] unless indeed he only assumed it. That is the proper inner state, and a man should not be seen by the gods to be either dissatisfied or complaining. For what evil is it to you, if you are now doing what is agreeable to your own nature, and are satisfied with that which at the moment is suitable to nature, since you are a human being placed at your post to endure whatever is for the common advantage?

14. Men despise one another, and flatter one another; and men wish to raise themselves above one another, and crouch before one another.

15. How unsound and insincere is he who says, "I have determined to deal with you in a fair way." What, do you have to give notice of fairness? It will show soon enough in action. Truth will be plainly written on your forehead. A man's character shows itself in his voice and eyes, just as lovers may read everything in each other's eyes. The man who is honest and good ought to be like a man who has a strong odor: anyone who comes near must smell whether he choose or not. But

---

[5] Possibly a reference to the Athenian statesman Phocion's charge to his son, before drinking the hemlock, "to bear no ill will against the Athenians."

the affectation of simplicity is like a crooked stick.[6] Nothing is more disgraceful than a wolfish friendship. Avoid this most of all. The good and simple and benevolent show all these things in the eyes, and there is no mistaking.

16. As to the perfecting of life, this power is in the soul, and it grows by being indifferent towards things which are indifferent. And it will be indifferent if it looks on each of these things separately and all together, and if it remembers that not one of them produces in us an opinion about itself, nor comes to us; but these things remain immovable, and it is we ourselves who produce the judgments about them, and, as we may say, write them on our minds, it being in our power not to write them, and it being in our power, if perchance these judgments have gained admission imperceptibly, to wipe them out. And the need for such discipline will be necessary only for a short time, and then life will be at an end. Why make a grievance out of doing this? For if these things are according to nature, rejoice in them, and they will be easy for you; but if contrary to nature, seek what is in harmony with your own nature and strive towards this, even if it bring no reputation; for every man is allowed to seek his own good.

17. Consider whence each thing comes, of what it consists, and into what it changes, what it will be like when changed, and that it will sustain no harm.

18. Consider these things: First, what is my relation to men; we are made for one another; or, in another view, I was made to be set over them, as a ram over a flock or a bull over a herd. But examine the question from first principles: If all things are not mere atoms, it is nature which orders all things; if this is so, the inferior things exist for the sake of the superior, and these for the sake of one another (II, 1; IX, 39; V, 16; III, 4).

---

[6] There is a Greek proverb, "You cannot make a crooked stick straight."

Second, consider how men are at table, in bed, and so forth; and particularly, under what compulsions they are with respect to opinions; and as to their acts, consider with what pride they do what they do (VIII, 14; IX, 34).

Third, that if men do rightly what they do, we ought not to be displeased; but if they do not right, it is plain that they do so involuntarily and in ignorance. For as every soul is unwillingly deprived of the truth, so also is it unwillingly deprived of the power of behaving to each man according to his deserts. Accordingly, men are pained when they are called unjust, ungrateful, and greedy, or charged with behaving wrongfully to their neighbors (VII, 62, 63; II, 1; VII, 26; VIII, 29).

Fourth, consider that you also do many things wrong, that you are a man like others; and even if you abstain from certain faults, you still have the disposition to commit them, though either through cowardice, or concern for reputation, or some such mean motive, you refrain from wrongdoing (I, 17).

Fifth, consider that you do not even know whether men are doing wrong or not, for many things are done with a certain reference to circumstances. In short, a man must learn a great deal to enable him to pass a correct judgment on another man's acts (IX, 38; IV, 51).

Sixth, consider when you are vexed or grieved that man's life is only a moment, and after a short time we all lie stretched in death (VII, 58; IV, 48).

Seventh, that it is not men's acts which disturb us, for those acts have their foundation in men's ruling principles, but it is our own opinions regarding them. Take away these opinions then, and resolve to dismiss your judgment about an act as if it were something grievous, and your anger is gone. How then shall you take away these opinions? By reflecting that no wrongful act of another brings shame on you; for since that which is shameful is alone bad, you must of necessity do all sorts of evil, become a robber and everything else (V, 25; VII, 16).

Eighth, consider how much more pain is brought on us by the anger and vexation caused by such acts than by the acts themselves, at which we are angry and vexed (IV, 39, 49; VII, 24).

Ninth, consider that benevolence is invincible if it be genuine, and not merely an affected smile and playing a part. For what will the most violent man do to you, if you continue to be of a benevolent disposition towards him and, as opportunity offers, gently admonish him and calmly correct his errors at the very time he is trying to do you harm, saying, "Not so, my child. We are constituted by nature for something else: I shall certainly not be injured, but you are injuring yourself, my child." And show him with gentle tact and by general principles that this is so, and that even bees do not as he does, nor any animals which are formed by nature to be gregarious. And do this neither with any double meaning, nor in the way of reproach, but affectionately and without rancor in your soul; and not as if you were lecturing him, or to show off before others, but quietly in his own ear, even if others are present.

Remember these nine rules, as if you had received them as a gift from the Muses, and begin at last to be a man so long as you live. But you must equally avoid flattering men and being vexed at them, for both are unsocial and lead to harm. And let this truth be present to you in the excitement of anger, that to be moved by passion is not manly, but that mildness and gentleness are more manly, just as they are more in conformity with human nature. And he who possesses these qualities possesses strength, nerves, and courage, and not the man who is subject to fits of passion and discontent. For in the same degree in which a man's mind is nearer to freedom from all passion, in the same degree also is it nearer to strength; and as the sense of pain is a characteristic of weakness, so also is anger. For he who yields to pain and he who yields to anger are both wounded, and both submit.

But if you will, receive also a tenth gift from Apollo, leader of the Muses, and it is this: That to expect bad men not to do wrong is madness, for he who expects this desires an impossibility. But to allow men to behave evilly to each other, and not to expect them to do you any wrong is irrational and tyrannical.

19. There are four principal aberrations of the superior faculty against which you should be constantly on guard, and when you have detected them you should wipe them out, saying on each occasion: This thought is not necessary; this tends to destroy social union; this which you are going to say comes not from your real thoughts—for you should consider it the most absurd of things for a man not to speak his real thoughts. But the fourth is when you reproach yourself for anything, for this is evidence of the diviner part within being overpowered and yielding to the less honorable and perishable part, the body, and to its gross pleasures (IV, 24; II, 16).

20. Your aerial part and all the fiery parts which are mingled in you, though by nature they have an upward tendency, still in obedience to the disposition of the universe they submit and keep their place in the compound mass. And also, the earthy and watery parts in you, whose tendency is downward, are raised up and keep a position which is not theirs by nature. In this manner then the elemental parts obey the universal, for when they have been fixed in any place they remain there until the universal sounds the signal for dissolution. Is it not then strange that your intelligent part alone should be disobedient with its own place? And yet no force is imposed on it, but only those things which are in harmony with its nature; even so, it does not submit, but is carried in the opposite direction. For the movement towards injustice and intemperance, anger, grief, and fear, is nothing else than the act of one who deviates from nature. And when the ruling faculty is discontented, then too it deserts its post; for it is constituted for piety and reverence towards the gods, no less than for justice. For these qualities also are comprehended under the generic term of contentment with the constitution of things, and indeed they are prior to acts of justice.

21. He who has not one and always the same object in life cannot be one and the same all through his life. But what I have said is not enough, unless this also is added, what this object ought to be. For as there is not the same opinion about all the things which in some way or other are considered by the majority to be good, but only about some certain things, that is, things which concern the common interest; so also ought we to propose to ourselves an aim which shall be of a social and political kind. For he who directs all his own efforts to this end, will make all his acts alike, and thus will always be the same.

22. Think of the country mouse and of the town mouse, and of the alarm and trepidation of the town mouse.[7]

23. Socrates used to call the opinions of the many by the name of "Lamiae," bugbears to frighten children.

24. The Lacedaemonians at their public spectacles used to set seats in the shade for strangers, but themselves sat down anywhere.

25. Socrates excused himself to Perdiccas [8] for not going to him, saying, "It is because I would not perish by the worst of all ends, that is, I would not receive a favor and then be unable to return to it."

26. In the writings of the Ephesians there was this precept, constantly to think of some one of the men of former times who practiced virtue.

27. The Pythagoreans bid us in the morning look to the heavens that we may be reminded of those bodies which con-

---

[7] The story is told by Horace in his *Satires* (II, 6), and by others since.

[8] Other writers say it was Archelaus, the son of King Perdiccas, who invited Socrates to Macedonia.

tinually do the same things and in the same manner perform their work, and also be reminded of their purity and nudity. For there is no veil over a star.

28. Consider what a man Socrates was when he dressed himself in a skin, after Xantippe had taken his cloak and gone out, and what Socrates said to his friends who were ashamed of him and drew back from him when they saw him dressed thus.

29. Neither in writing nor in reading will you be able to lay down rules for others before you shall have first learned to obey the rules yourself. Much more is this so in life.

30. A slave thou art: reason is not for thee!

31. And my heart laughed within! [9]

32. Virtue they will curse with harsh words. [10]

33. "To look for the fig in winter is a madman's act; such is he who looks for his child when the time is past." [11]

34. "When a man kisses his child he should whisper to himself, Tomorrow, perchance you may die." "But those are words of bad omen." "No word is of bad omen which expresses any work of nature; or if it is so it is also a word of bad omen to speak of the ears of corn being reaped."

35. "The unripe grape, the ripe bunch, the dried grape, are all changes, not into nothing, but into something which exists not yet."

36. "No man can rob us of our free will."

37. Epictetus also said, "A man must discover rules for giving his assent; and in respect to his movements he must be careful that they be made with regard to circumstances, consistent with social interests, and have regard to the value of the object; and as to sensual desire, he should keep from it

[9] Homer, *Odyssey*. See Classics Club edition, p. 113.

[10] Hesiod, *Works and Days*, 184.

[11] This quotation and the three following ones are paraphrases from the *Discourses* of Epictetus.

altogether; and as to aversion, he should show it with respect to things not in our power."

38. "The dispute then," he said, "is not about any common matter, but about being mad or not."

39. Socrates used to say: "What do you want—souls of rational or irrational men? If souls of rational men, what rational men? Sound or unsound?" "Sound." "Then why do you not seek them?" "Because we have them." "Why then do you fight and quarrel?"

XII

1. All those things to which you wish to attain sooner or later, you can have now, if you do not refuse them; if only you will take no notice of the past, and trust the future to providence, and direct the present in harmony with piety and justice. In harmony with piety that you may be content with the lot which is assigned to you, for nature designed it for you and you for it. In harmony with justice, that you may always speak the truth freely and without disguise, and do the things which are agreeable to law and according to the worth of each. And let neither another man's wickedness hinder you, nor opinion, nor voice, nor any persuasion of the flesh; for let that which suffers look to itself. If then, whatever the time may be when you shall be near your departure, you shall respect only your ruling faculty and the divinity within you, neglecting everything else, and if you are afraid—not that you shall some day cease to live but that you shall never have begun to live according to nature—then you will be a man worthy of the universe which has produced you, and you will cease to be a stranger in your native land, and to wonder at things which happen daily as if they were something unexpected and to be dependent on this event or that.

2. God sees the ruling principles of all men bared of the material vesture and rind and impurities. With his mental being he touches the intelligence which has flowed and been derived from himself into these bodies. If you accustom yourself to the same habit, you will rid yourself of much trouble. For he who looks not to his poor fleshly shell surely will not trouble himself by looking after raiment, houses, fame, and such externals and show.

3. You are composed of three things: body, life, intelligence. Of these the first two are yours, inasmuch as it is your duty to take care of them; but the third alone is really yours. Therefore if you will separate from yourself, that is, from your understanding, whatever others do or say, and whatever you have done or said yourself, and whatever future things trouble you because they may happen, and whatever in the body which envelops you or in the breath which is by nature associated with the body is attached to you independent of your will, and whatever the external circumfluent vortex whirls round, so that the intellectual power, exempt from the things of fate, can live pure and free by itself, doing what is just and accepting what happens and saying the truth; if you will separate, I say, from this ruling faculty the things which are attached to it by the impressions of sense, and the things of time to come and of time that is past, and will make yourself like Empedocles' sphere,

All round, and in its joyous rest reposing;

and if you strive to live only what is really your life, that is, the present—then you will be able to pass that portion of life which remains for you up to the time of your death, free from perturbations, nobly, and obedient to your own deity within (II, 13, 17; III, 5, 6; XI, 12).

4. I have often wondered how it is that every man loves himself more than all the rest of men, but yet sets less value on his own opinion of himself than on the opinion of others.

For if a god or a wise teacher should present himself to a man and bid him to think of nothing and to design nothing which he would not express as soon as he conceived it, he could not endure it even for a single day. So much more respect have we for what our neighbors think of us than for what we think of ourselves.

5. How can it be that the gods, after having arranged all things well and benevolently for mankind, have overlooked only this, that some men and very good men, and men who through pious acts and religious observances have had most intimate communion with the divinity, when they have once died should never exist again, but should be completely extinguished?

But if this is so, be assured that if it ought to have been otherwise, the gods would have done it. For if it were just, it would also be possible; and if it were according to nature, nature would have had it so. But because it is not so, if in fact it is not so, be assured that it ought not to have been so: for you see that in this inquiry you are disputing with the deity; and we could not thus dispute with the gods unless they were most excellent and just; but if this is so, they would not have allowed anything in the ordering of the universe to be neglected unjustly and irrationally.

6. Practice even at the things which you despair of accomplishing. For even the left hand, which is ineffectual for all other things for want of practice, holds the bridle more vigorously than the right hand; for it has been practiced in this.

7. Consider in what condition both in body and soul a man should be when he is overtaken by death; and consider the shortness of life, the boundless abyss of time past and future, the feebleness of all matter.

8. Contemplate the formative principles of things, bare of their coverings; the purposes of actions; consider what pain is, what pleasure is, and death, and fame; who is to himself the

cause of his uneasiness; how no man is hindered by another; that everything is opinion.

9. In the application of your principles you must be like the pancratiast,[1] not like the gladiator; for the gladiator lets fall the sword which he uses and is killed; but the other always has his hand, and needs to do nothing else than use it.

10. See what things are in themselves, dividing them into matter, form and purpose.

11. What a power man has to do nothing except what God will approve, and to accept all that God may give him.

12. With respect to that which happens in harmony with nature, we ought to blame neither gods, for they do nothing wrong either voluntarily or involuntarily, nor men, for they do nothing wrong, except involuntarily. Consequently we should blame nobody (II, 11, 12, 13; VII, 62; VIII, 17).

13. How ridiculous and how strange to be surprised at anything which happens in life!

14. Either there is a fatal necessity and invincible order, or a kind of providence, or a confusion without a purpose and without a director (IV, 27). If then there is an invincible necessity, why do you resist? But if there is a providence which allows itself to be propitiated, make yourself worthy of the help of the divinity. But if all is confusion without a governor, be content that in such a tempest you have in yourself a certain ruling intelligence. And even if the tempest carry you away, let it carry away the poor flesh, the breath, everything else; for the intelligence at least it will not sweep away.

15. Does the light of the lamp shine without losing its radiance until it is extinguished? Shall the truth and justice and temperance which is in you be extinguished?

16. When a man gives the impression of wrongdoing, say to yourself, "How do I know that it is a wrongful act?" And even if he has done wrong, how do I know that he has not con-

---

[1] A victor in the pancratium, a contest which included boxing and wrestling of all sorts.

demned himself—like the mourner tearing his own face? Remember that he who would not have the bad man do wrong is like one who would not have the fig tree bear juice in its figs and infants to cry and horses to neigh, and whatever else must of necessity be. For what must a man do who has such a character? If then you are irritable with a man, amend his disposition.

17. If it is not right, do not do it; if it is not true, do not say it.

18. In everything always observe what the thing is which produces an appearance, and resolve it by dividing it into the causal, the material, the purpose, and the time within which it must end.

19. Perceive at last that you have within you something better and more divine than the things which cause the various effects, and, as it were, pull you around by strings. What is there now in your mind? Is it fear, or suspicion, or desire, or anything of the kind? (v, 11).

20. First, do nothing thoughtlessly or without a purpose. Secondly, see that your acts are directed to a social end.

21. Consider that before long you will be nobody and nowhere, nor will any of the things exist which you now see, nor any of those who are now living. For all things are formed by nature to change and be turned and to perish in order that other things in continuous succession may exist (ix, 28).

22. Consider that everything is opinion, and opinion is in your power. Disown opinion when you choose; and like a mariner, who has doubled the promontory, you will find calm, still waters and a waveless bay.

23. Any one activity, whatever it may be, when it has ceased at its proper time, suffers no evil because it has ceased; nor he who has done this act, does he suffer any evil for this reason that the act has ceased. In like manner then the whole which consists of all the acts, which is our life, if it cease at its proper time, suffers no evil that it has ceased; nor he who has terminated this series at the proper time, has he been ill dealt with. But the proper time and the limit nature fixes, sometimes as in old age the peculiar nature of man, but always the universal nature, by the change of whose parts the whole universe continues ever young and perfect. And everything which is useful to the universal is always good and in season. Therefore the termination of life for every man is no evil, because it is nothing shameful, since it is both independent of the will and not opposed to the general interest, but it is good, since it is seasonable and profitable to the universal. For thus man becomes one with the deity, moved in the same manner with the deity in tendency and intent.

24. These three principles you must have in readiness. Do nothing either inconsiderately or otherwise than as justice herself would act; but with respect to what may happen to you from without, consider that it happens either by chance or according to providence, and you must neither blame chance nor accuse providence. Second, consider what every being is from the seed to the time of its receiving a soul, and from the reception of a soul to the giving back of the same, and of what things every being is compounded and into what things it is resolved. Third, if you should suddenly be raised up above the earth, and should look down on human things, and observe the variety of them how great it is, and at the same time also should see at a glance how great is the number of beings who dwell all around in the air and the ether, consider that as often as you should be raised up you would see the same things, sameness of form and shortness of duration. Are these things any ground for pride?

25. Cast away opinion: you are saved. Who hinders you from casting it away?

26. When you are troubled about anything, you have forgotten this, that all things happen according to the universal nature, and that a man's wrongful act is nothing to you; and further you have forgotten this, that everything which hap-

pens always happened so, and will happen so, and now happens so everywhere; forgotten this too, how close is the kinship between a man and the whole human race, for it is a community, not of a little blood or seed, but of intelligence. And you have forgotten this too, that every man's intelligence is a god, and is an efflux of the deity; and that nothing is a man's own, but that his child and his body and his very soul came from the deity; that everything is opinion; and lastly, that every man lives the present time only, and loses only this.

27. Constantly bring to your recollection those who have complained greatly about anything, those who have been most conspicuous by the greatest fame, or misfortunes and enmities, or fortunes of any kind; then think where are they all now? Smoke and ash and a tale and not even a tale. And let there be present to your mind also things of this sort, how Fabius Catullinus lived in the country, and Lucius Lupus in his gardens, and Stertinius at Baiae, and Tiberius at Capri, and Rufus at Velia; and, in short, think of the eager pursuit of anything joined together with pride; and how worthless everything is after which men strain violently; and how much more philosophical it is for a man in the opportunities presented to him to show himself just, temperate, obedient to the gods, and to do this with all simplicity: for the pride which is proud of its want of pride is the most intolerable of all.

28. To those who ask, "Where have you seen the gods and how do you know they exist, that you worship them as you do?" I answer: "In the first place, they may be seen even with the eyes;[2] in the second place, neither have I seen even my own soul and yet I honor it. Thus then with respect to the

---

[2] It is supposed that this may be explained by the Stoic doctrine that the universe is a god (IV, 23) and that the celestial bodies are gods (VIII, 19). But the emperor may mean that we know the gods exist, as he afterward states it, because we see what they do; as we know that man has intellectual powers, because we see what he does.

gods, from what I constantly experience of their power, from this I comprehend that they exist and I venerate them."

29. The safety of life is this, to examine everything all through, what it is itself, what is its material, what the causal part; and with all your soul to do justice and to speak the truth. What remains except to enjoy life by joining one good thing to another so as not to leave even the smallest gap between?

30. There is one light of the sun though it is distributed over walls, mountains, and other things infinite. There is one common substance, though it is distributed among countless bodies which have their several qualities. There is one soul, though it is distributed among infinite natures and individuals. There is one intelligent soul, though it seems to be divided. Now in the things which have been mentioned all the other parts, such as those which are air and substance, are without sensation and have no fellowship: and yet even these parts the intelligent principle holds together and they gravitate towards the same. But intellect in a peculiar manner tends to that which is of the same kin, and combines with it, and the feeling for communion is not interrupted.

31. What do you wish? To continue to exist? Well, do you wish to have sensation, movement, growth? And then again to cease to grow, to use speech, to think? What is there of all these things which seems to you worth desiring? But if it is easy to set little value on all these things, turn to that which remains, which is to follow reason and God. But it is inconsistent with honoring reason and God to be troubled because by death a man will be deprived of the other things.

32. How small a part of the boundless and unfathomable time is assigned to every man! In a moment it is swallowed up in the eternal. And how small a part of the whole substance, and how small a part of the universal soul! And on what a small clod of the whole earth you creep! Reflecting on all this, consider nothing to be great, except to act as your na-

ture leads you and to endure that which the common nature brings.

33. How does the ruling faculty make use of itself? For all lies in this. But everything else, whether it is in the power of your will or not, is only lifeless ashes and smoke.

34. This reflection is most adapted to move us to contempt of death, that even those who think pleasure to be a good and pain an evil still have despised it.

35. The man to whom that only is good which comes in due season, and to whom it is the same thing whether he has done more or fewer acts conformable to right reason, and to whom it makes no difference whether he contemplates the world for a longer or a shorter time—for this man neither is death a terrible thing (III, 7; VI, 23; X, 20; XII, 23).

36. Man, you have been a citizen in this great state (II, 16; III, 11; IV, 29): What difference does it make to you whether for five years or three? For that which is conformable to the laws is just for all. Where is the hardship then, if no tyrant nor yet an unjust judge sends you away from the state, but nature who brought you into it? The same as if a praetor who has employed an actor dismisses him from the stage. "But I have not finished the five acts, but only three of them." Good, but in life the three acts are the whole drama. For what shall constitute a complete drama is determined by him who first caused its composition, and now its dissolution: but you are the cause of neither. Depart then serenely, for he who releases you is also serene.

MARIUS THE
EPICUREAN[1]

XII

THE DIVINITY THAT DOTH
HEDGE A KING

But ah! Maecenas is yclad in claye,
And great Augustus long ygoe is dead,
And all the worthies liggen wrapt in lead,
That matter made for poets on to playe.

MARCUS AURELIUS who, though he had little relish for them
himself, had ever been willing to humor the taste of his people
for magnificent spectacles, was received back to Rome with
the lesser honors of the *Ovation*, conceded by the Senate (so
great was the public sense of deliverance) with even more
than the laxity which had become its habit under imperial
rule, for there had been no actual bloodshed in the late
achievement. Clad in the civic dress of the chief Roman
magistrate, and with a crown of myrtle upon his head, his

---

[1] Two chapters of Walter Pater's novel, *Marius the Epicurean*, are
introduced here, the first showing Marcus Aurelius performing his
official duties on his return from the war in the East, and the second
to present him at home in his intimate family circle.

colleague similarly attired walking beside him, he passed up
to the Capitol on foot, though in solemn procession along
the Sacred Way, to offer sacrifice to the national gods. The
victim, a goodly sheep, whose image we may still see between
the pig and the ox of the *Suovetaurilia*, filleted and stoled
almost like some ancient canon of the church, on a sculp-
tured fragment in the Forum, was conducted by the priests,
clad in rich white vestments, and bearing their sacred utensils
of massive gold, immediately behind a company of flute-
players, led by the great choir-master, or *conductor*, of the
day, visibly tetchy or delighted, according as the instruments
he ruled with his tuning-rod, rose, more or less adequately
amid the difficulties of the way, to the dream of perfect music
in the soul within him. The vast crowd, including the soldiers
of the triumphant army, now restored to wives and children,
all alike in holiday whiteness, had left their houses early in
the fine, dry morning, in a real affection for "the father of
his country," to await the procession, the two princes having
spent the preceding night outside the walls, at the old *Villa
of the Republic*. Marius, full of curiosity, had taken his position with much care; and stood to see the world's masters
pass by, at an angle from which he could command the view
of a great part of the processional route, sprinkled with fine
yellow sand, and punctiliously guarded from profane footsteps.

The coming of the pageant was announced by the clear
sound of the flutes, heard at length above the acclamations
of the people—*Salve Imperator!—Dii te servent!*—shouted in
regular time, over the hills. It was on the central figure, of
course, that the whole attention of Marius was fixed from
the moment when the procession came in sight, preceded by
the lictors with gilded *fasces*, the imperial image-bearers,
and the pages carrying lighted torches; a band of knights,
among whom was Cornelius in complete military array, following. Amply swathed about in the folds of a richly worked

toga, after a manner now long since become obsolete with
meaner persons, Marius beheld a man of about five-and-forty
years of age, with prominent eyes—eyes, which although
demurely downcast during this essentially religious ceremony, were by nature broadly and benignantly observant.
He was still, in the main, as we see him in the busts which
represent his gracious and courtly youth, when Hadrian
had playfully called him, not *Verus*, after the name of his
father, but *Verissimus*, for his candor of gaze, and the bland
capacity of the brow, which, below the brown hair, cluster-
ing thickly as of old, shone out low, broad, and clear, and
still without a trace of the trouble of his lips. You saw the
brow of one who, amid the blindness or perplexity of the
people about him, understood all things clearly; the dilemma,
to which his experience so far had brought him, between
Chance with meek resignation, and a Providence with boundless possibilities and hope, being for him at least distinctly
defined.

That outward serenity, which he valued so highly as a
point of manner or expression not unworthy the care of a
public minister—outward symbol it might be thought, of
the inward religious serenity it had been his constant purpose to maintain—was increased today by his sense of the
gratitude of his people; that his life had been one of such
gifts and blessings as made his person seem in very deed divine
to them. Yet the cloud of some reserved internal sorrow,
passing from time to time into an expression of fatigue and
effort, of loneliness amid the shouting multitude, might have
been detected there by the more observant—as if the sagacious
hint of one of his officers, "The soldiers can't understand you,
they don't know Greek," were applicable always to his re-
lationships with other people. The nostrils and mouth seemed
capable almost of peevishness; and Marius noted in them, as
in the hands, and in the spare body generally, what was new
to his experience—something of asceticism, as we say, of ₂

bodily gymnastic by which, although it told pleasantly in the clear blue humors of the eye, the flesh had scarcely been an equal gainer with the spirit. It was hardly the expression of "the healthy mind in the healthy body," but rather of a sacrifice of the body to the soul, its needs and aspirations, that Marius seemed to divine in this assiduous student of the Greek sages—a sacrifice, in truth, far beyond the demands of their very saddest philosophy of life.

Dignify thyself with modesty and simplicity for thine ornaments!—had been ever a maxim with this dainty and high-bred Stoic, who still thought *manners* a true part of *morals,* according to the old sense of the term, and who regrets now and again that he cannot control his thoughts equally well with his countenance. That outward composure was deepened during the solemnities of this day by an air of pontifical abstraction; which, though very far from being pride—nay, a sort of humility rather—yet gave, to himself, an air of unapproachableness, and to his whole proceeding, in which every minutest act was considered, the character of a ritual. Certainly, there was no haughtiness, social, moral, or even philosophic, in Aurelius, who had realized, under more trying conditions perhaps than anyone before, that no element of humanity could be alien from him. Yet, as he walked today, the center of ten thousand observers, with eyes discreetly fixed on the ground, veiling his head at times and muttering very rapidly the words of the "supplications," there was something many spectators may have noted as a thing new in their experience, for Aurelius, unlike his predecessors, took all this with absolute seriousness. The doctrine of the sanctity of kings, that, in the words of Tacitus, Princes are as Gods—*Principes instar deorum esse*—seemed to have taken a novel, because a literal, sense. For Aurelius, indeed, the old legend of his descent from Numa, from Numa who had talked with the gods, meant much. Attached in very early years to the service of the altars, like many another noble youth, he was "observed to perform all his sacerdotal functions with a constancy and exactness unusual at that age; was soon a master of the sacred music; and had all the forms and ceremonies by heart." And now, as the emperor, who had not only a vague divinity about his person, but was actually the chief religious functionary of the state, recited from time to time the forms of invocation, he needed not the help of the prompter, or *Ceremoniarius*, who then approached, to assist him by whispering the appointed words in his ear. It was that pontifical abstraction which then impressed itself on Marius as the leading outward characteristic of Aurelius; though to him alone, perhaps, in that vast crowd of observers, it was no strange thing, but a matter he had understood from of old.

Some fanciful writers have assigned the origin of these triumphal processions to the mythic pomps of Dionysus, after his conquests in the East; the very word *Triumph* being, according to this supposition, only *Thriambos*—the Dionysiac Hymn. And certainly the younger of the two imperial "brothers," who, with the effect of a strong contrast, walked beside Aurelius, and shared the honors of the day, might well have reminded people of the delicate Greek god of flowers and wine. This new conqueror of the East was now about thirty-six years old, but with his scrupulous care for all the advantages of his person, and a soft curling beard powdered with gold, looked many years younger. One result of the more genial element in the wisdom of Aurelius had been that, amid most difficult circumstances, he had known throughout life how to act in union with persons of character very alien from his own; to be more than loyal to the colleague, the younger brother in empire, he had too lightly taken to himself, five years before, then an uncorrupt youth, "skilled in manly exercises and fitted for war." When Aurelius thanks the gods that a brother had fallen to his lot, whose character was a stimulus to the proper care of his own,

one sees that this could only have happened in the way of
an example, putting him on his guard against insidious faults.
But it is with sincere amiability that the imperial writer,
who was indeed little used to be ironical, adds that the lively
respect and affection of the junior had often "gladdened"
him. To be able to make his use of the flower, when the
fruit perhaps was useless or poisonous: that was one of the
practical successes of his philosophy; and his people noted,
with a blessing, "the concord of the two Augusti."

The younger, certainly, possessed in full measure that
charm of a constitutional freshness of aspect which may
defy for a long time extravagant or erring habits of life; a
physiognomy healthy-looking, cleanly, and firm, which
seemed unassociable with any form of self-torment, and made
one think of the muzzle of some young hound or roe, such
as human beings invariably like to stroke—a physiognomy, in
effect, with all the goodliness of animalism of the finer sort,
though still wholly animal. The charm was that of the blond
head, the unshrinking gaze, the warm tints: neither more
nor less than one may see every English summer, in youth,
manly enough, and with the stuff which makes brave soldiers,
in spite of the natural kinship it seems to have with playthings
and gay flowers. But innate in Lucius Verus there was that
more than womanly fondness for fond things, which had
made the atmosphere of the old city of Antioch, heavy with
centuries of voluptuousness, a poison to him: he had come
to love his delicacies best out of season, and would have gilded
the very flowers. But with a wonderful power of self-
obliteration, the elder brother at the capital had directed his
procedure successfully, and allowed him, become now also
the husband of his daughter Lucilla, the credit of a "Con-
quest," though Verus had certainly not returned a conqueror over himself. He had returned, as we know, with
the plague in his company, along with many another strange
creature of his folly; and when the people saw him publicly

feeding his favorite horse *Fleet* with almonds and sweet grapes, wearing the animal's image in gold, and finally building it a tomb, they felt, with some unsentimental misgiving, that he might revive the manners of Nero.—What if, in the chances of war, he should survive the protecting genius of that elder brother?

He was all himself today: and it was with much wistful curiosity that Marius regarded him. For Lucius Verus was, indeed, but the highly expressive type of a class—the true son of his father, adopted by Hadrian. Lucius Verus the elder, also, had had the like strange capacity for misusing the adornments of life, with a masterly grace; as if such misusing were, in truth, the quite adequate occupation of an intelligence, powerful, but distorted by cynical philosophy or some disappointment of the heart. It was almost a sort of genius, of which there had been instances in the imperial purple: it was to ascend the throne, a few years later, in the person of one, now a hopeful little lad at home in the palace; and it had its following, of course, among the wealthy youth at Rome, who concentrated no inconsiderable force of shrewdness and tact upon minute details of attire and manner, as upon the one thing needful. Certainly, flowers were pleasant to the eye. Such things had even their sober use, as making the outside of human life superficially attractive, and thereby promoting the first steps towards friendship and social amity. But what precise place could there be for Verus and his peculiar charm, in that *Wisdom*, that Order of divine Reason "reaching from end to end, strongly and sweetly disposing all things," from the vision of which Aurelius came down, so tolerant of persons like him? Into such vision Marius too was certainly well-fitted to enter, yet, noting the actual perfection of Lucius Verus after his kind, his undeniable achievement of the select, in all minor things, felt, though with some suspicion of himself, that he entered into, and could understand, this other so dubious sort of character also. There was a voice in the theory he had brought to Rome with him which whispered "nothing is either great nor small"; as there were times when he could have thought that, as the "grammarian's" or the artist's ardor of soul may be satisfied by the perfecting of the theory of a sentence, or the adjustment of two colors, so his own life also might have been fulfilled by an enthusiastic quest after perfection—say, in the flowering and folding of a toga.

The emperors had burned incense before the image of Jupiter, arrayed in its most gorgeous apparel, amid sudden shouts from the people of *Salve Imperator!* turned now from the living princes to the deity, as they discerned his countenance through the great open doors. The imperial brothers had deposited their crowns of myrtle on the richly embroidered lapcloth of the gods; and, with their chosen guests sat down to a public feast in the temple itself. There followed what was, after all, the great event of the day: an appropriate discourse, a discourse almost wholly *de contemptu mundi*, delivered in the presence of the assembled Senate, by the emperor Aurelius, who had thus, on certain rare occasions, condescended to instruct his people, with the double authority of a chief pontiff and a laborious student of philosophy. In those lesser honors of the *Ovation*, there had been no attendant slave behind the emperors, to make mock of their effulgence as they went; and it was as if with the discretion proper to a philosopher, and in fear of a jealous Nemesis, he had determined himself to protest in time against the vanity of all outward success.

The Senate was assembled to hear the emperor's discourse in the vast hall of the *Curia Julia*. A crowd of high-bred youths idled around, or on the steps before the doors, with the marvelous toilets Marius had noticed in the *Via Nova;* in attendance, as usual, to learn by observation the minute points of senatorial procedure. Marius had already some acquaintance with them, and passing on found himself suddenly in the presence of what was still the most august assembly the world had seen. Under Aurelius, ever full of veneration for this ancient traditional guardian of public religion, the Senate had recovered all its old dignity and independence. Among its members many hundreds in number, visibly the most distinguished of them all, Marius noted the great sophists or rhetoricians of the day, in all their magnificence. The antique character of their attire, and the ancient mode of wearing it, still surviving with them, added to the imposing character of their persons, while they sat, with their staves of ivory in their hands, on their curule chairs—almost the exact pattern of the chair still in use in the Roman church when a Bishop *pontificates* at the divine offices—"tranquil and unmoved, with a majesty that seemed divine," as Marius thought, like the old Gaul of the Invasion. The rays of the early November sunset slanted full upon the audience, and made it necessary for the officers of the court to draw the purple curtains over the windows, adding to the solemnity of the scene. In the depth of those warm shadows, surrounded by her ladies, the empress Faustina was seated to listen. The beautiful Greek statue of Victory, which since the days of Augustus had presided over the assemblies of the Senate, had been brought into the hall, and placed near the chair of the emperor; who, after rising to perform a brief sacrificial service in its honor, bowing reverently to the assembled fathers left and right, took his seat and began to speak.

There was a certain melancholy grandeur in the very simplicity or triteness of the theme: as it were the very quintessence of all the old Roman epitaphs, of all that was monumental in that city of tombs, layer upon layer of dead things and people. As if in the very fervor of disillusion, he seemed to be composing the sepulchral titles of ages and whole peoples; nay! the very epitaph of the living Rome itself. The grandeur of the ruins of Rome—heroism in ruin: it was under the influence of an imaginative anticipation of this, that he appeared to be speaking. And though the impression of the actual greatness of Rome on that day was but enhanced by the strain of contempt, falling with an accent of pathetic conviction from the emperor himself, and gaining from his pontifical pretensions the authority of a religious intimation, yet the curious interest of the discourse lay in this, that Marius, for one, as he listened, seemed to foresee a grass-grown Forum, the broken ways of the Capitol, and the Palatine hill itself in humble occupation. That impression connected itself with what he had already noted of an actual change even then coming over Italian scenery. Throughout, he could trace something of a humor into which Stoicism at all times tends to fall, the tendency to cry, *Abase yourselves!* There was here the almost inhuman impassibility of one who had thought too closely on the paradoxical aspect of the love of posthumous fame. With the ascetic pride which lurks under all Platonism, resultant from its opposition of the seen to the unseen, as falsehood to truth—the imperial Stoic, like his true descendant, the hermit of the middle age, was ready, in no friendly humor, to mock, there in its narrow bed, the corpse which had made so much of itself in life. Marius could but contrast all that with his own Cyrenaic eagerness, just then, to taste and see and touch; reflecting on the opposite issues deducible from the same text. "The world, within me and without, flows away like a river," he had said; "therefore let me make the most of what is here and now."—"The world and the thinker upon it are consumed like a flame," said Aurelius, "therefore will I turn away my eyes from vanity; renounce; withdraw myself alike from all affections." He seemed tacitly to claim as a sort of personal dignity, that he was very familiarly versed in this view of things, and could discern a death's-head everywhere. Now and again Marius was reminded of the saying that "with the Stoics all people are the vulgar save themselves"; and at times the orator seemed to have forgotten his audience, and to be speaking only to himself.

"Art thou in love with men's praises, get thee into the very soul of them, and see!—see what judges they be, even in those matters which concern themselves. Wouldst thou have their praise after death, bethink thee, that they who shall come hereafter, and with whom thou wouldst survive by thy great name, will be but as these, whom here thou hast found so hard to live with. For of a truth, the soul of him who is aflutter upon renown after death, presents not this aright to itself, that of all whose memory he would have each one will likewise very quickly depart, until memory herself be put out, as she journeys on by means of such as are themselves on the wing but for a while, and are extinguished in their turn.—Making so much of those thou wilt never see! It is as if thou wouldst have had those who were before thee discourse fair things concerning thee.

"To him, indeed, whose wit hath been whetted by true doctrine, that well-worn sentence of Homer sufficeth, to guard him against regret and fear:

> *Like the race of leaves*
> *The race of man is:*
> *The wind in autumn strows*
> *The earth with old leaves, then the spring the woods with*
> *new endows.*

Leaves! little leaves!—thy children, thy flatterers, thine enemies! Leaves in the wind, those who would devote thee to darkness, who scorn or miscall thee here, even as they also whose great fame shall outlast them. For all these, and the like of them, are born indeed in the spring season and soon a wind hath scattered them, and thereafter the wood peopleth itself again with another generation of leaves. And what is common to all of them is but the littleness of their lives: and yet wouldst thou love and hate, as if these things should continue forever. In a little while thine eyes also will be closed, and he on whom thou perchance hast leaned thyself be himself a burden upon another.

"Bethink thee often of the swiftness with which the things that are, or are even now coming to be, are swept past thee: that the very substance of them is but the perpetual motion of water: that there is almost nothing which continueth: of that bottomless depth of time, so close at thy side. Folly! to be lifted up, or sorrowful, or anxious, by reason of things like these! Think of infinite matter, and thy portion—how tiny a particle, of it! of infinite time, and thine own brief point there; of destiny, and the jot thou art in it; and yield thyself readily to the wheel of Clotho, to spin of thee what web she will.

"As one casting a ball from his hand, the nature of things hath had its aim with every man, not as to the ending only, but the first beginning of his course, and passage thither. And hath the ball any profit of its rising, or loss as it descendeth again, or in its fall? or the bubble, as it groweth or breaketh on the air? or the flame of the lamp, from the beginning to the end of its brief story?

"All but at this present that future is, in which nature, who disposeth all things in order, will transform whatsoever thou now seest, fashioning from its substance somewhat else, and therefrom somewhat else in its turn, lest the world grow old. We are such stuff as dreams are made of—disturbing dreams. Awake, then! and see thy dream as it is, in comparison with that erewhile it seemed to thee.

"And for me, especially, it were well to mind those many mutations of empire in time past; therein peeping also upon the future, which must needs be of like species with what hath been, continuing ever within the rhythm and number of things which really are; so that in forty years one may note of man and of his ways little less than in a thousand. Ah! from this higher place, look we down upon the shipwrecks and the calm! Consider, for example, how the world went, under the emperor Vespasian. They are married and given in marriage, they breed children, love hath its way with them; they heap up riches for others or for themselves; they are murmuring at things as then they are; they are seeking for great place; crafty, flattering, suspicious, waiting upon the death of others; festivals, business, war, sickness, dissolution: and now their whole life is no longer anywhere at all. Pass on to the reign of Trajan; all things continue the same: and that life also is no longer anywhere at all. Ah! but look again, and consider, one after another, as it were the sepulchral inscriptions of all peoples and times, according to one pattern. What multitudes, after their utmost striving—a little afterwards! were dissolved again into their dust.

"Think again of life as it was far off in the ancient world; as it must be when we shall be gone; as it is now among the wild heathen. How many have never heard your names and mine, or will soon forget them! How soon may those who shout my name today begin to revile it, because glory, and the memory of men, and all things beside, are but vanity—a sand-heap under the senseless wind, the barking of dogs, the quarreling of children, weeping incontinently upon their laughter.

"This hasteth to be; that other to have been: of that which now cometh to be, even now somewhat hath been extinguished. And wilt thou make thy treasure of any one of these things? It were as if one set his love upon the swallow, as it passeth out of sight through the air!

"Bethink thee often, in all contentions public and private, of those whom men have remembered by reason of their anger and vehement spirit—those famous rages, and the occasions of them—the great fortunes, and misfortunes, of men's strife of old. What are they all now, and the dust of their battles? Dust and ashes indeed; a fable, a mythus, or not so much as that. Yes! Keep those before thine eyes who took this or that, the like of which happeneth to thee, so hardly; were so querulous, so agitated. And where again are they? Wouldst thou have it not otherwise with thee?

"Consider how quickly all things vanish away—their bodily structure into the general substance; the very memory of them into that great gulf and abysm of past thoughts. Ah! 'tis on a tiny space of earth thou art creeping through life—a pigmy soul carrying a dead body to its grave.

"Let death put thee upon the consideration both of thy body and thy soul: what an atom of all matter hath been distributed to thee; what a little particle of the universal mind. Turn thy body about, and consider what thing it is, and that which old age, and lust, and the languor of disease can make of it. Or come to its substantial and causal qualities, its very type: contemplate that in itself, apart from the accidents of matter, and then measure also the span of time for which the nature of things, at the longest, will maintain that special type. Nay! in the very principles and first constituents of things corruption hath its part—so much dust, humor, stench, and scraps of bone! Consider that thy marbles are but the earth's callosities, thy gold and silver its *faeces;* this silken robe but a worm's bedding, and thy purple an unclean fish. Ah! and thy life's breath is not otherwise, as it passeth out of matters like these, into the like of them again.

"For the one soul in things, taking matter like wax in the hands, molds and remolds—how hastily!—beast, and plant, and the babe, in turn: and that which dieth hath not slipped out of the order of nature, but, remaining therein, hath also its changes there, disparting into those elements of which nature herself, and thou too, art compacted. She changes without murmuring. The oaken chest falls to pieces with no more complaining than when the carpenter fitted it together. If one told thee certainly that on the morrow thou shouldst die, or at the furthest on the day after, it would be no great matter to thee to die on the day after tomorrow, rather than

tomorrow. Strive to think it a thing no greater that thou
wilt die—not tomorrow, but a year, or two years, or ten
years from today.

"I find that all things are now as they were in the days of
our buried ancestors—all things sordid in their elements, trite
by long usage, and yet ephemeral. How ridiculous, then, how
like a countryman in town, is he, who wonders at aught. Doth
the sameness, the repetition of the public shows, weary thee?
Even so doth that likeness of events in the spectacle of the
world. And so must it be with thee to the end. For the wheel
of the world hath ever the same motion, upward and downward, from generation to generation. When, when, shall time
give place to eternity?

"If there be things which trouble thee thou canst put them
away, inasmuch as they have their being but in thine own
notion concerning them. Consider what death is, and how,
if one does but detach from it the appearances, the notions,
that hang about it, resting the eye upon it as in itself it really
is, it must be thought of but as an effect of nature, and that
man but a child whom an effect of nature shall affright. Nay!
not function and effect of nature, only; but a thing profitable
also to herself.

"To cease from action—the ending of thine effort to think
and do: there is no evil in that. Turn thy thought to the ages
of man's life, boyhood, youth, maturity, old age: the change
in every one of these also is a dying, but evil nowhere. Thou
climbedst into the ship, thou hast made thy voyage and
touched the shore: go forth now! Be it into some other life:
the divine breath is everywhere, even there. Be it into forgetfulness forever; at least thou wilt rest from the beating of
sensible images upon thee, from the passions which pluck
thee this way and that like an unfeeling toy, from those long
marches of the intellect, from thy toilsome ministry to the
flesh.

"Art thou yet more than dust and ashes and bare bone—

a name only, or not so much as that, which also, is but whispering and a resonance, kept alive from mouth to mouth of dying abjects who have hardly known themselves; how much less thee, dead so long ago!

"When thou lookest upon a wise man, a lawyer, a captain of war, think upon another gone. When thou seest thine own face in the glass, call up there before thee one of thine ancestors—one of those old Caesars. Lo! everywhere, thy double before thee! Thereon, let the thought occur to thee: And where are they? anywhere at all, forever? And thou, thyself —how long? Art thou blind to that thou art—thy matter, how temporal; and thy function, the nature of thy business? Yet tarry, at least, till thou hast assimilated even these things to thine own proper essence, as a quick fire turneth into heat and light whatsoever be cast upon it.

"As words once in use are antiquated to us, so is it with the names that were once on all men's lips: Camillus, Volesus, Leonnatus: then, in a little while, Scipio and Cato, and then Augustus, and then Hadrian, and then Antoninus Pius. How many great physicians who lifted wise brows at other men's sickbeds, have sickened and died! Those wise Chaldeans, who foretold, as a great matter, another man's last hour, have themselves been taken by surprise. Aye! and all those others, in their pleasant places: those who doted on a Capreae like Tiberius, on their gardens, on the baths: Pythagoras and Socrates, who reasoned so closely upon immortality; Alexander, who used the lives of others as though his own should last forever—he and his mule-driver alike now!—one upon another. Well-nigh the whole court of Antoninus is extinct. Panthea and Pergamus sit no longer beside the sepulcher of their lord. The watchers over Hadrian's dust have slipped from his sepulcher. It were jesting to stay longer. Did they sit there still, would the dead feel it? or feeling it, be glad? or glad, hold those watchers forever? The time must come when they too shall be aged men and aged women, and decease, and fall from their places; and what shift were there then for imperial service? This too is but the breath of the tomb, and a skinful of dead men's blood.

"Think again of those inscriptions, which belong not to one soul only, but to whole families: *He was the last of his race*. Nay! of the burial of whole cities: Helice, Pompeii; of others, whose very burial place is unknown.

"Thou hast been a citizen in this wide city. Count not for how long, nor repine; since that which sends thee hence is no unrighteous judge, no tyrant, but Nature, who brought thee hither; as when a player leaves the stage at the bidding of the conductor who hired him. Sayest thou, 'I have not played five acts'? True! but in human life, three acts only make sometimes an entire play. That is the composer's business, not thine. Withdraw thyself with a good will; for that too hath, perchance, a good will which dismisseth thee from thy part."

The discourse ended almost in darkness, the evening having set in somewhat suddenly, with a heavy fall of snow. The torches, made ready to do him a useless honor, were of real service now, as the emperor was solemnly conducted home; one man rapidly catching light from another—a long stream of moving lights across the white Forum, up the great stairs, to the palace. And, in effect, that night winter began, the hardest that had been known for a lifetime. The wolves came from the mountains; and, led by the carrion scent, devoured the dead bodies which had been hastily buried during the plague, and, emboldened by their meal, crept, before the short day was well past, over the walls of the farmyards of the *Campagna*. The eagles were seen driving the flocks of smaller birds across the dusky sky. Only, in the city itself the winter was all the brighter for the contrast, among those who could pay for light and warmth. The habit-makers made a great sale of the spoil of all such furry creatures as had

escaped wolves and eagles, for presents at the *Saturnalia;* and
at no time had the winter roses from Carthage seemed more
lustrously yellow and red.

XIII

THE "MISTRESS AND MOTHER" OF PALACES

AFTER that sharp, brief winter, the sun was already at work,
softening leaf and bud, as you might feel by a faint sweetness
in the air; but he did his work behind an evenly white sky,
against which the abode of the Caesars, its cypresses and
bronze roofs, seemed like a picture in beautiful but melancholy color, as Marius climbed the long flights of steps to be
introduced to the emperor Aurelius. Attired in the newest
mode, his legs wound in dainty *fasciae* of white leather, with
the heavy gold ring of the *ingenuus,* and in his toga of ceremony, he still retained all his country freshness of complexion.
The eyes of the "golden youth" of Rome were upon him as
the chosen friend of Cornelius, and the destined servant of the
emperor; but not jealously. In spite of, perhaps partly because
of, his habitual reserve of manner, he had become "the
fashion," even among those who felt instinctively the irony
which lay beneath that remarkable self-possession, as of one
taking all things with a difference from other people, per-
ceptible in voice, in expression, and even in his dress. It was,
in truth, the air of one who, entering vividly into life, and
relishing to the full the delicacies of its intercourse, yet feels
all the while, from the point of view of an ideal philosophy,
that he is but conceding reality to suppositions, choosing of

his own will to walk in a daydream, of the illusiveness of
which he at least is aware.

In the house of the chief chamberlain Marius waited for
the due moment of admission to the emperor's presence. He
was admiring the peculiar decoration of the walls, colored like
rich old red leather. In the midst of one of them was depicted,
under a trellis of fruit you might have gathered, the figure
of a woman knocking at a door with wonderful reality of
perspective. Then the summons came; and in a few minutes,
the etiquette of the imperial household being still a simple
matter, he had passed the curtains which divided the central
hall of the palace into three parts—three degrees of approach
to the sacred person—and was speaking to Aurelius himself;
not in Greek, in which the emperor oftenest conversed with
the learned, but, more familiarly, in Latin, adorned however,
or disfigured, by many a Greek phrase, as now and again
French phrases have made the adornment of fashionable English. It was with real kindliness that Marcus Aurelius looked
upon Marius, as a youth of great attainments in Greek letters
and philosophy; and he liked also his serious expression, being,
as we know, a believer in the doctrine of physiognomy—that,
as he puts it, not love only, but every other affection of man's
soul, looks out very plainly from the window of the eyes.

The apartment in which Marius found himself was of ancient aspect, and richly decorated with the favorite toys of
two or three generations of imperial collectors, now finally
revised by the high connoisseurship of the Stoic emperor himself, though destined not much longer to remain together
there. It is the repeated boast of Aurelius that he had learned
from old Antoninus Pius to maintain authority without the
constant use of guards, in a robe woven by the handmaids of
his own consort, with no processional lights or images, and
"that a prince may shrink himself almost into the figure of a
private gentleman." And yet, again as at his first sight of him,
Marius was struck by the profound religiousness of the sur-

roundings of the imperial presence. The effect might have been due in part to the very simplicity, the discreet and scrupulous simplicity, of the central figure in this splendid abode; but Marius could not forget that he saw before him not only the head of the Roman religion, but one who might actually have claimed something like divine worship, had he cared to do so. Though the fantastic pretensions of Caligula had brought some contempt on that claim, which had become almost a jest under the ungainly Claudius, yet, from Augustus downwards, a vague divinity had seemed to surround the Caesars even in this life; and the peculiar character of Aurelius, at once a ceremonious polytheist never forgetful of his pontifical calling, and a philosopher whose mystic speculation encircled him with a sort of saintly halo, had restored to his person, without his intending it, something of that divine prerogative, or prestige. Though he would never allow the immediate dedication of altars to himself, yet the image of his *Genius*—his spirituality or celestial counterpart—was placed among those of the deified princes of the past; and his family, including Faustina and the young Commodus, was spoken of as the "holy" or "divine" house. Many a Roman courtier agreed with the barbarian chief, who, after contemplating a predecessor of Aurelius, withdrew from his presence with the exclamation: "I have seen a god today!" The very roof of his house, rising into a pediment or gable, like that of the sanctuary of a god, the laurels on either side its doorway, the chaplet of oak-leaves above, seemed to designate the place for religious veneration. And notwithstanding all this, the household of Aurelius was singularly modest, with none of the wasteful expense of palaces after the fashion of Lewis the Fourteenth; the palatial dignity being felt only in a peculiar sense of order, the absence of all that was casual, of vulgarity and discomfort. A merely official residence of his predecessors, the *Palatine* had become the favorite dwelling-place of Aurelius; its many-colored memories suiting, perhaps, his pensive character, and the crude splendors of Nero and Hadrian being now subdued by time. The windowless Roman abode must have had much of what to a modern would be gloom. How did the children, one wonders, endure houses with so little escape for the eye into the world outside? Aurelius, who had altered little else, choosing to *live* there, in a genuine homeliness, had shifted and made the most of the level lights, and broken out a quite medieval window here and there, and the clear daylight, fully appreciated by his youthful visitor, made pleasant shadows among the objects of the imperial collection. Some of these, indeed, by reason of their Greek simplicity and grace, themselves shone out like spaces of a purer, early light, amid the splendors of the Roman manufacture.

Though he looked, thought Marius, like a man who did not sleep enough, he was abounding and bright today, after one of those pitiless headaches, which since boyhood had been the "thorn in his side," challenging the pretensions of his philosophy to fortify one in humble endurances. At the first moment, to Marius, remembering the spectacle of the emperor in ceremony, it was almost bewildering to be in private conversation with him. There was much in the philosophy of Aurelius—much consideration of mankind at large, of great bodies, aggregates and generalities, after the Stoic manner—which, on a nature less rich than his, might have acted as an inducement to care for people in inverse proportion to their nearness to him. That has sometimes been the result of the Stoic cosmopolitanism. Aurelius, however, determined to beautify by all means, great or little, a doctrine which had in it some potential sourness, had brought all the quickness of his intelligence, and long years of observation, to bear on the conditions of social intercourse. He had early determined "not to make business an excuse to decline the offices of humanity—not to pretend to be too much occupied with important affairs to concede what life with others may hourly demand"; and with such success, that, in an age which made much of the finer points of that intercourse, it was felt that the mere honesty of his conversation was more pleasing than other men's flattery. His agreeableness to his young visitor today was, in truth, a blossom of the same wisdom which had made of Lucius Verus really a brother—the wisdom of not being exigent with men, any more than with fruit-trees (it is his own favorite figure) beyond their nature. And there was another person, still nearer to him, regarding whom this wisdom became a marvel, of equity—of charity.

The center of a group of princely children, in the same apartment with Aurelius, amid all the refined intimacies of a modern home, sat the empress Faustina, warming her hands over a fire. With her long fingers lighted up red by the glowing coals of the brazier Marius looked close upon the most beautiful woman in the world, who was also the great paradox of the age, among her boys and girls. As has been truly said of the numerous representations of her in art, so in life, she had the air of one curious, restless, to enter into conversation with the first comer. She had certainly the power of stimulating a very ambiguous sort of curiosity about herself. And Marius found this enigmatic point in her expression, that even after seeing her many times he could never precisely recall her features in absence. The lad of six years, looking older, who stood beside her, impatiently plucking a rose to pieces over the hearth, was, in outward appearance, his father—the young *Verissimus*—over again; but with a certain feminine length of feature, and with all his mother's alertness, or license, of gaze.

Yet rumor knocked at every door and window of the imperial house regarding the adulterers who knocked at them, or quietly left their lovers' garlands there. Was not that likeness of the husband, in the boy beside her, really the effect of a shameful magic, in which the blood of the murdered gladiator, his true father, had been an ingredient? Were the tricks for deceiving husbands which the Roman poet describes, really hers, and her household an efficient school of all the arts of furtive love? Or, was the husband too aware, like everyone beside? Were certain sudden deaths which happened there really the work of apoplexy or the plague?

The man whose ears, whose soul, those rumors were meant to penetrate, was, however, faithful to his sanguine and optimist philosophy, to his determination that the world should be to him simply what the higher reason preferred to conceive it; and the life's journey Aurelius had made so far, though involving much moral and intellectual loneliness had been ever in affectionate and helpful contact with other wayfarers, very unlike himself. Since his days of earliest childhood in the Lateran gardens, he seemed to himself, blessing the gods for it after deliberate survey, to have been always surrounded by kinsmen, friends, servants, of exceptional virtue. From the great Stoic idea, that we are all fellow citizens of one city, he had derived a tenderer, a more equitable estimate than was common among Stoics, of the eternal shortcomings of men and women. Considerations that might tend to the sweetening of his temper it was his daily care to store away, with a kind of philosophic pride in the thought that no one took more goodnaturedly than he the "oversights" of his neighbors. For had not Plato taught (it was not paradox, but simple truth of experience) that if people sin, it is because they know no better, and are "under the necessity of their own ignorance"? Hard to himself, he seemed at times, doubtless, to decline too softly upon unworthy persons. Actually, he came thereby upon many a useful instrument. The empress Faustina he would seem at least to have kept, by a constraining affection, from becoming altogether what most people have believed her, and won in her (we must take him at his word in the "Thoughts," abundantly confirmed by letters, on both sides, in his correspondence with Cornelius Fronto) a consolation, the more secure, perhaps, because misknown of others. Was the secret of her actual blamelessness, after all, with him who has at least screened her name? At all events, the one thing quite certain about her, besides her extraordinary beauty, is her sweetness to himself.

No! The wise, who had made due observation on the trees of the garden, would not expect to gather grapes of thorns or fig trees: and he was the vine, putting forth his genial fruit, by natural law, again and again, after his kind, whatever use people might make of it. Certainly, his actual presence never lost its power, and Faustina was glad in it today, the birthday of one of her children, a boy who stood at her knee holding in his fingers tenderly a tiny silver trumpet, one of his birthday gifts.—"For my part, unless I conceive my hurt to be such, I have no hurt at all,"—boasts the would-be apathetic emperor—"and how I care to conceive of the thing rests with me." Yet when his children fall sick or die, this pretense breaks down, and he is broken-hearted: and one of the charms of certain of his letters still extant, is his reference to those childish sicknesses.—"On my return to Lorium," he writes, "I found my little lady—*domnulam meam*—in a fever"; and again, in a letter to one of the most serious of men, "You will be glad to hear that our little one is better, and running about the room—*parvolam nostram melius valere et intra cubiculum discurrere.*"

The young Commodus had departed from the chamber, anxious to witness the exercises of certain gladiators, having a native taste for such company, inherited, according to popular rumor, from his true father—anxious also to escape from the too impressive company of the gravest and sweetest specimen of old age Marius had ever seen, the tutor of the imperial children, who had arrived to offer his birthday congratulations, and now, very familiarly and affectionately, made a part of the group, falling on the shoulders of the emperor, kissing the empress Faustina on the face, the little ones on the face and hands. Marcus Cornelius Fronto, the "Orator," fa-

vorite teacher of the emperor's youth, afterwards his most
trusted counselor, and now the undisputed occupant of the
sophistic throne, whose equipage, elegantly mounted with
silver, Marius had seen in the streets of Rome, had certainly
turned his many personal gifts to account with a good fortune, remarkable even in that age, so indulgent to professors
or rhetoricians. The gratitude of the emperor Aurelius, always generous to his teachers, arranging their very quarrels
sometimes, for they were not always fair to one another, had
helped him to a really great place in the world. But his
sumptuous appendages, including the villa and gardens of
Maecenas, had been borne with an air perfectly becoming, by
the professor of a philosophy which, even in its most accomplished and elegant phase, presupposed a gentle contempt for
such things. With an intimate practical knowledge of manners, physiognomies, smiles, disguises, flatteries, and courtly
tricks of every kind—a whole accomplished rhetoric of daily
life—he applied them all to the promotion of humanity, and
especially of men's family affection. Through a long life of
now eighty years, he had been, as it were, surrounded by the
gracious and soothing air of his own eloquence—the fame,
the echoes, of it—like warbling birds, or murmuring bees.
Setting forth in that fine medium the best ideas of matured
pagan philosophy, he had become the favorite "director" of
noble youth.

Yes! it was the one instance Marius, always eagerly on the
lookout for such, had yet seen of a perfectly tolerable, perfectly beautiful, old age—an old age in which there seemed,
to one who perhaps habitually overvalued the expression of
youth, nothing to be regretted, nothing really lost, in what
years had taken away. The wise old man, whose blue eyes and
fair skin were so delicate, uncontaminate and clear, would
seem to have replaced carefully and consciously each natural
trait of youth, as it departed from him, by an equivalent grace
of culture; and had the blitheness, the placid cheerfulness, as

he had also the infirmity, the claim on stronger people, of a delightful child. And yet he seemed to be but awaiting his exit from life—that moment with which the Stoics were almost as much preoccupied as the Christians, however differently—and set Marius pondering on the contrast between a placidity like this, at eighty years, and the sort of desperateness he was aware of in his own manner of entertaining that thought. His infirmities nevertheless had been painful and long-continued, with losses of children, of pet grandchildren. What with the crowd, and the wretched streets, it was a sign of affection which had cost him something, for the old man to leave his own house at all that day; and he was glad of the emperor's support, as he moved from place to place among the children he protests so often to have loved as his own.

For a strange piece of literary good fortune, at the beginning of the present century, has set free the long-buried fragrance of this famous friendship of the old world, from below a valueless later manuscript, in a series of letters, wherein the two writers exchange, for the most part their evening thoughts, especially at family anniversaries, and with entire intimacy, on their children, on the art of speech, on all the various subtleties of the "science of images"—rhetorical images—above all, of course, on sleep and matters of health. They are full of mutual admiration of each other's eloquence, restless in absence till they see one another again, noting, characteristically, their very dreams of each other, expecting the day which will terminate the office, the business or duty, which separates them—"as superstitious people watch for the star, at the rising of which they may break their fast." To one of the writers, to Aurelius, the correspondence was sincerely of value. We see him once reading his letters with genuine delight on going to rest. Fronto seeks to deter his pupil from writing in Greek.—Why buy, at great cost, a foreign wine, inferior to that from one's own vineyard? Aurelius, on the other hand, with an extraordinary innate susceptibility to words—

la parole pour la parole, as the French say—despairs, in presence of Fronto's rhetorical perfection.

Like the modern visitor to the Capitoline and some other museums, Fronto had been struck, pleasantly struck, by the family likeness among the Antonines; and it was part of his friendship to make much of it, in the case of the children of Faustina. "Well! I have seen the little ones," he writes to Aurelius, then, apparently, absent from them: "I have seen the little ones—the pleasantest sight of my life; for they are as like yourself as could possibly be. It has well repaid me for my journey over that slippery road, and up those steep rocks; for I beheld you, not simply face to face before me, but, more generously, whichever way I turned, to my right and my left. For the rest, I found them, Heaven be thanked! with healthy cheeks and lusty voices. One was holding a slice of white bread, like a king's son; the other a crust of brown bread, as becomes the offspring of a philosopher. I pray the gods to have both the sower and the seed in their keeping; to watch over this field wherein the ears of corn are so kindly alike. Ah! I heard too their pretty voices, so sweet that in the childish prattle of one and the other I seemed somehow to be listening—yes! in that chirping of your pretty chickens—to the limpid and harmonious notes of your own oratory. Take care! you will find me growing independent, having those I could love in your place—love, on the surety of my eyes and ears."

"*Magistro meo salutem!*" replies the Emperor, "I too have seen my little ones in your sight of them; as, also, I saw yourself in reading your letter. It is that charming letter forces me to write thus:" with reiterations of affection, that is, which are continual in these letters, on both sides, and which may strike a modern reader perhaps as fulsome; or, again, as having something in common with the old Judaic unction of friendship. They were certainly sincere.

To one of those children Fronto had now brought the

birthday gift of the silver trumpet, upon which he ventured to blow softly now and again, turning away with eyes delighted at the sound, when he thought the old man was not listening. It was the well-worn, valetudinarian subject of sleep, on which Fronto and Aurelius were talking together. Aurelius always feeling it a burden, Fronto a thing of magic capacities, so that he had written an *encomium* in its praise, and often by ingenious arguments recommends his imperial pupil not to be sparing of it. Today, with his younger listeners in mind, he had a story to tell about it:

"They say that our father Jupiter, when he ordered the world at the beginning, divided time into two parts exactly equal: the one part he clothed with light, the other with darkness: he called them Day and Night; and he assigned rest to the night and to day the work of life. At that time Sleep was not yet born and men passed the whole of their lives awake; only, the quiet of the night was ordained for them, instead of sleep. But it came to pass, little by little, being that the minds of men are restless, that they carried on their business alike by night as by day, and gave no part at all to repose. And Jupiter, when he perceived that even in the nighttime they ceased not from trouble and disputation, and that even the courts of law remained open (it was the pride of Aurelius, as Fronto knew, to be assiduous in those courts till far into the night) resolved to appoint one of his brothers to be the overseer of the night and have authority over man's rest. But Neptune pleaded in excuse the gravity of his constant charge of the seas, and Father Dis the difficulty of keeping in subjection the spirits below; and Jupiter, having taken counsel with the other gods, perceived that the practice of nightly vigils was somewhat in favor. It was then, for the most part, that Juno gave birth to her children: Minerva, the mistress of all art and craft, loved the midnight lamp: Mars delighted in the darkness for his plots and sallies; and the favor of Venus and Bacchus was with those who roused by night. Then it was that Jupiter formed the design of creating Sleep; and he added him to the number of the gods, and gave him the charge over night and rest, putting into his hands the keys of human eyes. With his own hands he mingled the juices wherewith Sleep should soothe the hearts of mortals—herb of Enjoyment and herb of Safety, gathered from a grove in Heaven; and, from the meadows of Acheron, the herb of Death: expressing from it one single drop only, no bigger than a tear one might hide. 'With this juice,' he said, 'pour slumber upon the eyelids of mortals. So soon as it hath touched them they will lay themselves down motionless, under thy power. But be not afraid: they shall revive, and in a while stand up again upon their feet.' Thereafter, Jupiter gave wings to Sleep, attached, not, like Mercury's, to his heels, but to his shoulders, like the wings of Love. For he said, 'It becomes thee not to approach men's eyes as with the noise of chariots, and the rushing of a swift courser, but in placid and merciful flight, as upon the wings of a swallow—nay! with not so much as the flutter of the dove.' Besides all this, that he might be yet pleasanter to men, he committed to him also a multitude of blissful dreams, according to every man's desire. One watched his favorite actor; another listened to the flute, or guided a charioteer in the race: in his dream, the soldier was victorious, the general was borne in triumph, the wanderer returned home. Yes!—and sometimes those dreams come true!"

Just then Aurelius was summoned to make the birthday offerings to his household gods. A heavy curtain of tapestry was drawn back; and beyond it Marius gazed for a few moments into the *Lararium*, or imperial chapel. A patrician youth, in white habit, was in waiting, with a little chest in his hand containing incense for the use of the altar. On richly carved *consoles*, or sideboards, around this narrow chamber, were arranged the rich apparatus of worship and the golden or gilded images, adorned today with fresh flowers, among them that image of Fortune from the apartment of Antoninus

Pius, and such of the emperor's own teachers as were gone to their rest. A dim fresco on the wall commemorated the ancient piety of Lucius Albinius, who in flight from Rome on the morrow of a great disaster, overtaking certain priests on foot with their sacred utensils, descended from the wagon in which he rode and yielded it to the ministers of the gods. As he ascended into the chapel the emperor paused, and with a grave but friendly look at his young visitor, delivered a parting sentence, audible to him alone: *Imitation is the most acceptable part of worship: the gods had much rather mankind should resemble than flatter them. Make sure that those to whom you come nearest be the happier by your presence!*

It was the very spirit of the scene and the hour—the hour Marius had spent in the imperial house. How temperate, how tranquilizing! what humanity! Yet, as he left the eminent company concerning whose ways of life at home he had been so youthfully curious, and sought, after his manner, to determine the main trait in all this, he had to confess that it was a sentiment of mediocrity, though of a mediocrity for once really golden.

PART II

Lucian of Samosata, Skeptic

INTRODUCTION

THE satirist Lucian was born about the year 125 A.D. in Samosata, an Oriental town on the Euphrates, in the northeastern corner of Syria, then a province of the Roman Empire. In this eastern end of the Empire had arisen many diverse sects and philosophies. Lucian grew to maturity in the midst of a veritable hotbed of clashing cults and spent the greater portion of his adult life satirizing them and the society which supported them, with such vigor and wit that his words are stingingly alive today. Like other arch-skeptics with whom he is often compared—Swift, Voltaire and Rabelais—he could not endure the pretensions of those who claimed that their philosophies or their beliefs represented the only truth. And like those three fellow-spirits of later centuries, he attained a literary skill that places him among the great masters of literature. In his development of the dialogue as a literary form, he is in the direct Socratic line, and like Socrates, used this instrument to stimulate straight thinking on numerous aspects of contemporary life. Like Socrates too, he held up for laughter many permanent weaknesses of humankind. In one of his *Letters to Dead Authors*, Andrew Lang addresses him thus: "Yes, Lucian, we are the same vain creatures of doubt and dread, of unbelief and credulity, of avarice and pretense that you knew, at whom you smile." Lucian indeed makes us feel ourselves akin to the Romans and the people they were governing in the second century after Christ.

The period was one of great intellectual flux, of restless probing. Side by side in Rome—as well as in the cultural centers of Greece and Asia Minor—there lived sincere and devout pagans, such as the Emperor Marcus Aurelius; skeptics, who neglected the old schools of philosophy and the old religions, preferring what we would call agnosticism; and those men of the new faith which was spreading—in spite of scorn and persecution—through the Empire from Galilee.

In certain of its features, Lucian's life makes us think of a modern "success story." It wears the familiar pattern of a poor boy rising to fame and riches. He started as a humble, uncouth colonial who, before he could pass as an educated man, had to master the language of culture as a foreign tongue, and who nevertheless attained sufficient stature to attack the favorite philosophy of the emperor himself. There is also a contemporary sound to his choice of vocations. He was, first, a popular lecturer who made an excellent living by amusing and even shocking his audiences, then, in later life, a comfortably-placed civil official, serving the interests of the imperial government in Egypt. Quite apart from his writings, which are full of the spirit of modern agnosticism, these two biographical details seem to link Lucian of Samosata to our own times.

The known facts of Lucian's life are few, and may be quickly recounted. His parents chose for him the respectable career of statuary or stone-cutter, and he was apprenticed to an uncle. The first day ended disastrously: Lucian broke a valuable piece of marble and was sent home. But this accident proved a blessing in disguise, for it turned his mother's thoughts to other and higher callings. It was at length decided that the bright boy should be trained for the profession of scholar or rhetorician, and Lucian left home to achieve this ambition. He was at the time, he tells us somewhere, a "barbarian" unacquainted with Greek, and garbed in Oriental fashion. But ten years among the Sophists in the Ionian cities of Asia Minor and in Greece put a high polish on the rough diamond. He mastered the Greek language, studied all the great Greek writers, and prepared himself for the fields of rhetoric and law. A rhetorician in those days had a number of employments open to him. He might plead cases for a client in court; write speeches for other men to deliver; teach, and eventually become the head of a school; or he might follow the career of public lecturer. How many of these activities Lucian engaged in we do not know, but we have ample data as to his success as a lecturer. It was the custom for lecturers to speak often extemporaneously on whatever subject was proposed by a member of the audience, and to this training we may attribute Lucian's quickness of wit and readiness of tongue.

At all events, it is known that he lived for a time at Rome in the reign of Marcus Aurelius and that he traveled widely in Trans-Alpine Gaul and other corners of the Empire, achieving prestige and prosperity. We can envisage him as an emissary of free thought, carrying advanced ideas from the centers of learning into the more backward hinterland. There is a record of his meeting in Antioch with Lucius Verus, Marcus Aurelius' coadjutor and half-brother, which would seem to indicate that his talents were recognized in the highest circles. In middle life, however, he settled down in Athens, having brought his father and family from Asia Minor to live with him there. He now turned his attention to serious work as a writer, particularly to the development of the form for which he is most famous—the satiric dialogue. Later he returned to popular lecturing. At the time of his death about 200 A.D., he was, as we have said, a government official in Egypt.

Although our knowledge of the events of his life is scanty, we may glean much from his writings of his interests and impulses. Many, too, of the people he knew are clearly, even mercilessly, portrayed in his dialogues. Expert as Lucian was in the art of rhetoric, when in middle age he abandoned rhetoric for dialectic, we may assume he no longer cared only to win arguments, which was the business of rhetoricians and lawyers, but to present some view of truth, which was the aim of dialectic or the dialogue. The best of the dialogues

have come down through the centuries to enkindle other
minds. His penetrating observation of human foibles, his fan-
tasy and lightness of touch are qualities which his admirers
prize. He was a crusader particularly against hypocrisy and
sham, a shatterer of idols, and no respecter of official cults. In
fact, one of his *bêtes noirs* was the Stoic school, which enjoyed the support and patronage of Marcus Aurelius. He took
pains also to ridicule Platonic doctrines of the immortality and transmigration of souls; even Aristotle did not escape
his caustic criticisms.

Lucian's titles have a strangely modern sound. There is an
essay called "The Illiterate Bibliophile" which today's dealers
in rare books may read with delight. "The Encomium on a
Fly" suggests Charles Lamb in its delicate whimsicality. "The
Cult of Sigma versus Tau" and "The Purist Purized" are
philological fooling at a high level. "The Sale of Creeds" and
"The Way to Write History" are full of wit and malice. In
the "Dialogues of the Hetaerae" the pitiful trivia of trivial
minds are emptied out in a way to remaind us of silly girls'
gossip about boy-friends today. "The Dependent Scholar"
also has a contemporary application, depicting as it does the
plight of the "kept" mind. The "Dialogues of the Gods,"
"The Gods in Council," and several others of the kind, surely
helped to give the death-blow to faith in Zeus and his turbu-
lent Olympian family. The parasite, the legacy-seeker, the
dealers in marvels and miracles, oracles and warnings, are
among Lucian's favorite targets.

More than sixty of his critical essays and dialogues have
come down to us. Two dialogues were chosen for inclusion
in this volume. "Hermotimus or the Rival Philosophies" is
one of the longest. In it Lucian, in the person of Lycinus, a
cognomen he frequently used when expressing his own
point of view, has excellent sport with Hermotimus, the perpetual student, and in the course of the conversation, takes
occasion to challenge most of the prevailing schools of phi-

losophy. The second dialogue, the "Icaromenippus," or in other words, "The Flying Menippus," is a saucy mockery of the traditional gods of Olympus, as well as of the philosophers. Icarus, we may remember, was the earliest recorded aviator. Lucian's lesson here, as elsewhere, is to do one's thinking for oneself. He had no pity for man's delusions, errors, and aspirations; to that Christian virtue he was a stranger.

The translation here used is that which H. W. and F. G. Fowler made from the Greek.

HERMOTIMUS, OR THE
RIVAL PHILOSOPHIES

Lycinus. Hermotimus

Ly. Good morning, Hermotimus; I guess by your book and the pace you are going at that you are on your way to lecture, and a little late. You were conning over something as you walked, your lips working and muttering, your hand flung out this way and that as you got a speech into order in your mind; you were doubtless inventing one of your crooked questions, or pondering some tricky problem; never a vacant mind, even in the streets; always on the stretch and in earnest, bent on advancing in your studies.

Her. I admit the impeachment; I was running over the details of what he said in yesterday's lecture. One must lose no chance, you know; the Coan doctor[1] spoke so truly: *ars longa, vita brevis*.[2] And what *he* referred to was only physic—a simpler matter. As to philosophy, not only will you never attain it, however long you study, unless you are wide awake all the time, contemplating it with intense eager gaze; the stake is so tremendous, too—whether you shall rot miserably with the vulgar herd, or be counted among philosophers and reach Happiness.

Ly. A glorious prize, indeed! however, you cannot be far off it now, if one may judge by the time you have given to philosophy, and the extraordinary vigor of your long pursuit. For twenty years now, I should say, I have watched you perpetually going to your professors, generally bent over a book taking notes of past lectures, pale with thought and emaciated in body. I suspect you find no release even in your dreams,

---
[1] Hippocrates. [2] Art is long, life is short.

you are so wrapped up in the thing. With all this you must surely get hold of Happiness soon, if indeed you have not found it long ago without telling us.

Her. Alas, Lycinus, I am only just beginning to get an inkling of the right way. Very far off dwells Virtue, as Hesiod says, and long and steep and rough is the way thither, and travelers must bedew it with sweat.

Ly. And you have not yet sweated and traveled enough?

Her. Surely not; else should I have been on the summit, with nothing left between me and bliss; but I am only starting yet, Lycinus.

Ly. Ah, but Hesiod, your own authority, tells us, Well begun is half done; so we may safely call you half-way by this time.

Her. Not even there yet; that would indeed have been much.

Ly. Where *shall* we put you, then?

Her. Still on the lower slopes, just making an effort to get on; but it is slippery and rough, and needs a helping hand.

Ly. Well, your master can give you that; from his station on the summit, like Zeus in Homer with his golden cord, he can let you down his discourse, and therewith haul and heave you up to himself and to the Virtue which he has himself attained this long time.

Her. The very picture of what he is doing; if it depended on him alone, I should have been hauled up long ago; it is my part that is still wanting.

Ly. You must be of good cheer and keep a stout heart; gaze at the end of your climb and the Happiness at the top, and remember that he is working with you. What prospect does he hold out? when are you to be up? does he think you will be on the top next year—by the Great Mysteries, or the Panathenaea,[3] say?

---

[3] Two festivals of this name were celebrated in Athens, the lesser annually, the greater every fourth year.

Her. Too soon, Lycinus.

Ly. By next Olympiad, then?

Her. All too short a time, even that, for habituation to Virtue and attainment of Happiness.

Ly. Say two Olympiads, then, for an outside estimate. You may fairly be found guilty of laziness, if you cannot get it done by then; the time would allow you three return trips from the Pillars of Heracles to India, with a margin for exploring the tribes on the way instead of sailing straight and never stopping. How much higher and more slippery, pray, is the peak on which your Virtue dwells than that Aornos crag which Alexander stormed in a few days?

Her. There is no resemblance, Lycinus. This is not a thing, as you conceive it, to be compassed and captured quickly, though ten thousand Alexanders were to assault it; in that case, the scalers would have been legion. As it is, a good number begin the climb with great confidence, and do make progress, some very little indeed, others more; but when they get half-way, they find endless difficulties and discomforts, lose heart, and turn back, panting, dripping, and exhausted. But those who endure to the end reach the top, to be blessed thenceforth with wondrous days, looking down from their height upon the ants which are the rest of mankind.

Ly. Dear me, what tiny things you make us out—not so big as the Pygmies even, but positively groveling on the face of the earth. I quite understand it; your thoughts are up aloft already. And we, the common men that walk the earth, shall mingle you with the Gods in our prayers; for you are translated above the clouds, and gone up whither you have so long striven.

Her. If but that ascent might be, Lycinus! but it is far yet.

Ly. But you have never told me *how* far, in terms of time.

Her. No; for I know not precisely myself. My guess is that it will not be more than twenty years; by that time I shall surely be on the summit.

Ly. Mercy upon us, you take long views!

Her. Ay; but, as the toil, so is the reward.

Ly. That may be; but about these twenty years—have you your master's promise that you will live so long, is he prophet as well as philosopher, or is it a soothsayer or Chaldean expert that you trust? Such things are known to them, I understand. You would never, of course, if there were any uncertainty of your life's lasting to the Virtue-point, slave and toil night and day like this; why, just as you were close to the top, your fate might come upon you, lay hold of you by the heel, and lug you down with your hopes unfulfilled.

Her. God forbid! these are words of ill omen, Lycinus; may life be granted me, that I may grow wise, and have if it be but one day of Happiness!

Ly. For all these toils will you be content with your one day?

Her. Content? yes, or with the briefest moment of it.

Ly. But is there indeed Happiness up there—and worth all the pains? How can you tell? You have never been up yourself.

Her. I trust my master's word; and he knows well; is he not on the topmost height?

Ly. Oh, do tell me what he says about it; what is Happiness like? wealth, glory, pleasures incomparable?

Her. Hush, friend! all these have nought to do with the Virtuous life.

Ly. Well, if these will not do, what *are* the good things he offers to those who carry their course right through?

Her. Wisdom, courage, true beauty, justice, full and firm knowledge of all things as they are; but wealth and glory and pleasure and all bodily things—these a man strips off and abandons before he mounts up, like Heracles burning on Mount Oeta before deification; he too cast off whatever of the human he had from his mother, and soared up to the Gods with his divine part pure and unalloyed, sifted by the fire.

Even so those I speak of are purged by the philosophic fire of all that deluded men count admirable, and reaching the summit have Happiness with never a thought of wealth and glory and pleasure—except to smile at any who count them more than phantoms.

Ly. By Heracles (and his death on Oeta), they quit themselves like men, and have their reward, it seems. But there is one thing I should like to know: are they allowed to come down from their elevation sometimes, and have a taste of what they left behind them? or when they have once got up, must they stay there, conversing with Virtue, and smiling at wealth and glory and pleasure?

Her. The latter, assuredly; more than that, a man once admitted of Virtue's company will never be subject to wrath or fear or desire any more; no, nor can he feel pain, nor any such sensation.

Ly. Well, but—if one might dare to say what one thinks— but no—let me keep a good tongue in my head—it were irreverent to pry into what wise men do.

Her. Nay, nay; let me know your meaning.

Ly. Dear friend, I have not the courage.

Her. Out with it, my good fellow; we are alone.

Ly. Well, then—most of your account I followed and accepted—how they grow wise and brave and just, and the rest—indeed I was quite fascinated by it; but then you went on to say they despised wealth and glory and pleasure; well, just there (quite between ourselves, you know) I was pulled up; I thought of a scene t'other day with—shall I tell you whom? Perhaps we can do without a name?

Her. No, no; we must have that too.

Ly. Your own professor himself, then,—a person to whom all respect is due, surely, not to mention his years.

Her. Well?

Ly. You know the Heracleot, quite an old pupil of his in philosophy by this time—red-haired—likes an argument?

Her. Yes; Dion, he is called.

Ly. Well, I suppose he had not paid up punctually; anyhow the other day the old man haled him before the magistrate, with a halter made of his own coat; he was shouting and fuming, and if some friends had not come up and got the young man out of his hands, he would have bitten off his nose, he was in such a temper.

Her. Ah, *he* is a bad character, always an unconscionable time paying his debts. There are plenty of others who owe the professor money, and he has never treated any of them so; they pay him his interest punctually.

Ly. Not so fast. What in the world does it matter to him, if they do not pay up? he is purified by philosophy, and has no further need of the cast clothes of Oeta.

Her. Do you suppose his interest in such things is selfish? no, but he has little ones; his care is to save them from indigence.

Ly. Whereas he ought to have brought them up to Virtue too, and let them share his inexpensive Happiness.

Her. Well, I have no time to argue it, Lycinus. I must not be late for lecture, lest in the end I find myself left behind.

Ly. Don't be afraid, my duteous one; today is a holiday; I can save you the rest of your walk.

Her. What do you mean?

Ly. You will not find him just now, if the notice is to be trusted; there was a tablet over the door announcing in large print, No meeting this day. I hear he dined yesterday with the great Eucrates, who was keeping his daughter's birthday. He talked a good deal of philosophy over the wine, and lost his temper a little with Euthydemus the Peripatetic; they were debating the old Peripatetic objections to the Porch. His long vocal exertions (for it was midnight before they broke up) gave him a bad headache, with violent perspiration. I fancy he had also drunk a little too much, toasts being the order of the day, and eaten more than an old man should.

When he got home, he was very ill, they said, just managed
to check and lock up carefully the slices of meat which he
had conveyed to his servant at table, and then, giving orders
that he was not at home, went to sleep, and has not waked
since. I overheard Midas his man telling this to some of his
pupils; there were a number of them coming away.

Her. Which had the victory, though, he or Euthydemus
—if Midas said anything about that?

Ly. Why, at first, I gathered, it was very even between
them; but you Stoics had it in the end, and your master was
much too hard for him. Euthydemus did not even get off
whole; he had a great cut on his head. He was pretentious,
insisted on proving his point, would not give in, and proved
a hard nut to crack; so your excellent professor, who had a
goblet as big as Nestor's in his hand, brought this down on
him as he lay within easy reach, and the victory was his.

Her. Good; so perish all who will not yield to their betters!

Ly. Very reasonable, Hermotimus; what was Euthydemus
thinking of, to irritate an old man who is purged of wrath and
master of his passions, when he had such a heavy goblet in his
hand?

But we have time to spare—you might tell a friend like me
the story of your start in philosophy; then I might perhaps, if
it is not too late, begin now and join your school; you are
my friends; you will not be exclusive?

Her. If only you would, Lycinus! you will soon find out
how much you are superior to the rest of men. I do assure
you, you will think them all children, you will be so much
wiser.

Ly. Enough for me, if after twenty years of it, I am where
you are now.

Her. Oh, I was about your age when I started on philosophy; I was forty; and you must be about that.

Ly. Just that; so take and lead me on the same way; that
is but right. And first tell me—do you allow learners to criti-

cize, if they find difficulties in your doctrines, or must juniors abstain from that?

Her. Why, yes, they must; but *you* shall have leave to ask questions and criticize; you will learn easier that way.

Ly. I thank you for it, Hermotimus, by your name-God Hermes.

Now, is there only one road to philosophy—the Stoic way? they tell me there are a great many other philosophers; is that so?

Her. Certainly—Peripatetics, Epicureans, Platonists, followers of Diogenes, Antisthenes, Pythagoras, and more yet.

Ly. Quite so; numbers of them. Now, are their doctrines the same, or different?

Her. Entirely different.

Ly. But the truth, I presume, is bound to be in one of them, and not in all, as they differ?

Her. Certainly.

Ly. Then, as you love me, answer this: when you first went in pursuit of philosophy, you found many gates wide open; what induced you to pass the others by, and go in at the Stoic gate? Why did you assume that that was the only true one, which would set you on the straight road to Virtue, while the rest all opened on blind alleys? What was the test you applied *then*? Please abolish your present self, the self which is now instructed, or half-instructed, and better able to distinguish between good and bad than we outsiders, and answer in your then character of a layman, with no advantage over me as I am now.

Her. I cannot tell what you are driving at.

Ly. Oh, there is nothing recondite about it. There are a great many philosophers—let us say Plato, Aristotle, Antisthenes, and your spiritual fathers, Chrysippus, Zeno, and all the rest of them; what was it that induced you, leaving the rest alone, to pick out the school you did from among them all, and pin your philosophic faith to it? Were you

favored like Chaerephon with a revelation from Apollo? Did
he tell you the Stoics were the best of men, and send you to
their school? I dare say he recommends different philosophers
to different persons, according to their individual needs?

Her. Nothing of the kind, Lycinus; I never consulted him
upon it.

Ly. Why? was it not a *dignus vindice nodus?*[4] or were
you confident in your own unaided discrimination?

Her. Why, yes; I was.

Ly. Then this must be my first lesson from you—how one
can decide out of hand which is the best and the true philosophy to be taken, and the others left.

Her. I will tell you: I observed that it attracted most disciples, and thence inferred that it was superior.

Ly. Give me figures; how many more of them than of Epicureans, Platonists, Peripatetics? Of course you took a sort of
show of hands.

Her. Well, no; I didn't count; I just guessed.

Ly. Now, now! you are not teaching, but hoaxing me;
judge by guesswork and impression, indeed, on a thing of this
importance! You are hiding the truth.

Her. Well, that was not my only way; everyone told me
the Epicureans were sensual and self-indulgent, the Peripatetics avaricious and contentious, the Platonists conceited and
vain; about the Stoics, on the contrary, many said they had
fortitude and an open mind; he who goes their way, I heard,
was the true king and millionaire and wise man, alone and all
in one.

Ly. And, of course, it was other people who so described
them; you would not have taken their own word for their
excellences.

Her. Certainly not; it was others who said it.

Ly. Not their rivals, I suppose?

[4] A difficulty great enough to demand a deliverer.

Her. Oh, no.

Ly. Laymen, then?

Her. Just so.

Ly. There you are again, cheating me with your irony; you take me for a blockhead, who will believe that an intelligent person like Hermotimus, at the age of forty, would accept the word of laymen about philosophy and philosophers, and make his own selection on the strength of what they said.

Her. But you see, Lycinus, I did not depend on their judgment entirely, but on my own too. I saw the Stoics going about with dignity, decently dressed and groomed, ever with a thoughtful air and a manly countenance, as far from effeminacy as from the utter repulsive negligence of the Cynics, bearing themselves, in fact, like moderate men; and everyone admits that moderation is right.

Ly. Did you ever see them behaving like your master, as I described him to you just now? Lending money and clamoring for payment, losing their tempers in philosophic debates, and making other exhibitions of themselves? Or perhaps these are trifles, so long as the dress is decent, the beard long, and the hair close-cropped? We are provided for the future, then, with an infallible rule and balance, guaranteed by Hermotimus? It is by appearance and walk and haircutting that the best men are to be distinguished; and whosoever has not these marks, and is not solemn and thoughtful, shall be condemned and rejected?

Nay, do not play with me like this; you want to see whether I shall catch you at it.

Her. Why do you say that?

Ly. Because, my dear sir, this appearance test is one for statues; *their* decent orderly attire has it easily over the Stoics, because Phidias or Alcamenes or Myron designed them to be graceful. However, granting as much as you like that these are the right tests, what is a blind man to do, if he wants to

take up philosophy? how is he to find the man whose principles are right, when he cannot see his appearance or gait?

Her. I am not teaching the blind, Lycinus; I have nothing
to do with them.

Ly. Ah, but, my good sir, there ought to have been some
universal criterion, in a matter of such great and general use.
Still, if you will have it so, let the blind be excluded from philosophy, as they cannot see—though, by the way, they are
just the people who most need philosophy to console them for
their misfortune; but now, the people who *can* see—give them
the utmost possible acuity of vision, and what can they detect
of the spiritual qualities from this external shell?

What I mean is this: was it not from admiration of their
spirit that you joined them, expecting to have your own spirit
purified?

Her. Assuredly.

Ly. How could you possibly discern the true philosopher
from the false, then, by the marks you mentioned? It is not
the way of such qualities to come out like that; they are hidden
and secret; they are revealed only under long and patient
observation, in talk and debate and the conduct they inspire.
You have probably heard of Momus'[5] indictment of Hephaestus; if not, you shall have it now. According to the myth,
Athene, Poseidon, and Hephaestus had a match in inventive-
ness. Poseidon made a bull, Athene planned a house, Hephaestus constructed a man; when they came before Momus, who
was to judge, he examined their productions; I need not
trouble you with his criticisms of the other two; but his objec-
tion to the man, and the fault he found with Hephaestus, was
this: he should have made a window in his chest, so that,
when it was opened, his thoughts and designs, his truth or
falsehood, might have been apparent. Momus must have been
blear-eyed, to have such ideas about men; but you have
sharper eyes than Lynceus, and pierce through the chest to

[5] Son of night, and god of criticism.

what is inside; all is patent to you, not merely any man's wishes and sentiments, but the comparative merits of any pair.

Her. You trifle, Lycinus. I made a pious choice, and do not repent it; that is enough for me.

Ly. And will you yet make a mystery of it to your friend, and let him be lost with the vulgar herd?

Her. Why, you will not accept anything I say.

Ly. On the contrary, my good sir, it is you who will not say anything I can accept. Well, as you refuse me your confidence, and are so jealous of my becoming a philosopher and your equal, I must even do my best to find out the infallible test and learn to choose safely for myself. And you may listen, if you like.

Her. That I will, Lycinus; you will very likely hit on some good idea.

Ly. Then attend, and do not mock me, if my inquiry is quite unscientific; it is all I can do, as you, who know better, will not give me any clearer light.

I conceive Virtue, then, under the figure of a State whose citizens are happy—as your professor, who is one of them, phrases it,—absolutely wise, all of them brave, just, and self-controlled, hardly distinguishable, in fact, from Gods. All sorts of things that go on here, such as robbery, assault, unfair gain, you will never find attempted there, I believe; their relations are all peace and unity; and this is quite natural, seeing that none of the things which elsewhere occasion strife and rivalry, and prompt men to plot against their neighbors, so much as come in their way at all. Gold, pleasures, distinctions, they never regard as objects of dispute; they have banished them long ago as undesirable elements. Their life is serene and blissful, in the enjoyment of legality, equality, liberty, and all other good things.

Her. Well, Lycinus? Must not all men yearn to belong to a State like that, and never count the toil of getting there, nor lose heart over the time it takes? Enough that one day they will arrive, and be naturalized, and given the franchise.

Ly. In good truth, Hermotimus, we should devote all our efforts to this, and neglect everything else; we need pay little heed to any claims of our earthly country; we should steel our hearts against the clingings and cryings of children or parents, if we have them; it is well if we can induce them to go with us; but, if they will not or cannot, shake them off and march straight for the city of bliss, leaving your coat in their hands, if they lay hold of it to keep you back, in your hurry to get there; what matter for a coat? You will be admitted there without one.

I remember hearing a description of it all once before from an old man, who urged me to go there with him. He would show me the way, enroll me when I got there, introduce me to his own circles, and promise me a share in the universal Happiness. But I was stiff-necked, in my youthful folly (it was some fifteen years ago); else might I have been in the outskirts, nay, haply at the very gates, by now. Among the noteworthy things he told me, I seem to remember these: all the citizens are aliens and foreigners, not a native among them; they include numbers of barbarians, slaves, cripples, dwarfs, and poor; in fact anyone is admitted; for their law does not associate the franchise with income, with shape, size, or beauty, with old or brilliant ancestry; these things are not considered at all; anyone who would be a citizen needs only understanding, zeal for the right, energy, perserverance, fortitude and resolution in facing all the trials of the road; whoever proves his possession of these by persisting till he reaches the city is *ipso facto* a full citizen, regardless of his antecedents. Such distinctions as superior and inferior, noble and common, bond and free, simply do not exist there, even in name.

Her. There, now; you see I am not wasting my pains on trifles; I yearn to be counted among the citizens of that fair and happy State.

Ly. Why, your yearning is mine too; there is nothing I would sooner pray for. If the city had been near at hand and plain for all to see, be assured I would never have doubted, nor needed prompting; I would have gone thither and had my franchise long ago; but as you tell me—you and your bard Hesiod—that it is set exceeding far off, one must find out the way to it, and the best guide. You agree?

Her. Of course that is the only thing to do.

Ly. Now, so far as promises and professions go, there is no lack of guides; there are numbers of them waiting about, all representing themselves as from there. But instead of one single road there seem to be many different and inconsistent ones. North and south, east and west, they go; one leads through meadows and vegetation and shade, and is well watered and pleasant, with never a stumbling-block or inequality; another is rough and rocky, threatening heat and drought and toil. Yet all these are supposed to lead to the one city, though they take such different directions.

That is where my difficulty lies; whichever of them I try, there is sure to be a most respectable person stationed just at the entrance, with a welcoming hand and an exhortation to go his way; each of them says he is the only one who knows the straight road; his rivals are all mistaken, have never been themselves, nor learnt the way from competent guides. I go to his neighbor, and he gives the same assurances about *his* way, abusing the other respectable persons; and so the next, and the next, and the next. This multiplicity and dissimilarity of the roads gives me searchings of heart, and still more the assertiveness and self-satisfaction of the guides. I really cannot tell which turning or whose directions are most likely to bring me to the city.

Her. Oh, but I can solve that puzzle for you. You cannot go wrong, if you trust those who have been already.

Ly. Which do you mean? those who have been by which

road, and under whose guidance? It is the old puzzle in a new form; you have only substituted men for measures.

Her. How do you mean?

Ly. Why, the man who has taken Plato's road and traveled with him will recommend that road; so with Epicurus and the rest; and *you* will recommend your own. How else, Hermotimus? It must be so.

Her. Well, of course.

Ly. So you have not solved my puzzle; I know just as little as before which traveler to trust; I find that each of them, as well as his guide, has tried one only, which he now recommends and will have to be the only one leading to the city. Whether he tells the truth I have no means of knowing; that he has attained *some* end, and seen *some* city, I may perhaps allow; but whether he saw the right one, or whether, Corinth being the real goal, he got to Babylon and thought he had seen Corinth—that is still undecided; for surely everyone who has seen a city has not seen Corinth, unless Corinth is the only city there is. But my greatest difficulty of all is the absolute certainty that the true road is one; for Corinth is one, and the other roads lead anywhere but to Corinth, though there may be people deluded enough to suppose that the north road and the south road lead equally to Corinth.

Her. But that is absurd, Lycinus; they go opposite ways, you see.

Ly. Then, my dear good man, this choice of roads and guides is quite a serious matter; we can by no means just follow our noses; we shall be discovering that we are well on the way to Babylon or Bactria instead of to Corinth. Nor is it advisable to toss up, either, on the chance that we may hit upon the right way if we start upon any one at a venture. That is no impossibility; it may have come off once and again in a cycle; but I cannot think we ought to gamble recklessly with such high stakes, nor commit our hopes to a frail craft, like the wise men who went to sea in a bowl; we should have no fair complaint against Fortune, if her arrow or dart did not precisely hit the center; the odds are ten thousand to one against her; just so the archer in Homer—Teucer, I suppose it was—when he meant to hit the dove, only cut the string, which held it; of course it is infinitely more likely that the point of the arrow will find its billet in one of the numberless other places, than just in that particular central one. And as to the perils of blundering into one of the wrong roads instead of the right one, misled by a belief in the discretion of Fortune, here is an illustration: it is no easy matter to turn back and get safe into port when you have once cast loose your moorings and committed yourself to the breeze; you are at the mercy of the sea, frightened, sick and sorry with your tossing about, most likely. Your mistake was at the beginning: before leaving, you should have gone up to some high point, and observed whether the wind was in the right quarter, and of the right strength for a crossing to Corinth, not neglecting, by the way, to secure the very best pilot obtainable, and a seaworthy craft equal to so high a sea.

Her. Much better so, Lycinus. However, I know that, if you go the whole round, you will find no better guides or more expert pilots than the Stoics; if you mean ever to get to Corinth, you will follow them, in the tracks of Chrysippus and Zeno. It is the only way to do it.

Ly. Ah, many can play at the game of assertion. Plato's fellow traveler, Epicurus' follower, and all the rest, will tell me just what you do, that I shall never get to Corinth except with whichever of them it is. So I must either believe them all, or disbelieve impartially. The latter is much the safest, until we have found out the truth.

Put a case, now: just as I am, as uncertain as ever which of the whole number has the truth, I choose your school; I rely on you, who are my friend, but who still know only the Stoic doctrine, and have not traveled any way but that. Now some God brings Plato, Pythagoras, Aristotle, and the rest to life again; they gather round and cross-examine me, or actually sue me in court for constructive defamation; "Good Lycinus," they say, "what possessed or who induced you to exalt Chrysippus and Zeno at our expense? we are far older established; they are mere creatures of yesterday; yet you never gave us a hearing, nor inquired into our statements at all." Well, what am I to plead? will it avail me to say I trusted my friend Hermotimus? I feel sure they will say, "We know not this Hermotimus, who he is, nor he us; you had no right to condemn us all, and give judgment by default against us, on the authority of a man who knew only one of the philosophic roads, and even that, perhaps, imperfectly. These are not the instructions issued to juries, Lycinus; they are not to hear one party, and refuse the other permission to say what he deems advisable; they are to hear both sides alike, with a view to the better sifting of truth from falsehood by comparison of the arguments; if they fail in these duties, the law allows an appeal to another court." That is what we may expect them to say.

Then one of them might proceed to question me like this: "Suppose, Lycinus, that an Ethiopian who had never been abroad in his life, nor seen other men like us, were to state categorically in an Ethiopian assembly that there did not exist on earth any white or yellow men—nothing but blacks —would his statement be accepted? Or would some Ethiopian elder remark, How do you know, my confident friend? you have never been in foreign parts, nor had any experience of other nations." Shall I tell him the old man's question was justified? what do you advise, my counsel?

Her. Say that, certainly; I consider the old man's rebuke quite reasonable.

Ly. So do I. But I am not so sure you will approve what comes next; as for me, I have as little doubt of that as of the other.

Her. What is it?

Ly. The next step will be the application; my questioner will say, "Now Lycinus, let us suppose an analogue, in a person acquainted only with the Stoic doctrine, like your friend Hermotimus; he has never traveled in Plato's country, or to Epicurus, or any other land; now, if he were to state that there was no such beauty or truth in those many countries as there is in the Porch and its teaching, would you not be justified in considering it bold of him to give you his opinion about them all, whereas he knew only one, having never set foot outside the bounds of Ethiopia?" What reply do you advise to that?

Her. The perfectly true one, of course, that it is indeed the Stoic doctrine that we study fully, being minded to sink or swim with that, but still we do know what the others say also; our teacher rehearses the articles of their beliefs to us incidentally, and demolishes them with his comments.

Ly. Do you suppose the Platonists, Pythagoreans, Epicureans, and other schools, will let that pass? Or will they laugh out loud and say, "What remarkable methods your friend has, Lycinus! he accepts our adversaries' character of us, and gathers our doctrines from the description of people who do not know, or deliberately misrepresent them. If he were to see an athlete getting his muscles in trim by kicking high, or hitting out at empty space as though he were getting a real blow home, would he (in the capacity of umpire) at once proclaim him victor, because he *could not help winning?* No; he would reflect that these displays are easy and safe, when there is no defense to be reckoned with, and that the real decision must wait till he has beaten and mastered his opponent, and the latter has had enough. Well then, do not let Hermotimus suppose from his teachers' sparrings with our shadows (for *we* are not there) that they have the victory, or that our doctrines are so easily upset; tell him the business is too like the sand houses which children, having built them weak, have no difficulty in overturning, or, to change the figure, like people practicing archery; they make a straw target, hang it to a post, plant it a little way off, and then let fly at it; if they hit and get through the straw, they burst into a shout, as if it were a great triumph to have driven through the dry stuff. That is not the way the Persians take, or those Scythian tribes which use the bow. Generally, when *they* shoot, in the first place they are themselves mounted and in motion, and secondly, they like the mark to be moving too; it is not to be stationary, waiting for the arrival of the arrow, but passing at full speed; they can usually kill beasts, and their marksmen hit birds. If it ever happens that they want to test the actual impact on a target, they set up one of stout wood, or a shield of raw hide; piercing that, they reckon that their shafts will go through armor too. So, Lycinus, tell Hermotimus from us that his teachers pierce straw targets, and then say they have disposed of armed men; or paint up figures of us, spar at them, and, after a not surprising success, think they have beaten us. But we shall severally quote against them Achilles' words against Hector:

> *They dare not face the nodding of my plume.*"

So say all of them, one after the other.

I suspect that Plato, with his intimate knowledge of Sicily, will add an anecdote from there. Gelo of Syracuse had disagreeable breath, but did not find it out himself for a long time, no one venturing to mention such a circumstance to a tyrant. At last a foreign woman who had a connection with him dared to tell him; whereupon he went to his wife and scolded her for never having, with all her opportunities of knowing, warned him of it; she put in the defense that, as she had never been familiar or at close quarters with any other man, she had supposed all men were like that. So Hermotimus (Plato will say) after his exclusive association with Stoics, cannot be expected to know the savor of other people's mouths. Chrysippus, on the other hand, might say as much or more if I were to put *him* out of court and betake myself to Platonism, in reliance upon someone who had conversed with Plato alone. And in a word, as long as it is uncertain which is the true philosophic school, I choose none; choice of one is insult to the rest.

Her. For heaven's sake, Lycinus, let us leave Plato, Aristotle, Epicurus, and the rest of them alone; to argue with them is not for me. Why not just hold a private inquiry, you and I, whether philosophy is what I say it is? As for the Ethiopians and Gelo's wife, what a long way you have brought them on none of their business!

Ly. Away with them, then, if you find their company superfluous. And now do you proceed; my expectations are high.

Her. Well, it seems to me perfectly possible, Lycinus, after studying the Stoic doctrines alone, to get at the truth from them, without going through a course of all the others too. Look at it this way: if anyone tells you simply, Twice two is four, need you go round all the mathematicians to find out whether there is one who makes it five, or seven; or would you know at once that the man was right?

Ly. Certainly I should.

Her. Then why should you think it impossible for a man who finds, without going further, that the Stoics make true statements, to believe them and dispense with further witness? He knows that four can never be five, though ten thousand Platos or Pythagorases said it was.

Ly. Not to the point. You compare accepted with disputed facts, whereas they are completely different. Tell me, did you ever meet a man who said twice two was seven or eleven?

Her. Not I; anyone who did not make four of it must be mad.

Ly. But on the other hand—try to tell the truth, I adjure you—, did you ever meet a Stoic and an Epicurean who did *not* differ about principles or ends?

Her. No.

Ly. You are an honest man; now ask yourself whether you are trapping a friend with false logic. We are trying to find out with whom philosophic truth lies; and you beg the question and make a present of that same truth to the Stoics; for you say (what is quite unproved) that they are the people who make twice two four; the Epicureans or Platonists would say that *they* bring out that result, whereas you get five or seven. Does it not amount to that, when your school reckons goodness the only end, and the Epicureans pleasure? or again when you say everything is material, and Plato recognizes an immaterial element also in all that exists? As I said, you lay hold of the thing in dispute, as though it were the admitted property of the Stoics, and put it into their hands, though the others claim it and maintain that it is theirs; why, it is the very point at issue. If it is once established that Stoics have the monopoly of making four out of twice two, it is time for the rest to hold their tongues; but as long as they refuse to yield that point, we must hear all alike, or be prepared for people's calling us partial judges.

Her. It seems to me, Lycinus, you do not understand what I mean.

Ly. Very well, put it plainer, if it is something different from that.

Her. You will see in a minute. Let us suppose two people have gone into the temple of Aesculapius or Dionysus, and subsequently one of the sacred cups is missing. Both of them will have to be searched, to see which has it about him.

Ly. Clearly.

Her. Of course one of them has it.

Ly. Necessarily, if it is missing.

Her. Then, if you find it on the first, you will not strip the other; it is clear he has not got it.

Ly. Quite.

Her. And if we fail to find it on the first, the other certainly has it; it is unnecessary to search him that way either.

Ly. Yes, he has it.

Her. So with us; if we find the cup in the possession of the Stoics, we shall not care to go on and search the others; we have what we were looking for; why trouble further?

Ly. There is no why, if you really find it, and can be certain it is the missing article, the sacred object being unmistakable. But there are some differences in this case, friend; the temple-visitors are not two, so that if one has not got the booty the other has, but many; and the identity of the missing object is also uncertain; it may be cup, or bowl, or garland; every priest gives a different description of it; they do not agree even about the material; bronze, say these, silver, say those—anything from gold to tin. So there is nothing for it but to strip the visitors, if you want to find it; even if you discover a gold cup on the first man, you must go on to the others.

Her. What for?

Ly. Because it is not certain that the thing was a cup. And even if that is generally admitted, they do not all agree that it was gold; and if it is well known that a gold cup is missing, and you find a gold cup on your first man, even so you are not quit of searching the others; it is not clear that this is *the* sacred cup; do you suppose there is only one gold cup in the world?

Her. No, indeed.

Ly. So you will have to go the round, and then collect all your finds together and decide which of them is most likely to be divine property.

For the source of all the difficulty is this: everyone who is stripped has something or other on him, one a bowl, one a cup, one a garland, which again may be bronze, gold, or silver; but whether the one he has is the sacred one, is not yet clear. It is absolutely impossible to know which man to accuse of sacrilege; even if all the objects were similar, it would be uncertain who had robbed the God; for such things may be private property too. Our perplexity, of course, is simply due to the fact that the missing cup—assume it to be a cup—has no inscription; if either the God's or the donor's name had been on it, we should not have had all this trouble; when we found the inscribed one, we should have stopped stripping and inconveniencing other visitors. I suppose, Hermotimus, you have often been at athletic meetings?

Her. You suppose right; and in many places too.

Ly. Did you ever have a seat close by the judges?

Her. Dear me, yes; last Olympia, I was on the left of the stewards; Euandridas of Elis had got me a place in the Elean enclosure; I particularly wanted to have a near view of how things are done there.

Ly. So you know how they arrange ties for the wrestling or the pancratium?

Her. Yes.

Ly. Then you will describe it better than I, as you have seen it so close.

Her. In old days, when Heracles presided, bay leaves——

Ly. No old days, thank you; tell me what you saw with your own eyes.

Her. A consecrated silver urn is produced, and into it are thrown little lots about the size of a bean, with letters on them. Two are marked alpha,[6] two beta, two more gamma, and so on, if the competitors run to more than that—two lots always to each letter. A competitor comes up, makes a prayer to Zeus, dips his hand into the urn, and pulls out one lot; then another does the same; there is a policeman to each drawer, who holds his hand so that he cannot see what letter he has drawn. When all have drawn, the chief police officer, I think it is, or one of the stewards themselves—I cannot quite remem-

---

[6] The Greek alphabet runs: alpha, beta, gamma, delta, epsilon, zeta, eta, theta, iota, kappa, lambda, mu, nu, xi, omicron, pi, rho, sigma, tau, upsilon, phi, chi, psi, omega.

ber this detail—goes round and examines the lots while they
stand in a circle, and puts together the two alphas for the
wrestling or pancratium, and so for the two betas, and the
rest. That is the procedure when the number of competitors
is even, as eight, four, or twelve. If it is five, seven, nine, or
other odd number, an odd letter is marked on one lot, which
is put in with the others, not having a duplicate. Whoever
draws this is a bye, and waits till the rest have finished their
ties; no duplicate turns up for him, you see; and it is a considerable advantage to an athlete, to know that he will come
fresh against tired competitors.

Ly. Stop there; that is just what I wanted. There are nine
of them, we will say, and they have all drawn, and the lots
are in their hands. You go round—for I promote you from
spectator to steward—examining the letters; and I suppose
you will not know who is the bye till you have been to them
all and paired them.

Her. How do you mean?

Ly. It is impossible for you to hit straight upon the letter
which indicates the bye; at least, you may hit upon the letter,
but you will not know about the bye; it was not announced
beforehand that kappa or mu or iota had the appointment in
its gift; when you find alpha, you look for the holder of the
other alpha, whom finding, you pair the two. Again finding
beta, you inquire into the whereabouts of the second beta
which matches it; and so all through, till there is no one left
but the holder of the single unpaired letter.

Her. But suppose you come upon it first or second, what
will you do then?

Ly. Never mind me; I want to know what *you* will do,
Mr. Steward. Will you say at once, Here is the bye? or will
you have to go round to all, and see whether there is a duplicate to be found, it being impossible to know the bye till you
have seen all the lots?

Her. Why, Lycinus, I shall know quite easily; nine being

the number, if I find the epsilon first or second, I know the
holder of it for the bye.

Ly. But how?

Her. How? Why, two of them must have alpha, two beta,
and of the next two pairs one has certainly drawn gammas
and the other deltas, so that four letters have been used up
over eight competitors. Obviously, then, the next letter,
which is epsilon, is the only one that can be odd, and the
drawer of it is the bye.

Ly. Shall I extol your intelligence, or would you rather
I explained to you my own poor idea, which differs?

Her. The latter, of course, though I cannot conceive how
you can reasonably differ.

Ly. You have gone on the assumption that the letters are
taken in alphabetical order, until at a particular one the number of competitors runs short; and I grant you it may be done
so at Olympia. But suppose we were to pick out five letters
at random, say chi, sigma, zeta, kappa, theta, and duplicate
the other four on the lots for eight competitors, but put a
single zeta on the ninth, which we meant to indicate the bye
—what then would you do if you came on the zeta first? How
can you tell that its holder is the bye till you have been all
round and found no counterpart to it? for you could not
tell by the alphabetical order, as at Olympia.

Her. A difficult question.

Ly. Look at the same thing another way. Suppose we put
no letters at all on the lots, but, instead of them, signs and
marks such as the Egyptians use for letters, men with dogs' or
lions' heads. Or no, those are rather too strange; let us avoid
hybrids, and put down simple forms, as well as our draughts-
manship will allow—men on two lots, horses on two, a pair of
cocks, a pair of dogs, and let a lion be the mark of the ninth.
Now, if you hit upon the lion at the first try, how can you tell
that this is the bye-maker, until you have gone all round and
seen whether any one else has a lion to match?

Her. Your question is too much for me.

Ly. No wonder; there is no plausible answer. Consequently, if we mean to find either the man who has the sacred cup, or the bye, or our best guide to the famous city of Corinth, we must absolutely go to and examine them all, trying them carefully, stripping and comparing them; the truth will be hard enough to find, even so. If I am to take anyone's advice upon the right philosophy to choose, I insist upon his knowing what they all say; everyone else I disqualify; I will not trust him while there is one philosophy he is unacquainted with; that one may possibly be the best of all. If someone were to produce a handsome man, and state that he was the handsomest of mankind, we should not accept that, unless we knew he had seen all men; very likely his man is handsome, but whether the handsomest, he has no means of knowing without seeing all. Now we are looking not simply for beauty, but for the greatest beauty, and if we miss that, we shall account ourselves no further than we were; we shall not be content with chancing upon some sort of beauty; we are in search of a definite thing, the supreme beauty, which must necessarily be *one*.

Her. True.

Ly. Well then, can you name me a man who has tried every road in philosophy? one who, knowing the doctrine of Pythagoras, Plato, Aristotle, Chrysippus, Epicurus, and the rest, has ended by selecting one out of all these roads, because he has proved it genuine, and had found it by experience to be the only one that led straight to Happiness? If we can meet with such a man, we are at the end of our troubles.

Her. Alas, that is no easy matter.

Ly. What shall we do, then? I do not think we ought to despair, in the momentary absence of such a guide. Perhaps the best and safest plan of all is to set to work oneself, go through every system, and carefully examine the various doctrines.

Her. That is what seems to be indicated. I am afraid, though, there is an obstacle in what you said just now: it is not easy, when you have committed yourself with a spread of canvas to the wind, to get home again. How can a man try all the roads, when, as you said, he will be unable to escape from the first of them?

Ly. My notion is to copy Theseus, get dame Ariadne to give us a skein, and go into one labyrinth after another, with the certainty of getting out by winding it up.

Her. Who is to be our Ariadne? Where shall we find the skein?

Ly. Never despair; I fancy I have found something to hold on to and escape.

Her. And what is that?

Ly. It is not original; I borrow it from one of the wise men: "Be sober and doubt all things," says he. If we do not believe everything we are told, but behave like jurymen who suspend judgment till they have heard the other side, we may have no difficulty in getting out of the labyrinths.

Her. A good plan; let us try it.

Ly. Very well, which shall we start with? However, that will make no difference; we may begin with whomsoever we fancy, Pythagoras, say; how long shall we allow for learning the whole of Pythagoreanism? and do not omit the five years of silence; including those, I suppose thirty altogether will do; or, if you do not like that, still we cannot put it lower than twenty.

Her. Put it at that.

Ly. Plato will come next with as many more, and then Aristotle cannot do with less.

Her. No.

Ly. As to Chrysippus, I need not ask you; you have told me already that forty is barely enough.

Her. That is so.

Ly. And we have still Epicurus and the others. I am not

taking high figures, either, as you will see if you reflect upon the number of octogenarian Stoics, Epicureans, and Platonists who confess that they have not yet completely mastered their own systems. Or, if they did not confess it, at any rate Chrysippus, Aristotle, and Plato would for them; still more Socrates, who is as good as they; he used to proclaim to all comers that, so far from knowing all, he knew nothing whatever, except the one fact of his own ignorance. Well, let us add up. Twenty years we gave Pythagoras, the same to Plato, and so to the others. What will the total come to, if we assume only ten schools?

Her. Over two hundred years.

Ly. Shall we deduct a quarter of that, and say a hundred and fifty will do? or can we halve it?

Her. You must decide about that; but I see that, at the best, it will be but few who will get through the course, though they begin philosophy and life together.

Ly. In that case, what are we to do? Must we withdraw our previous admission, that no one can choose the best out of many without trying all? We thought selection without experiment a method of inquiry savoring more of divination than of judgment, did we not?

Her. Yes.

Ly. Without such longevity, then, it is absolutely impossible for us to complete the series—experiment, selection, philosophy, Happiness. Yet anything short of that is a mere game of blindman's-buff; whatever we knock against and get hold of we shall be taking for the thing we want, because the truth is hidden from us. Even if a mere piece of luck brings us straight to it, we shall have no grounded conviction of our success; there are so many similar objects, all claiming to be the real thing.

Her. Ah, Lycinus, your arguments seem to me more or less logical, but—but—to be frank with you—I hate to hear you going through them and wasting your acuteness. I suspect it was in an evil hour that I came out today and met you; my hopes were almost in my grasp; and now here are you plunging me into a slough of despond with your demonstrations; truth is undiscoverable, if the search needs so many years.

Ly. My dear friend, it would be much fairer to blame your parents, Menecrates and whatever your mother's name may have been—or indeed to go still further back to human nature. Why did not they make you a Tithonus for years and durability? instead of which, they limited you like other men to a century at the outside. As for me, I have only been helping you to deduce results.

Her. No, no; it is just your way; you want to crow over me; you detest philosophy—I cannot tell why—and poke fun at philosophers.

Ly. Hermotimus, I cannot show what truth is, so well as wise people like you and your professor; but one thing I do know about it, and that is that it is not pleasant to the ear; falsehood is far more esteemed; it is prettier, and therefore pleasanter; while Truth, conscious of its purity, blurts out downright remarks, and offends people. Here is a case of it: even you are offended with me for having discovered (with your assistance) how this matter really stands, and shown that our common object is hard of attainment. Suppose you had been in love with a statue and hoped to win it, under the impression that it was human, and I had realized that it was only bronze or marble, and given you a friendly warning that your passion was hopeless—you might just as well have thought I was your enemy then, because I would not leave you a prey to extravagant and impracticable delusions.

Her. Well, well; are we to give up philosophy, then, and idle our lives away like the common herd?

Ly. What have I said to justify that? My point is not that we are to give up philosophy, but this: whereas we are to pursue philosophy, and whereas there are many roads, each professing to lead to philosophy and Virtue, and whereas it is uncertain which of these is the true road, therefore the selection shall be made with care. Now we resolved that it was impossible out of many offers to choose the best, unless a man should try all in turn; and then the process of trial was found to be long. What do *you* propose?—It is the old question again. To follow and join philosophic forces with whomsoever you first fall in with, and let him thank Fortune for his proselyte?

Her. What is the good of answering your questions? You say no one can judge for himself, unless he can devote the life of a phoenix to going round experimenting; and on the other hand you refuse to trust either previous experience or the multitude of favorable testimony.

Ly. Where is your multitude, with knowledge and experience *of all*? Never mind the multitude; one man who answers the description will do for me. But if you mean the people who do *not* know, their mere numbers will never persuade me, as long as they pronounce upon all from knowledge of, at the most, one.

Her. Are you the only man who has found the truth, and are all the people who go in for philosophy fools?

Ly. You wrong me, Hermotimus, when you imply that I put myself above other people, or rank myself at all with those who know. You forget what I said; I never claimed to know the truth better than others, only confessed that I was as ignorant of it as everyone else.

Her. Well, but, Lycinus, it may be all very well to insist on going the round, testing the various statements, and eschewing any other method of choice; but it is ridiculous to spend so many years on each experiment, as though there were no such thing as judging from samples. That device seems to me quite simple, and economical of time. There is a story that some sculptor, Phidias, I think, seeing a single claw, calculated from it the size of the lion, if it were modeled proportionally. So, if someone were to let you see a man's hand, keeping the rest of his body concealed, you would know at once that what was behind was a man, without seeing his whole body. Well, it is easy to find out in a few hours the essential points of the various doctrines, and, for selecting the best, these will suffice, without any of your scrupulous exacting investigation.

Ly. Upon my word, how confident you are in your faculty of divining the whole from the parts! and yet I remember being told just the opposite—that knowledge of the whole includes that of the parts, but not vice versa. Well, but tell me; when Phidias saw the claw, would he ever have known it for a lion's, if he had never seen a lion? Could you have said the hand was a man's, if you had never known or seen a man? Why are you dumb? Let me make the only possible answer for you—that you could *not*; I am afraid Phidias has modeled his lion all for nothing; for it proves to be neither here nor there. What resemblance is there? What enabled you and Phidias to recognize the parts was just your knowledge of the wholes—the lion and the man. But in philosophy—the Stoic, for instance—how will the part reveal the other parts to you, or how can you conclude that they are beautiful? You do not know the whole to which the parts belong.

Then you say it is easy to hear in a few hours the essentials of all philosophy—meaning, I suppose, their principles and ends, their accounts of God and the soul, their views on the material and the immaterial, their respective identification of pleasure or goodness with the desirable and the Happy; well, it is easy—it is quite a trifle—to deliver an opinion after such a hearing; but really to *know* where the truth lies will be work, I suspect, not for a few hours, but for a good many days. If not, what can have induced them to enlarge on these rudiments to the tune of a hundred or a thousand volumes apiece? I imagine they only wanted to establish the truth of those few points which you thought so easy and intelligible.

If you refuse to spend your time on a conscientious selection, after personal examination of each and all, in sum and in detail, it seems to me you will still want your soothsayer to choose the best for you. It would be a fine short cut, with no meanderings or wastings of time, if you sent for him, listened to the summaries, and killed a victim at the end of each; by indicating in its liver which is the philosophy for you, the God would save you a pack of troubles.

Or, if you like, I can suggest a still simpler way. You need not shed all this blood in sacrifice to any God, nor employ an expensive priest; put into an urn a set of tablets, each marked with a philosopher's name, and tell a boy (he must be quite young, and his parents both be living) to go to the urn and pick out whichever tablet his hand first touches; and live a philosopher ever after, of the school which then comes out triumphant.

Her. This is buffoonery, Lycinus; I should not have expected it of you. Now tell me, did you ever buy wine? in person, I mean.

Ly. Many a time.

Her. Well, did you go to every wine vault in town, one after another, tasting and comparing?

Ly. Certainly not.

Her. No; as soon as you find good sound stuff, you have only to get it sent home.

Ly. To be sure.

Her. And from that little taste you could have answered for the quality of the whole?

Ly. Yes.

Her. Now suppose you had gone to all the wine-merchants and said: I want to buy a pint of wine; I must ask you, gentlemen, to let me drink the whole of the cask which each of you has on tap; after that exhaustive sampling, I shall know which of you keeps the best wine, and is the man for my money. If you had talked like that, they might have laughed at you, and, if you persisted in worrying them, have tried how you liked water.

Ly. Yes; it would be no more than my deserts.

Her. Apply this to philosophy. What need to drink the whole cask, when you can judge the quality of the whole from one little taste?

Ly. What an adept at evasion you are, Hermotimus! How you slip through one's fingers! However, it is all the better this time; you fancied yourself out, but you have flopped into the net again.

Her. What do you mean?

Ly. You take a thing whose nature is self-evident and universally admitted, like wine, and argue from it to perfectly unlike things, whose nature is obscure and generally debated. In fact I cannot tell what analogy you find between philosophy and wine; there *is* just one, indeed: philosophers and wine-merchants both sell their wares, mostly resorting to adulteration, fraud, and false measures, in the process. But let us look into your real meaning. You say all the wine in a cask is of the same quality—which is perfectly reasonable; further, that anyone who draws and tastes quite a small quantity will know at once the quality of the whole—of which the same may be said; I should never have thought of objecting. But mark what comes now: do philosophy and its professors (your own, for instance) give you every day the same remarks on the same subjects, or do they vary them? They vary them a great deal, friend; you would never have stuck to your master through your twenty years' wandering—quite a philosophic Odyssey—if he had always said the same thing; one hearing would have been enough.

Her. So it would.

Ly. How could you have known the whole of his doctrines from the first taste, then? They were not homogeneous, like the wine; novelty today, and novelty tomorrow on the top of it. Consequently, dear friend, short of drinking the whole cask, you might soak to no purpose; Providence seems to me to have hidden the philosophic Good right at the bottom, underneath the lees. So you will have to drain it dry, or you will never get to that nectar for which I know you have so long thirsted. According to your idea, it has such virtue that, could you once taste it and swallow the very least drop, you would straightway have perfect wisdom; so they say the Delphian prophetess is inspired by one draught of the sacred spring with answers for those who consult the oracle. But it seems not to be so; you have drunk more than half the cask; yet you told me you were only beginning yet.

Now see whether this is not a better analogy. You shall keep your merchant, and your cask; but the contents of the latter are not to be wine, but assorted seeds. On the top is wheat, next beans, then barley, below that lentils, then peas— and other kinds yet. You go to buy seeds, and he takes some wheat out of that layer, and puts it in your hand as a sample; now, could you tell by looking at that whether the peas were sound, the lentils tender, and the beans full?

Her. Impossible.

Ly. No more can you tell the quality of a philosophy from the first statements of its professor; it is not uniform, like the wine to which you compared it, claiming that it must resemble the sample glass; it is heterogeneous, and it had better not be cursorily tested. If you buy bad wine, the loss is limited to a few pence; but to rot with the common herd (in your own words) is not so light a loss. Moreover, your man who wants to drink up the cask as a preliminary to buying a pint will injure the merchant, with his dubious sampling; but philosophy knows no such danger; you may drink your fill, but this cask grows no emptier, and its owner suffers no loss. It is cut and come again here; we have the converse of the Danaids' cask; that would not hold what was put into it; it ran straight through; but here, the more you take away, the more remains.

And I have another similar remark to make about these specimen drops of philosophy. Do not fancy I am libeling it, if I say it is like hemlock, aconite, or other deadly poison. Those too, though they have death in them, will not kill if a man scrapes off the tiniest particle with the edge of his nail and tastes it; if they are not taken in the right quantity, the right manner, and the right vehicle, the taker will not die; you were wrong in claiming that the least possible quantity is enough to base a generalization on.

Her. Oh, have it your own way, Lycinus. Well then, we have got to live a hundred years, and go through all this trouble? There is no other road to philosophy?

Ly. No, none; and we need not complain; as you very truly said, *ars longa, vita brevis*. But I do not know what has come over you; you now make a grievance of it, if you cannot before set of sun develop into a Chrysippus, a Plato, a Pythagoras.

Her. You trap me, and drive me into a corner, Lycinus; yet I never provoked you. It is all envy, I know, because I have made some progress in my studies, whereas you have neglected yourself, when you were old enough to know better.

Ly. Seest, then, thy true course? Never mind me, but leave me as a lunatic to my follies, and you go on your way and accomplish what you have intended all this time.

Her. But you are so masterful, you will not let me make a choice, till I have proved all.

Ly. Why, I confess, you will never get me to budge from that. But when you call me masterful, it seems to me you blame the blameless, as the poet says; for I am myself being dragged along by reason, until you bring up some other reason to release me from durance. And here is reason about to talk more masterfully still, you will see; but I suppose you will exonerate it, and blame me.

Her. What can it be? I am surprised to hear it still has anything in reserve.

Ly. It says that seeing and going through all philosophies will not suffice, if you want to choose the best of them; the most important qualification is still missing.

Her. Indeed? Which?

Ly. Why (bear with me), a critical investigating faculty, mental acumen, intellectual precision and independence equal to the occasion; without this, the completest inspection will be useless. Reason insists that the owner of it must further be allowed ample time; he will collect the rival candidates together, and make his choice with long, lingering, repeated deliberation; he will give no heed to the candidate's age, appearance, or repute for wisdom, but perform his functions like the Areopagites,[7] who judge in the darkness of night, so that they must regard not the pleaders, but the pleadings. Then and not till then will you be able to make a sound choice and live a philosopher.

Her. Live? an after life, then. No mortal span will meet your demands; let me see: go the whole round, examine each with care, on that examination form a judgment, on that judgment make a choice, on that choice be a philosopher; so and no otherwise you say the truth may be found.

Ly. I hardly dare tell you—even that is not exhaustive. I am afraid, after all, the solid basis we thought we had found was imaginary. You know how fishermen often let down their nets, feel a weight, and pull them up expecting a great haul; when they have got them up with much toil, behold, a stone, or an old pot full of sand. I fear our catch is one of those.

Her. I don't know what this particular net may be; your nets are all round me, anyhow.

Ly. Well, try and get through; providentially, you are as good a swimmer as can be. Now, this is it: granted that we

---

[7] Ancient Athenian councilors and judges.

go all round experimenting, and get it done at last, too, I do not believe we shall have solved the elementary question, whether *any* of them has the much-desired; perhaps they are all wrong together.

Her. Oh, come now! not one of *them* right either?

Ly. I cannot tell. Do you think it impossible they may all be deluded, and the truth be something which none of them has yet found?

Her. How can it possibly be?

Ly. This way: take a correct number, twenty; suppose, I mean, a man has twenty beans in his closed hand, and asks ten different persons to guess the number; they guess seven, five, thirty, ten, fifteen—various numbers, in short. It is possible, I suppose, that one may be right?

Her. Yes.

Ly. It is not impossible, however, that they may all guess different incorrect numbers, and not one of them suggest twenty beans. What say you?

Her. It is not impossible.

Ly. In the same way, all philosophers are investigating the nature of Happiness; they get different answers, one Pleasure, another Goodness, and so through the list. It is probable that Happiness *is* one of these; but it is also not improbable that it is something else altogether. We seem to have reversed the proper procedure, and hurried on to the end before we had found the beginning. I suppose we ought first to have ascertained that the truth has actually been discovered, and that some philosopher or other has it, and only then to have gone on to the next question, *which* of them is to be believed.

Her. So that, even if we go all through all philosophy, we shall have no certainty of finding the truth even then; that is what you say.

Ly. Please, please do not ask *me*; once more, apply to reason itself. Its answer will perhaps be that there can be no certainty yet—as long as we cannot be sure that it is one or other of the things they say it is.

Her. Then, according to you, we shall never finish our quest nor be philosophers, but have to give it up and live the life of laymen. What you say amounts to that: philosophy is impossible and inaccessible to a mere mortal; for you expect the aspirant first to choose the best philosophy; and you considered that the only guarantee of such choice's being correct was to go through all philosophy before choosing the truest. Then in reckoning the number of years required by each you spurned all limits, extended the thing to several generations, and made out the quest of truth too long for the individual life; and now you crown all by proving success doubtful even apart from all that; you say it is uncertain whether the philosophers have ever found truth at all.

Ly. Could you state on oath that they have?

Her. Not on oath, no.

Ly. And yet there is much that I have intentionally spared you, though it merits careful examination too.

Her. For instance?

Ly. Is it not said that, among the professed Stoics, Platonists, and Epicureans, some do know their respective doctrines, and some do not (without prejudice to their general respectability)?

Her. That is true.

Ly. Well, don't you think it will be a troublesome business to distinguish the first, and know them from the ignorant professors?

Her. Very.

Ly. So, if you are to recognize the best of the Stoics, you will have to go to most, if not all, of them, make trial, and appoint the best your teacher, first going through a course of training to provide you with the appropriate critical faculty; otherwise you might mistakenly prefer the wrong one. Now reflect on the additional time this will mean; I purposely left it out of account, because I was afraid you might be angry; all the same, it is the most important and necessary thing of all in questions like this—so uncertain and dubious, I mean. For the discovery of truth, your one and only sure or well-founded hope is the possession of this power: you *must* be able to judge and sift truth from falsehood; you must have the assayer's sense for sound and true or forged coin; if you could have come to your examination of doctrines equipped with a technical skill like that, I should have nothing to say; but without it there is nothing to prevent their severally leading you by the nose; you will follow a dangled bunch of carrots like a donkey; or, better still, you will be water spilt on a table, trained whichever way one chooses with a finger-tip; or again, a reed growing on a river's bank, bending to every breath, however gentle the breeze that shakes it in its passage.

If you could find a teacher, now, who understood demonstration and controversial method, and would impart his knowledge to you, you would be quit of your troubles; the best and the true would straightway be revealed to you, at the bidding of this art of demonstration, while falsehood would stand convicted; you would make your choice with confidence; judgment would be followed by philosophy; you would reach your long-desired Happiness, and live in its company, which sums up all good things.

Her. Thank you, Lycinus; that is a much better hearing; there is more than a glimpse of hope in that. We must surely look for a man of that sort, to give us discernment, judgment, and, above all, the power of demonstration; then all will be easy and clear, and not too long. I am grateful to you already for thinking of this short and excellent plan.

Ly. Ah, no, I cannot fairly claim gratitude yet. I have not discovered or revealed anything that will bring you nearer your hope. On the contrary, we are further off than ever; it is a case of much cry and little wool.

Her. Bird of ill omen, pessimist, explain yourself.

Ly. Why, my friend, even if we find someone who claims to know this art of demonstration, and is willing to impart it, we shall surely not take his word for it straight off; we shall look about for another man to resolve us whether the first is telling the truth. Finding number two, we shall still be uncertain whether our guarantor really knows the difference between a good judge and a bad, and shall need a number three to guarantee number two; for how can we possibly know ourselves how to select the best judge? You see how far this must go; the thing is unending; its nature does not allow us to draw the line and put a stop to it; for you will observe that all the demonstrations that can possibly be thought of are themselves unfounded and open to dispute; most of them struggle to establish their certainty by appealing to facts as questionable as themselves; and the rest produce certain truisms with which they compare, quite illegitimately, the most speculative theories, and then say they have demonstrated the latter: our eyes tell us there are altars to the Gods; therefore there must be Gods; that is the sort of thing.

Her. How unkindly you treat me, Lycinus, turning my treasure into ashes; I suppose all these years are to have been lost labor.

Ly. At least your chagrin will be considerably lessened by the thought that you are not alone in your disappointment; practically all who pursue philosophy do no more than disquiet themselves in vain. Who could conceivably go through all the stages I have rehearsed? You admit the impossibility yourself. As to your present mood, it is that of the man who cries and curses his luck because he cannot climb the sky, or plunge into the depths of the sea at Sicily and come up at Cyprus, or soar on wings and fly within the day from Greece to India; what is responsible for his discontent is his basing of hopes on a dream-vision or his own wild fancy, without ever asking whether his aspirations were realizable or consistent with humanity. You too, my friend, have been having a long and marvelous dream; and now reason has stuck a pin into you and startled you out of your sleep; your eyes are only half open yet, you are reluctant to shake off a sleep which has shown you such fair visions, and so you scold. It is just the condition of the day-dreamer; he is rolling in gold, digging up treasure, sitting on his throne, or somehow at the summit of bliss; for dame How-I-wish is a lavish facile Goddess, that will never turn a deaf ear to her votary, though he have a mind to fly, or change statures with Colossus, or strike a gold-reef; well, in the middle of all this, in comes his servant with some every-day question, wanting to know where he is to get bread, or what he shall say to the landlord, tired of waiting for his rent; and then he flies into a temper, as though the intrusive questioner had robbed him of all his bliss, and is ready to bite the poor fellow's nose off.

As you love me, do not treat me like that. I see you digging up treasure, spreading your wings, nursing extravagant ideas, indulging impossible hopes; and I love you too well to leave you to the company of a lifelong dream—a pleasant one, if you will, but yet a dream. I beseech you to get up and take to some every-day business, such as may direct the rest of your life's course by common sense. Your acts and your thoughts up to now have been no more than Centaurs, Chimeras, Gorgons, or what else is figured by dreams and poets and painters, chartered libertines all, who reck not of what has been or may be. Yet the common folk believe them, bewitched by tale and picture just because they are strange and monstrous.

I fancy you hearing from some teller of tales how there is a certain lady of perfect beauty, beyond the Graces themselves or the Heavenly Aphrodite, and then, without ever an inquiry whether his tale is true, and such a person to be found on earth, falling straight in love with her, like Medea in the story enamoured of a dream-Jason. And what most drew you on to love, you and the others who worship the same phantom, was, if I am not mistaken, the consistent way in which the inventor of the lady added to his picture, when once he had got your ear. That was the only thing you all looked to, with that he turned you about as he would, having got his first hold upon you, averring that he was leading you the straight way to your beloved. After the first step, you see, all was easy; none of you ever looked round when he came to the entrance, and inquired whether it was the right one, or whether he had accidentally taken the wrong; no, you all followed in your predecessors' footsteps, like sheep after the bell-wether, whereas the right thing was to decide at the entrance whether you should go in.

Perhaps an illustration will make my meaning clearer: when one of those audacious poets affirms that there was once a three-headed and six-handed man, if you accept that quietly without questioning its possibility, he will proceed to fill in the picture consistently—six eyes and ears, three voices talking at once, three mouths eating, and thirty fingers instead of our poor ten all told; if he has to fight, three of his hands will have a buckler, wicker targe, or shield apiece, while of the other three one swings an axe, another hurls a spear, and the third wields a sword. It is too late to carp at these details, when they come; they are consistent with the beginning; it was about that that the question ought to have been raised whether it was to be accepted and passed as true. Once grant that, and the rest comes flooding in, irresistible, hardly now susceptible of doubt, because it is consistent and accordant with your initial admissions. That is just your case; your love-yearning would not allow you to look into the facts at each entrance, and so you are dragged on by consistency; it never occurs to you that a thing may be self-consistent and yet false; if a man says twice five is seven, and you take his word for it without checking the sum, he will naturally deduce that four times five is fourteen, and so on *ad libitum*. This is the way that weird geometry proceeds: it sets before beginners certain strange assumptions, and insists on their granting the existence of inconceivable things, such as points having no parts, lines without breadth, and so on, builds on these rotten foundations a superstructure equally rotten, and pretends to go on to a demonstration which is true, though it starts from premises which are false.

Just so you, when you have granted the principles of any school, believe in the deductions from them, and take their consistency, false as it is, for a guarantee of truth. Then with some of you, hope travels through, and you die before you have seen the truth and detected your deceivers, while the rest, disillusioned too late, will not turn back for shame: what, confess at their years that they have been abused with toys all this time? So they hold on desperately, putting the best face upon it and making all the converts they can, to have the consolation of good company in their deception; they are well aware that to speak out is to sacrifice the respect and superiority and honor they are accustomed to; so they will not do it if it may be helped, knowing the height from which they will fall to the common level. Just a few are found with the courage to say they were deluded, and warn other aspirants. Meeting such a one, call him a good man, a true and an honest; nay, call him philosopher, if you will; to my mind, the name is his or no one's; the rest either have no knowledge of the truth, though they think they have, or else have knowledge and hide it, shamefaced cowards clinging to reputation.

But now for goodness' sake let us drop all this, cover it up with an amnesty, and let it be as if it had not been said; let us assume that the Stoic philosophy, and no other, is correct; then we can examine whether it is practicable and possible, or its disciples wasting their pains; it makes wonderful promises, I am told, about the Happiness in store for those who reach the summit; for none but they shall enter into full possession of the true Good. The next point you must help me with— whether you have ever met such a Stoic, such a pattern of Stoicism, as to be unconscious of pain, untempted by pleasure, free from wrath, superior to envy, contemptuous of wealth, and, in one word, Happy; such should the example and model of the Virtuous life be; for anyone who falls short in the slightest degree, even though he is better than other men at all points, is not complete, and in that case not yet Happy.

Her. I never saw such a man.

Ly. I am glad you do not palter with the truth. But what are your hopes in pursuing philosophy, then? You see that neither your own teacher, nor his, nor his again, and so on to the tenth generation, has been absolutely wise and so attained Happiness. It will not serve you to say that it is enough to get near Happiness; that is no good; a person on the doorstep is just as much outside and in the air as another a long way off, though with the difference that the former is tantalized by a nearer view. So it is to get into the neighborhood of Happiness—I will grant you so much—that you toil like this, wearing yourself away, letting this great portion of your life slip from you, while you are sunk in dullness and wakeful weariness; and you are to go on with it for twenty more years at the least, you tell me, to take your place when you are eighty—always assuming someone to assure you that length of days—in the ranks of the not yet Happy. Or perhaps you reckon on being the exception; you are to crown your pursuit by attaining what many a good man before you, swifter far, has pursued and never overtaken.

Well, overtake it, if that is your plan, grasp it and have it whole, this something, mysterious to me, of which the possession is sufficient reward for such toils; this something which I wonder how long you will have the enjoyment of, old man that you will be, past all pleasure, with one foot in the grave; ah, but perhaps, like a brave soul, you are getting ready for another life, that you may spend it the better when you come to it, having learned how to live: as though one should take so long preparing and elaborating a superlative dinner that he fainted with hunger and exhaustion!

However, there is another thing I do not think you have observed: Virtue is manifested, of course, in action, in doing what is just and wise and manly; but you—and when I say you, I mean the most advanced philosophers—you do not seek these things and ensue them, but spend the greater part of your life conning over miserable sentences and demonstrations and problems; it is the man who does best at these that you hail a glorious victor. And I believe that is why you admire this experienced old professor of yours: he nonplusses his associates, knows how to put crafty questions and inveigle you into pitfalls; so you pay no attention to the fruit—which consists in action—but are extremely busy with the husks, and smother each other with the leaves in your debates; come now, Hermotimus, what else are you about from morning to night?

Her. Nothing; that is what it comes to.

Ly. Is it wronging you to say that you hunt the shadow or the snake's dead slough, and neglect the solid body or the creeping thing itself? You are no better than a man pouring water into a mortar and braying it with an iron pestle; he thinks he is doing a necessary useful job, whereas, let him bray till all's blue (excuse the slang), the water is as much water as ever it was.

And here let me ask you whether, putting aside his discourse, you would choose to resemble your master, and be as passionate, as sordid, as quarrelsome, ay, and as addicted to pleasure (though that trait of his is not generally known). Why no answer, Hermotimus? Shall I tell you a plea for philosophy which I lately heard? It was from the mouth of an old, old man, who has quite a company of young disciples. He was angrily demanding his fees from one of these; they were long overdue, he said; the day stated in the agreement was the first of the month, and it was now the fifteenth.

The youth's uncle was there, a rustic person without any notion of your refinements; and by way of stilling the storm,

"Come, come, sir," says he, "you need not make such a fuss because we have bought words of you and not yet settled the bill. As to what you have sold us, you have got it still; your stock of learning is none the less; and in what I really sent the boy to you for, you have not improved him a bit; he has carried off and seduced neighbor Echecrates' daughter, and there would have been an action for assault, only Echecrates is a poor man; but the prank cost me a couple of hundred. And the other day he struck his mother; she had tried to stop him when he was smuggling wine out of the house, for one of his club-dinners, I suppose. As to temper and conceit and impudence and brass and lying, he was not half so bad twelve months ago as he is now. That is where I should have liked him to profit by your teaching; and we could have done without his knowing the stuff he reels off at table every day: 'a crocodile seized hold of a baby,' says he, 'and promised to give it back if its father could answer'—the Lord knows what; or how, 'day being, night cannot be'; and sometimes his worship twists round what we say somehow or other, till there we are with horns on our heads! We just laugh at it—most of all when he stuffs up his ears and repeats to himself what he calls temperaments and conditions and conceptions and impressions, and a lot more like that. And he tells us God is not in heaven, but goes about in everything, wood and stone and animals—the meanest of them, too; and if his mother asks him why he talks such stuff, he laughs at her and says if once he gets the 'stuff' pat off, there will be nothing to prevent him from being the only rich man, the only king, and counting everyone else slaves and offscourings."

When he had finished, mark the reverend philosopher's answer. "You should consider," he said, "that if he had never come to me, he would have behaved far worse—very possibly have come to the gallows. As it is, philosophy and the respect he has for it have been a check upon him, so that you find he keeps within bounds and is not quite unbearable; the philo-

sophic system and name tutor him with their presence, and
the thought of disgracing them shames him. I should be quite
justified in taking your money, if not for any positive improvement I have effected, yet for the abstentions due to his
respect for philosophy; the very nurses will tell you as much:
children should go to school, because, even if they are not old
enough to learn, they will at least be out of mischief there.
My conscience is quite easy about him; if you like to select
any of your friends who are acquainted with Stoicism and
bring him here tomorrow you shall see how the boy can
question and answer, how much he has learnt, how many
books he has read on axioms, syllogisms, conceptions, duty,
and all sorts of subjects. As for his hitting his mother or se-
ducing girls, what have I to do with that? Am I his keeper?"

A dignified defense of philosophy for an old man! Perhaps
you will say too that it is a good enough reason for pursuing
it, if it will keep us from worse employments. Were our original expectations from philosophy at all of a different nature,
by the way? did they contemplate anything beyond a more
decent behavior than the average? Why this obstinate silence?

Her. Oh, why but that I could cry like a baby? It cuts me
to the heart, it is all so true; it is too much for me, when I
think of my wretched, wasted years—paying all that money
for my own labor, too! I am sober again after a debauch, I see
what the object of my maudlin affection is like, and what it
has brought upon me.

Ly. No need for tears, dear fellow; that is a very sensible
fable of Aesop's. A man sat on the shore and counted the
waves breaking; missing count, he was excessively annoyed.
But the fox came up and said to him: "Why vex yourself,
good sir, over the past ones? You should let them go, and
begin counting afresh." So you, since this is your mind, had
better reconcile yourself now to living like an ordinary man;
you will give up your extravagant haughty hopes and put
yourself on a level with the commonalty; if you are sensible,

you will not be ashamed to unlearn in your old age, and change your course for a better.

Now I beg you not to fancy that I have said all this as an anti-Stoic, moved by any special dislike of your school; my arguments hold against all schools. I should have said just the same if you had chosen Plato or Aristotle, and condemned the others unheard. But, as Stoicism was your choice, the argument has seemed to be aimed at that, though it had no such special application.

Her. You are quite right. And now I will be off to metamorphose myself. When we next meet, there will be no long, shaggy beard, no artificial composure; I shall be natural, as a gentleman should. I may go as far as a fashionable coat, by way of publishing my renunciation of nonsense. I only wish there were an emetic that would purge out every doctrine they have instilled into me; I assure you, if I could reverse Chrysippus' plan with the hellebore,[8] and drink forgetfulness, not of the world but of Stoicism, I would not think twice about it. Well, Lycinus, I owe you a debt indeed; I was being swept along in a rough turbid torrent, unresisting, drifting with the stream; when lo, you stood there and fished me out, a true *deus ex machina*.[9] I have good enough reason, I think, to shave my head like the people who get clear off from a wreck; for I am to make votive offerings today for the dispersion of that thick cloud which was over my eyes. Henceforth, if I meet a philosopher on my walks (and it will not be with my will), I shall turn aside and avoid him as I would a mad dog.

---

[8] An herb from which a poisonous drink was distilled.
[9] Literally, a god from the machine, an allusion to the practice in classical tragedies of bringing a god on stage by machinery to solve a difficulty.

ICAROMENIPPUS, AN
AERIAL EXPEDITION

Menippus and a Friend

Me. Let me see, now. First stage, Earth to Moon, 350 miles.
Second stage, up to the Sun, 500 leagues. Then the third, to
the actual Heaven and Zeus' citadel, might be put at a day's
journey for an eagle in light marching order.

Fr. In the name of goodness, Menippus, what are these
astronomical sums you are doing under your breath? I have
been dogging you for some time, listening to your suns and
moons, queerly mixed up with common earthly stages and
leagues.

Me. Ah, you must not be surprised if my talk is rather
exalted and ethereal; I was making out the mileage of my
journey.

Fr. Oh, I see; using stars to steer by, like the Phoenicians?

Me. Oh no, traveling among them.

Fr. Well, to be sure, it must have been a longish dream, if
you lost yourself in it for whole leagues.

Me. Dream, my good man? I am just come straight from
Zeus. Dream, indeed!

Fr. How? What? Our Menippus a literal godsend from
Heaven?

Me. 'Tis even so; from very Zeus I come this day, eyes and
ears yet full of wonders. Oh, doubt, if you will. That my
fortune should pass belief makes it only the more gratifying.

Fr. Nay, my worshipful Olympian, how should I, "a man
begotten, treading this poor earth," doubt him who trans-

cends the clouds, a "denizen of Heaven," as Homer says? But vouchsafe to tell me how you were uplifted, and where you got your mighty tall ladder. There is hardly enough of Ganymede in your looks to suggest that you were carried off by the eagle for a cupbearer.

Me. I see you are bent on making a jest of it. Well, it *is* extraordinary; you could not be expected to see that it is not a romance. The fact is, I needed neither ladder nor amorous eagle; I had wings of my own.

Fr. Stranger and stranger! This beats Daedalus. What, you turned into a hawk or a crow on the sly?

Me. Now that is not a bad shot; it was Daedalus' wing trick that I tried.

Fr. Well, talk of foolhardiness! Did you like the idea of falling into the sea, and giving us a *Mare Menippeum* after the precedent of the *Icarium*?

Me. No fear. Icarus' feathers were fastened with wax, and of course, directly the sun warmed this, he molted and fell. No wax for me, thank you.

Fr. How did you manage, then? I declare I shall be believing you soon, if you go on like this.

Me. Well, I caught a fine eagle, and also a particularly powerful vulture, and cut off their wings above the shoulder-joint. . . . But no; if you are not in a hurry, I may as well give you the enterprise from the beginning.

Fr. Do, do; I am rapt aloft by your words already, my mouth open for your *bonne bouche*;[1] as you love me, leave me not in those upper regions hung up by the ears!

Me. Listen, then; it would be a sorry sight, a friend deserted, with his mouth open, and *sus. per aures.*[2]—Well, a very short survey of life had convinced me of the absurdity and meanness and insecurity that pervade all human objects, such

---

[1] Good mouthful, French slang.
[2] Suspended by the ears.

as wealth, office, power. I was filled with contempt for them, realized that to care for them was to lose all chance of what deserved care, and determined to grovel no more, but fix my gaze upon the great All. Here I found my first problem in what wise men call the universal order; I could not tell how it came into being, who made it, what was its beginning, or what its end. But my next step, which was the examination of details, landed me in yet worse perplexity. I found the stars dotted quite casually about the sky, and I wanted to know what the sun was. Especially the phenomena of the moon struck me as extraordinary, and quite passed my comprehension; there must be some mystery to account for those many phases, I conjectured. Nor could I feel any greater certainty about such things as the passage of lightning, the roll of thunder, the descent of rain and snow and hail.

In this state of mind, the best I could think of was to get at the truth of it all from the people called philosophers; they of course would be able to give it me. So I selected the best of them, if solemnity of visage, pallor of complexion and length of beard are any criterion—for there could not be a moment's doubt of their soaring words and heaven-high thoughts—and in their hands I placed myself. For a considerable sum down, and more to be paid when they should have perfected me in wisdom, I was to be made an airy metaphysician and instructed in the order of the universe. Unfortunately, so far from dispelling my previous ignorance, they perplexed me more and more, with their daily drenches of beginnings and ends, atoms and voids, matters and forms. My greatest difficulty was that, though they differed among themselves, and all they said was full of inconsistency and contradiction, they expected me to believe them, each pulling me in his own direction.

Fr. How absurd that wise men should quarrel about facts, and hold different opinions on the same things!

Me. Ah, but keep your laughter till you have heard something of their pretentious mystifications. To begin with, their feet are on the ground; they are no taller than the rest of us "men that walk the earth"; they are no sharper-sighted than their neighbors, some of them purblind, indeed, with age or indolence; and yet they say they can distinguish the limits of the sky, they measure the sun's circumference, take their walks in the supra-lunar regions, and specify the sizes and shapes of the stars as though they had fallen from them; often one of them could not tell you correctly the number of miles from Megara to Athens, but has no hesitation about the distance in feet from the sun to the moon. How high the atmosphere is, how deep the sea, how far it is round the earth —they have the figures for all that; and moreover, they have only to draw some circles, arrange a few triangles and squares, add certain complicated spheres, and lo, they have the cubic contents of Heaven.

Then, how reasonable and modest of them, dealing with subjects so debatable, to issue their views without a hint of uncertainty; thus it must be and it shall be; *contra gentes* [3] they will have it so; they will tell you on oath the sun is a molten mass, the moon inhabited, and the stars water-drinkers, moisture being drawn up by the sun's rope and bucket and equitably distributed among them.

How their theories conflict is soon apparent; next-door neighbors? No, they are miles apart. In the first place, their views of the world differ. Some say it had no beginning, and cannot end; others boldly talk of its creator and his procedure; what particularly entertained me was that these latter set up a contriver of the universe, but fail to mention where he came from, or what he stood on while about his elaborate task, though it is by no means obvious how there could be place or time before the universe came into being.

---

[3] Contrary to or against the people.

Fr. You really do make them out very audacious conjurers.

Me. My dear fellow, I wish I could give you their lucubrations on ideas and incorporeals, on finite and infinite. Over that point, now, there is fierce battle; some circumscribe the All, others will have it unlimited. At the same time they declare for a plurality of worlds, and speak scornfully of others who make only one. And there is a bellicose person who maintains that war is the father of the universe.[4]

As to Gods, I need hardly deal with that question. For some of them God is a number; some swear by dogs and geese and plane trees.[5] Some again banish all other Gods, and attribute the control of the universe to a single one; I got rather depressed on learning how small the supply of divinity was. But I was comforted by the lavish souls who not only make many, but classify; there was a First God, and second and third classes of divinity. Yet again, some regard the divine nature as unsubstantial and without form, while others conceive it as a substance. Then they were not all disposed to recognize a Providence; some relieve the Gods of all care, as we relieve the superannuated of their civic duties; in fact, they treat them exactly like supernumeraries on the stage. The last step is also taken, of saying that Gods do not exist at all, and leaving the world to drift along without a master or a guiding hand.

Well, when I heard all this, I dared not disbelieve people whose voices and beards were equally suggestive of Zeus. But I knew not where to turn for a theory that was not open to exception, nor combated by one as soon as propounded by another. I found myself in the state Homer has described;

---

[4] Variously attributed to Heraclitus, who denies the possibility of repose, and insists that all things are in a state of flux; and to Empedocles, who makes all change and becoming depend on the interaction of the two principles, attraction and repulsion.

[5] Socrates made a practice of substituting these for the names of Gods in his oaths.

many a time I would vigorously start believing one of these gentlemen;

But then came second thoughts.

So in my distress I began to despair of ever getting any knowledge about these things on earth; the only possible escape from perplexity would be to take to myself wings and go up to Heaven. Partly the wish was father to the thought; but it was confirmed by Aesop's Fables, from which it appears that Heaven is accessible to eagles, beetles, and sometimes camels. It was pretty clear that I could not possibly develop feathers of my own. But if I were to wear vulture's or eagle's wings—the only kinds equal to a man's weight—I might perhaps succeed. I caught the birds, and effectually amputated the eagle's right, and the vulture's left wing. These I fastened together, attached them to my shoulders with broad thick straps, and provided grips for my hands near the end of the quill-feathers. Then I made experiments, first jumping up and helping the jump by flapping my hands, or imitating the way a goose raises itself without leaving the ground and combines running with flight. Finding the machine obedient, I next made a bolder venture, went up the Acropolis, and launched myself from the cliff right over the theater.

Getting safely to the bottom that time, my aspirations shot up aloft. I took to starting from Parnes or Hymettus, flying to Geranea, thence to the top of the Acrocorinthus, and over Pholoë and Erymanthus to Taÿgetus. The training for my venture was now complete; my powers were developed, and equal to a lofty flight; no more fledgling essays for me. I went up Olympus, provisioning myself as lightly as possible. The moment was come; I soared skywards, giddy at first with that great void below, but soon conquering this difficulty. When I approached the Moon, long after parting from the clouds, I was conscious of fatigue, especially in the left or vulture's wing. So I alighted and sat down to rest, having a bird's-eye view of the Earth, like the Homeric Zeus,

> *Surveying now the Thracian horsemen's land,*
> *Now Mysia,*

and again, as the fancy took me, Greece or Persia or India. From all which I drew a manifold delight.

Fr. Oh well, Menippus, tell me all about it. I do not want to miss a single one of your travel experiences; if you picked up any stray information, let me have that too. I promise myself a great many facts about the shape of the Earth, and how everything on it looked to you from your point of vantage.

Me. And you will not be disappointed there, friend. So do your best to get up to the Moon, with my story for traveling companion and showman of the terrestrial scene.

Imagine yourself first descrying a tiny Earth, far smaller than the Moon looks; on turning my eyes down, I could not think for some time what had become of our mighty mountains and vast sea. If I had not caught sight of the Colossus of Rhodes and the Pharus [6] tower, I assure you I should never have made out the Earth at all. But their height and projection, with the faint shimmer of Ocean in the sun, showed me it must be the Earth I was looking at. Then, when once I had got my sight properly focused, the whole human race was clear to me, not merely in the shape of nations and cities, but the individuals, sailing, fighting, plowing, going to law; the women, the beasts, and in short every breed "that feedeth on earth's foison."

Fr. Most unconvincing and contradictory. Just now you were searching for the Earth, it was so diminished by distance, and if the Colossus had not betrayed it, you would have taken it for something else; and now you develop sud-

---

[6] An island off the coast of Egypt, on which was a famous lighthouse.

denly into a Lynceus, and distinguish everything upon it, the men, the beasts, one might almost say the gnat-swarms. Explain, please.

Me. Why, to be sure! how did I come to leave out so essential a particular? I had made out the Earth, you see, but could not distinguish any details; the distance was so great, quite beyond the scope of my vision; so I was much chagrined and baffled. At this moment of depression—I was very near tears —who should come up behind me but Empedocles the physicist? His complexion was like charcoal variegated with ashes, as if he had been baked. I will not deny that I felt some tremors at the sight of him, taking him for some lunar spirit. But he said: "Do not be afraid, Menippus;

A mortal I, no God; how vain thy dreams.

I am Empedocles the physicist. When I threw myself into the crater in such a hurry, the smoke of Etna whirled me off up here; and now I live in the Moon, doing a good deal of high thinking on a diet of dew. So I have come to help you out of your difficulty; you are distressed, I take it, at not being able to see everything on the Earth." "Thank you so much, you good Empedocles," I said; "as soon as my wings have brought me back to Greece, I will remember to pour libations to you up the chimney, and salute you on the first of every month with three moonward yawns." "Endymion be my witness," he replied, "I had no thought of such a bargain; I was touched by the sight of your distress. Now, what do you think is the way to sharpen your sight?"

"I have no idea, unless you were to remove the mist from my eyes for me; the sight seems quite bleared." "Oh, you can do without me; the thing that gives sharp sight you have brought with you from Earth." "Unconsciously, then; what is it?" "Why, you know that you have on an eagle's right wing?" "Of course I do; but what have wings and eyes to

do with one another?" "Only this," he said; "the eagle is far
the strongest-eyed of all living things, the only one that can
look straight at the sun; the test of the true royal eagle is, his
meeting its rays without blinking." "So I have heard; I wish
I had taken out my own eyes when I was starting, and substituted the eagle's. I am an imperfect specimen now I am
here, not up to the royal standard at all, but like the rejected
bastards." "Well, you can very soon acquire one royal eye.
If you will stand up for a minute, keep the vulture wing still,
and work the other, your right eye, corresponding to that
wing, will gain strength. As for the other, its dimness cannot possibly be obviated, as it belongs to the inferior member." "Oh, I shall be quite content with aquiline vision for
the right eye only," I said; "I have often observed that car-
penters in ruling their wood find one better than two." So
saying, I proceeded to carry out my instructions at once.
Empedocles began gradually to disappear, and at last vanished
in smoke.

I had no sooner flapped the wing than a flood of light enveloped me, and things that before I had not even been aware
of became perfectly clear. I turned my eyes down earthwards,
and with ease discerned cities, men, and all that was going on,
not merely in the open, but in the fancied security of houses.
There was Ptolemy in his sister's arms, the son of Lysimachus
plotting against his father, Seleucus' son Antiochus making
signs to his step-mother Stratonice, Alexander of Pherae being
murdered by his wife, Antigonus corrupting his daughter-
in-law, the son of Attalus putting the poison in his cup;
Arsaces was in the act of slaying his mistress, while the eunuch
Arbaces drew his sword upon him; the guards were dragging
Spatinus the Mede out from the banquet by foot, with the
lump on his brow from the golden cup. Similar sights were to
be seen in the palaces of Libya and Scythia and Thrace—
adulteries, murders, treasons, robberies, perjuries, suspicions,
and monstrous betrayals.

Such was the entertainment afforded me by royalty; private life was much more amusing; for I could make that out too. I saw Hermodorus the Epicurean perjuring himself for £40, Agathocles the Stoic suing a pupil for his fees, lawyer Clinias stealing a bowl from the temple of Aesculapius, and Herophilus the Cynic sleeping in a brothel. Not to mention the multitude of burglars, litigants, usurers, duns; oh, it was a fine representative show!

Fr. I must say, Menippus, I should have liked the details here too; it all seems to have been very much to your taste.

Me. I could not go through the whole of it, even to please you; to take it in with the eyes kept one busy. But the main divisions were very much what Homer gives from the shield of Achilles: here junketings and marriages, there courts and councils, in another compartment a sacrifice, and hard by a mourning. If I glanced at Getica, I would see the Getae at war; at Scythia, there were the Scythians wandering about on their wagons; half a turn in another direction gave me Egyptians at the plow, or Phoenicians chaffering, Cilician pirates, Spartan flagellants, Athenians at law.

All this was simultaneous, you understand; and you must try to conceive what a queer jumble it all made. It was as if a man were to collect a number of choristers, or rather of choruses,[7] and then tell each individual to disregard the others and start a strain of his own; if each did his best, went his own way, and tried to drown his neighbor, can you imagine what the musical effect would be?

Fr. A very ridiculous confusion.

Me. Well, friend, such are the earthly dancers; the life of man is just such a discordant performance; not only are the voices jangled, but the steps are not uniform, the motions not concerted, the objects not agreed upon—until the impresario dismisses them one by one from the stage, with a "not

---

[7] The Greek chorus combined singing with dancing.

wanted." Then they are all alike, and quiet enough, confound-
ing no longer their undisciplined rival strains. But as long as
the show lasts in its marvelous diversity, there is plenty of
food for laughter in its vagaries.

The people who most amused me, however, were those
who dispute about boundaries, or pride themselves on culti-
vating the plain of Sicyon, or holding the Oenoë side of Mara-
thon, or a thousand acres at Acharnae. The whole of Greece,
as I then saw it, might measure some four inches; how much
smaller Athens on the same scale. So I realized what sort of
sized basis for their pride remains to our rich men. The widest-
acred of them all, methought, was the proud cultivator of
an Epicurean atom. Then I looked at the Peloponnese, my
eyes fell on the Cynurian district, and the thought occurred
that it was for this little plot, no broader than an Egyptian
lentil, that all those Argives and Spartans fell in a single day.
Or if I saw a man puffed up by the possession of seven or
eight gold rings and half as many gold cups, again my lungs
would begin to crow; why, Pangaeus with all its mines was
about the size of a grain of millet.

Fr. You lucky man! what a rare sight you had! And how
big, now, did the towns and the people look from there?

Me. You must often have seen a community of ants, some
of them a seething mass, some going abroad, others coming
back to town. One is a scavenger, another a bustling porter
loaded with a bit of bean-pod or half a wheat grain. They no
doubt have, on their modest myrmecic scale, their architects
and politicians, their magistrates and composers and philosophers. At any rate, what men and cities suggested to me was
just so many ant-hills. If you think the similitude too disparag-
ing, look into the Thessalian legends, and you will find that
the most warlike tribe there was the Myrmidons, or ants
turned men. Well, when I had had enough of contemplation
and laughter, I roused myself and soared

To join the Gods, where dwells the Lord of storms.

I had only flown a couple of hundred yards, when Selene's [8] feminine voice reached me: "Menippus, do me an errand to Zeus, and I will wish you a pleasant journey." "You have only to name it," I said, "provided it is not something to carry." "It is a simple message of entreaty to Zeus. I am tired to death, you must know, of being slandered by these philosophers; they have no better occupation than impertinent curiosity about me—What am I? how big am I? why am I halved? why am I gibbous? I am inhabited; I am just a mirror hung over the sea; I am—whatever their latest fancy suggests. It is the last straw when they say my light is stolen, sham, imported from the sun, and keep on doing their best to get up jealousy and ill feeling between brother and sister. They might have been contented with making *him* out a stone or a red-hot lump.

"These gentry who in the day look so stern and manly, dress so gravely, and are so revered by common men, would be surprised to learn how much I know of their vile nightly abominations. I see them all, though I never tell; it would be too indecent to make revelations, and show up the contrast between their nightly doings and their public performances; so, if I catch one of them in adultery or theft or other nocturnal adventure, I pull my cloud veil over me; I do not want the vulgar to see old men disgracing their long beards and their virtuous calling. But they go on giving tongue and worrying me all the same, and, so help me Night, I have thought many a time of going a long, long way off, out of reach of their impertinent tongues. Will you remember to tell Zeus all this? and you may add that I cannot remain at my post unless he will pulverize the physicists, muzzle the logicians, raze the Porch, burn the Academy, and put an end to strolling

8 Selene was goddess of the moon.

in the Lyceum. That might secure me a little peace from these daily mensurations."

"I will remember," said I, and resumed my upward flight to Heaven, through

> *A region where nor ox nor man had wrought.*

For the Moon was soon but a small object, with the Earth entirely hidden behind it. Three days' flight through the stars, with the Sun on my right hand, brought me close to Heaven; and my first idea was to go straight in as I was; I should easily pass unobserved in virtue of my half-eagleship; for of course the eagle was Zeus' familiar; on second thoughts, though, my vulture wing would very soon betray me. So, thinking it better not to run any risks, I went up to the door and knocked. Hermes opened, took my name, and hurried off to inform Zeus. After a brief wait I was asked to step in; I was now trembling with apprehension, and I found that the Gods, who were all seated together, were not quite easy themselves. The unexpected nature of the visit was slightly disturbing to them, and they had visions of all mankind arriving at my heels by the same conveyance.

But Zeus bent upon me a Titanic glance, awful, penetrating, and spoke:

> *Who art thou? where thy city? who thy kin?*

At the sound, I nearly died of fear, but remained upright, though mute and paralyzed by that thunderous voice. I gradually recovered, began at the beginning, and gave a clear account of myself—how I had been possessed with curiosity about the heavens, had gone to the philosophers, found their accounts conflicting, and grown tired of being logically rent in twain; so I came to my great idea, my wings, and ultimately to Heaven; I added Selene's message. Zeus smiled and slightly unbent his brow. "What of Otus and Ephialtes now?" he said; "here is Menippus scaling Heaven! Well, well, for today consider yourself our guest. Tomorrow we will treat with you of your business, and send you on your way." And therewith he rose and walked to the acoustic center of Heaven, it being prayer time.

As he went, he put questions to me about earthly affairs, beginning with, What was wheat a quarter in Greece? had we suffered much from cold last winter, and did the vegetables want more rain? Then he wished to know whether any of Phidias' kin were alive, why there had been no Diasia [9] at Athens all these years, whether his Olympeum [10] was ever going to be completed, and had the robbers of his temple at Dodona been caught? I answered all these questions, and he proceeded: "Tell me, Menippus, what are men's feelings towards me?" "What should they be, Lord, but those of absolute reverence, as to the King of all Gods?" "Now, now, chaffing as usual," he said; "I know their fickleness very well, for all your dissimulation. There was a time when I was their prophet, their healer, and their all,

And Zeus filled every street and gathering-place.

In those days Dodona [11] and Pisa [12] were glorious and farfamed, and I could not get a view for the clouds of sacrificial steam. But now Apollo has set up his oracle at Delphi, Aesculapius his temple of health at Pergamum, Bendis and Anubis and Artemis their shrines in Thrace, Egypt, Ephesus; and to these all run; theirs the festal gatherings and the hecatombs. As for me, I am superannuated; they think themselves very generous if they offer me a victim at Olympia at four-year intervals. My altars are cold as Plato's *Laws* or Chrysippus' *Syllogisms*."

---

[9] Festival of Zeus.

[10] A temple of Zeus at Athens, begun in the time of Pisistratus and finished 600 years later, in the reign of Hadrian.

[11] Oracle of Zeus in Epirus.

[12] A town in Elis, near which the Olympic games were held.

So talking, we reached the spot where he was to sit and listen to the prayers. There was a row of openings with lids like well-covers, and a chair of gold by each. Zeus took his seat at the first, lifted off the lid and inclined his ear. From every quarter of Earth were coming the most various and contradictory petitions; for I too bent down my head and listened. Here are specimens. "O Zeus, that I might be king!" "O Zeus, that my onions and garlic might thrive!" "Ye Gods, a speedy death for my father!" Or again, "Would that I might succeed to my wife's property!" "Grant that my plot against my brother be not detected." "Let me win my suit." "Give me an Olympic garland." Of those at sea, one prayed for a north, another for a south wind; the farmer asked for rain, the fuller for sun. Zeus listened, and gave each prayer careful consideration, but without promising to grant them all;

Our Father this bestowed, and that withheld.

Righteous prayers he allowed to come up through the hole, received and laid them down at his right, while he sent the unholy ones packing with a downward puff of breath, that Heaven might not be defiled by their entrance. In one case I saw him puzzled; two men praying for opposite things and promising the same sacrifices, he could not tell which of them to favor, and experienced a truly Academic suspense of judgment, showing a reserve and equilibrium worthy of Pyrrho [13] himself.

The prayers disposed of, he went on to the next chair and opening, and attended to oaths and their takers. These done with, and Hermodorus the Epicurean annihilated, he proceeded to the next chair to deal with omens, prophetic voices, and auguries. Then came the turn of the sacrifice aperture, through which the smoke came up and communicated to Zeus the name of the devotee it represented. After that, he was free

---
[13] Pyrrho was founder of the Skeptics.

to give his wind and weather orders: Rain for Scythia today, a thunderstorm for Libya, snow for Greece. The north wind he instructed to blow in Lydia, the west to raise a storm in the Adriatic, the south to take a rest; a thousand bushels of hail to be distributed over Cappadocia.

His work was now pretty well completed, and as it was just dinner time, we went to the banquet hall. Hermes received me, and gave me my place next to a group of Gods whose alien origin left them in a rather doubtful position—Pan, the Corybants, Attis, and Sabazius. I was supplied with bread by Demeter, wine by Dionysus, meat by Heracles, myrtle-blossoms by Aphrodite, and sprats by Poseidon. But I also got a sly taste of ambrosia and nectar; good-natured Ganymede, as often as he saw that Zeus' attention was engaged elsewhere, brought round the nectar and indulged me with a half-pint or so. The Gods, as Homer (who I think must have had the same opportunities of observation as myself) somewhere says, neither eat bread nor drink the ruddy wine; they heap their plates with ambrosia, and are nectar-bibbers; but their choicest dainties are the smoke of sacrifice ascending with rich fumes, and the blood of victims poured by their worshipers round the altars. During dinner, Apollo harped, Silenus danced his wild measures, the Muses uprose and sang to us from Hesiod's *Birth of Gods*, and the first of Pindar's odes. When we had our fill and had well drunken, we slumbered, each where he was.

> *Slept all the Gods, and men with plumed helms,*
> *That livelong night; but me kind sleep forsook;*

for I had much upon my mind; most of all, how came it that Apollo, in all that time, had never grown a beard? And how was night possible in Heaven, with the sun always there taking his share of the good cheer? So I had but a short nap of it. And in the morning Zeus arose, and bade summon an assembly.

When all were gathered, he thus commenced: "The immediate occasion of my summoning you is the arrival of this stranger yesterday. But I have long intended to take counsel with you regarding the philosophers, and now, urged by Selene and her complaints, I have determined to defer the consideration of the question no longer. There is a class which has recently become conspicuous among men; they are idle, quarrelsome, vain, irritable, lickerish, silly, puffed up, arrogant, and, in Homeric phrase, vain cumberers of the earth. These men have divided themselves into bands, each dwelling in a separate word-maze of its own construction, and call themselves Stoics, Epicureans, Peripatetics, and more farcical names yet. Then they take to themselves the holy name of Virtue, and with uplifted brows and flowing beards exhibit the deceitful semblance that hides immoral lives; their model is the tragic actor, from whom if you strip off the mask and the gold-spangled robe, there is nothing left but a paltry fellow hired for a few shillings to play a part.

"Nevertheless, quite undeterred by their own characters, they scorn the human and travesty the divine; they gather a company of guileless youths, and feed them with solemn chatter upon Virtue and quibbling verbal puzzles; in their pupils' presence they are all for fortitude and temperance, and have no words bad enough for wealth and pleasure: when they are by themselves, there is no limit to their gluttony, their lechery, their licking of dirty pence. But the head and front of their offending is this: they neither work themselves nor help others' work; they are useless drones,

Of no avail in council nor in war;

which notwithstanding, they censure others; they store up poisoned words, they con invectives, they heap their neighbors with reproaches; their highest honors are for him who shall be loudest and most overbearing and boldest in abuse.

"Ask one of these brawling bawling censors, And what do *you* do? in God's name, what shall we call *your* contribution to progress? and he would reply, if conscience and truth were anything to him: I consider it superfluous to sail the sea or till the earth or fight for my country or follow a trade; but I have a loud voice and a dirty body; I eschew warm water and go barefoot through the winter; I am a Momus who can always pick holes in other people's coats; if a rich man keeps a costly table or a mistress, I make it my business to be properly horrified; but if my familiar friend is lying sick, in need of help and care, I am not aware of it. Such, your Godheads, is the nature of this vermin.

"There is a special insolence in those who call themselves Epicureans; these go so far as to lay their hands on our character; we take no interest in human affairs, they say, and in fact have nothing to do with the course of events. And this is a serious question for you; if once they infect their generation with this view, you will learn what hunger means. Who will sacrifice to you, if he does not expect to profit by it? As to Selene's complaints, you all heard them yesterday from this stranger's lips. And now decide upon such measures as shall advantage mankind and secure your own safety."

Zeus had no sooner closed his speech than clamor prevailed, all crying at once: "Blast! burn! annihilate! to the pit with them! to Tartarus! to the Giants!" Zeus ordered silence again, and then, "Your wishes," he said, "shall be executed; they shall all be annihilated, and their logic with them. But just at present chastisement is not lawful; you are aware that we are now in the four months of the long vacation; the formal notice has lately been issued. In the spring of next year, the baleful levin-bolt shall give them the fate they deserve."

He spake, and sealed his word with lowering brows.

"As to Menippus," he added, "my pleasure is this. He shall be deprived of his wings, and so incapacitated for repeating his visit, but shall today be conveyed back to Earth by Hermes." So saying, he dismissed the assembly. The Cyllenian accordingly lifted me up by the right ear, and yesterday evening deposited me in the Ceramicus. And now, friend, you have all the latest from Heaven. I must be off to the Poecile,[14] to let the philosophers loitering there know the luck they are in.

---

[14] The Poecile was another name for the painted porch in which the Stoics held their school.

PART III

Justin Martyr, Christian

INTRODUCTION

In the time of Marcus Aurelius Rome had become a great cosmopolitan capital, where men of many races, languages and customs jostled one another in the streets and the circus. Many of these foreigners had brought their religions with them and the shrines and mysteries of the Egyptian goddess Isis and the Persian god Mithras drew worshipers from every rank of Roman society. As a rule, these religions, being polytheistic, like the old religion of Rome, were tolerant of one another. There was room in their heavens for as many gods as one chose to believe in. But to this rule two monotheistic sects from the East, Judaism and Christianity, were exceptions. In particular, the Christians aggressively and openly denounced all pagan divinities as devils and refused to offer the customary sacrifices before the images of the deified Caesars, which represented the majesty of the Roman state. To many pagans, therefore, they seemed to be dangerous enemies not only to all the familiar ancestral faiths but also to the whole established peaceable order of things and even to the Roman government itself.

How long before Marcus' time Christianity had been legally a forbidden religion there are no records extant to tell us. In Trajan's reign (98-117 A.D.) there was a law of some kind against it, though apparently not often enforced. Under Hadrian (117-138 A.D.) the resentment of the pagan populace against the disloyal "atheists" in their midst was beginning to show itself and rumors of Christian secret orgies and black conspiracies against the community were spreading fast. In a few places popular clamor compelled the authorities to arrest and punish persons guilty of the proscribed faith. Hadrian's letter to the proconsul of Asia, appended to Justin's

"First Apology," reveals the Emperors' concern to have the law applied justly and with moderation.

Under Hadrian appeared the first of the Christian apologies or defenses against the pagan accusations. Educated converts took up their pens to protest that the lurid slanders against them were totally false. It was true that they called the immoral gods of the old mythologies demons, who masqueraded as divine in order deliberately to corrupt the human race, and that they themselves worshiped only the one Father, the God of goodness and truth. But that was their sole offense. As citizens, they lived dutiful, obedient, and peaceful lives. They were charitable and chaste, and patient under persecution and injustice. To any unprejudiced mind, they said, they could prove the truth of their faith by its fulfillment of prophecies uttered long since by inspired men of old. At certain points also it resembled the teachings of the noblest Greek philosophers, and through its doctrine of eternal rewards and punishments it offered the strongest possible incentives to goodness in everyday living now.

Under Antoninus Pius (138-161 A.D.) there was a lull in the persecutions, a "peace of the church," but by the time of Marcus Aurelius (161-180 A.D.) the Christians had so increased in numbers, especially in the cities of the Empire, that popular feeling against these enemies of the gods was growing more violent than ever and officials in many places were forced by mob excitement to act with vigor. We hear of Christians executed in Asia Minor, in Africa, and on the Rhone, as well as in Rome itself. How far Marcus, the humane philosopher, approved these persecutions we cannot be sure. In his *Meditations*, he refers once to the Christians, with evident distaste for their fanatical behavior, but he was not by nature a persecutor. He may not even have known what was going on. He had things far more important to think of than an occasional, small-scale religious fuss, which his officials were quite competent to handle. He probably read none of the Christian apologies, not even those addressed to himself. They may never have reached his hands.

Lucian, the sharp-eyed cynical observer of the human scene, knew considerably more about the Christians than the Emperor did. The hero of one of his dialogues, "The Death of Peregrinus," was a professional villain and cheat from Armenia known as Peregrinus, who lived by exploiting the credulity of simple-minded folk and found some of his easiest victims among the guileless, tender-hearted Christians of Syria. From their teachers he picked up, Lucian says, enough of their queer notions to be accepted by them as a prophet and president of their assemblies. "He expounded their books, commented on them and wrote some himself. . . . The Christians, you know, worship to this day that enchanter who was crucified in Palestine for founding their weird sect."

Peregrinus eventually got himself arrested as a Christian and thrown into prison, whereupon his fellow believers near and far sent food, money, and friends to comfort him. "These deluded creatures, you see, have persuaded themselves that they are immortal and will live forever, which explains the contempt of death and willing self-sacrifice so common among them. It was impressed on them too by their lawgiver that from the moment they are converted, deny the gods of Greece, worship the crucified sage, and live after his laws, they are all brothers. They take his instructions completely on faith, with the result that they despise all worldly goods and hold them in common ownership. So any adroit, unscrupulous fellow, who knows the world, has only to get among these simple souls and his fortune is quickly made; he plays with them." Peregrinus, however, ran no danger of death. The Roman governor himself cut short any dream he might have had of playing the glorious martyr by setting him tamely free.

To Marcus, the ruler, then, the Christians seem to have appeared chiefly as irritating petty nuisances in the path of smooth administration, and to Lucian, the Skeptic, as a joke. A contemporary of theirs, however, called Justin, a Syrian philosopher of Greek descent, was converted to Christianity, wrote several defenses and explanations of his faith, and was put to death for it at last in Rome under Marcus. From him we get some idea of the appeal Christianity had for another type of thoughtful man and why, when the test came, he preferred to die rather than forsake it. Authors disagree as to the date of Justin's birth, some placing it at the end of the first and others at the beginning of the second century after Christ. The place was Neapolis, a city of Samaria, in northern Palestine, then of course a province of Rome. Justin's family was of Greek origin, descendants, it is thought of a colony of Greeks which had settled there some time earlier. As a Greek, Justin must have grown up quite outside the native culture of Samaria, unfamiliar with the Hebrew language, religion, and law. He had, however, an unusually thorough education under excellent tutors and traveled considerably as a young man. Like many another in this period of intellectual ferment, he decided to investigate for himself the various schools of philosophy. He studied with the Stoics, the Aristotelians, the Pythagoreans, and, finally, with an eminent Platonist.

To Plato and his ideas he became strongly attached, but his attachment was not strong enough to resist the moral and intellectual appeal of Christianity, as presented to him, first,—according to Justin's own account—by a venerable teacher whom he met on a solitary walk. There is reason to suppose that he had previously witnessed the martyrdom of several Christians and been impressed by their courage and fortitude. He now saw in the Hebrew prophets of the Old Testament the inspired precursors of the Christ. Far back in the dim beginnings of human history, long before Plato, they had "glorified the Creator, the God and Father of all things and proclaimed his son the Christ. Straightway," he writes, "a flame was kindled in my soul, and a love of the prophets and of those who are the friends of Christ. I found this philosophy alone to be safe and profitable." In another place he writes, "Think not, O ye Greeks, that I have rashly and without judgment and deliberation departed from the rites of your religion. But I could find in it nothing really sacred and worthy of divine acceptance."

The influence of Plato, however, and of Justin's Greek philosophic training shows in all his writing as a Christian, and he is eager to point out the concepts they have in common, such as the creation of the world by God, and the immortality of the soul. Socrates too taught the moral dignity of man and his obligation to stand under all circumstances true to what he believed to be right. The Stoic doctrine of the freedom and importance of the human will also finds an important place in Justin's Christianity. As a matter of fact, he insists, every noble Greek principle of knowledge and conduct, whether contained in Homer, in the Greek dramatists, or in the philosophers, may be found stated earlier in the Christian Scriptures. "Whatever all men have uttered aright, then, belongs to us Christians." The Logos or Divine Word is everywhere among all men and always at work. But now with Christ has come fullness of light and the assurance of eternal life that the philosophers never had. For in Christ, the teacher, Justin sees the supreme Reason incarnate of God, whereas in the poets and philosophers there was only the seed of reason which is the natural endowment of all men. Christianity is thus to Justin "the oldest, the truest, the most divine of philosophies."

Justin's conversion took place about 132, not long after a Jewish uprising in Palestine against Roman rule, led by the rabbi Simon Bar Hochba, who claimed to be the true, expected Messiah. The Roman legion in Jerusalem was driven from its camp, and the rebellion was with some difficulty put down. Perhaps because of the disturbed conditions in Palestine, Justin soon after his conversion traveled to Rome. He still wore the traditional coarse cloak of the philosopher, whether to give him a philosopher's immunity from interference or because he regarded himself still as a true philosopher, we cannot know. Antoninus Pius had then become emperor. It was a time of expansion for the new sect, and temporary rest from the sporadic outbursts against it. At the moment, it was the Jews who were regarded as the chief troublemakers in the Empire.

In Rome, although Justin received no regular ordination as a preacher, he became a prominent figure in at least one of the groups that met weekly on the Day of the Sun. With tireless zeal he argued and wrote, winning souls to the faith, disputing with learned pagans and Jews, teaching the ignorant, fighting heretics inside the church as well as enemies outside. He called himself a "disciple of the apostles," a modest claim, for he was a leader of conspicuous talent. The faith had need of just such skilled speakers and writers if it was to make itself heard through the welter of older, more sophisticated religions and philosophies. Justin, so far as is known, was the first trained philosopher to desert his philosophy for Christianity. His appeals, accordingly, were addressed not so much to simple, childlike minds as to persons of education in the upper levels of society. His "First Apology," the ablest and most systematic of the early defenses of the faith, was written especially to interest two other philosophers—the emperor Antoninus Pius and the emperor-to-be, Marcus Aurelius.

This work is of interest not only as an example of the way a cultivated Christian, a little over a hundred years after Christ's death, could prove by reasoning the truth of his beliefs but also as a picture of life among the group of Christians at Rome in that early time and of the growth of the church and its services. To themselves they still seemed to be living in the afterglow of the ardor of the apostles' day, united closely with one another and sharing wealth and resources as children of their common Lord. Already the liturgy of their worship was taking form. In the Sunday assemblies, held wherever a place could be found, after the reading of the Scripture lesson, there followed in order the sermon by the presiding bishop or priest, then the general prayer for all men, the offertory, the presiding member's prayer of thanksgiving, the consecration of the bread and wine, and the communion. The rites of baptism and the eucharist had already taken on the character of sacraments. By the water of baptism the soul was purified from all past and inherited sin and born anew. The elements blessed by the consecrating prayer became the blood and flesh of that Jesus who was made flesh, and a food of immortality for the soul.

Later, Justin returned to Asia Minor for a time and established a school of Christian teaching at Ephesus. It was here, presumably, that he wrote his "Dialogue with Trypho the Jew," which contains the account of his own conversion, as well as a long argument based on the Old Testament, to persuade Jewish readers that Christ was their long-anticipated Messiah. Whether Trypho was a literary creation or an actual Jew with whom Justin held a debate, we do not know. But the dialogue shows his skill in handling an adversary of no mean parts.

When at length, under Marcus Aurelius, Justin returned to Rome things were not going so well for the Christians. The imperial interdict against them was being enforced more stringently. When not put to death they were frequently despoiled of their property. The brief, anonymous account of the trial and death of Justin and several companions, which in this book follows his "Apology," is probably contemporary and authentic.

The version of Justin's writings used here, and the account of his martyrdom, is based on the translation from the Greek in *The Ante-Nicene Fathers*, Vol. 1, which has been revised in the interests of clarity and readability.

DIALOGUE OF JUSTIN, THE PHILOSOPHER AND MARTYR, WITH TRYPHO, A JEW

1. As I was strolling one morning in the walks of the Xystus,[1] a man in a group with others met me, and said, "Hail, O philosopher!" And so saying, he turned around and walked along with me; his friends likewise followed him. And I in turn said to him, "What is on your mind?"

And he replied, "I was taught by Corinthus of the school of Socrates in Argos that I ought not to despise or look with indifference on those who wear your dress,[2] but show them all friendliness, and associate with them, as perhaps some advantage would spring from our intercourse either to them or to myself. It is good for both if either one be benefited. So on this account, whenever I see anyone in your costume, I gladly approach him. And now, for this same reason, I have eagerly accosted you; and these my friends accompany me, in the expectation of hearing something profitable from you."

"But who are you, most excellent of mortal men?" I answered in jest.[3]

Then he told me frankly both his name and race. "Trypho," said he, "I am called; and I am a Hebrew of the circumcision, and having escaped the recent war there,[4] I am spending my days in Greece, chiefly at Corinth."

---

[1] Probably at Ephesus.
[2] Justin wore the traditional mantle of the philosophers.
[3] In jest, no doubt, because quoting a line from Homer's *Iliad*, VI, 123.
[4] The Jews of Palestine under the rabbi, Simon Bar Hochba, had attempted another unsuccessful revolt against the Roman rule.

"And how," said I, "would you be profited by philosophy so much as by your own lawgiver and your prophets?"

"Why not?" he replied. "Do not the philosophers discourse always on God? Are they not continually discussing questions of his unity and providence? Is not this the duty of philosophy—to investigate the Deity?"

"Assuredly," said I, "so we too have believed. But most of them [5] do not consider whether there be one or more gods, and whether they have a regard for each of us or no, as if this knowledge contributed nothing to our happiness; nay, they even attempt to persuade us that God takes care of the universe with its genera and species, but not of me and you and every individual, since otherwise we would surely be praying to Him night and day. And it is not difficult to understand the effect of this attitude; for rash and reckless speaking result from maintaining these opinions; men do and say whatever they choose, neither dreading punishment nor hoping for any benefit from God. For how could they? They say that things will always be the same; and further that you and I will live again as now, having become neither better nor worse. And there are others,[6] who do take the soul to be immortal and immaterial, but believe that even though they do evil, they will not suffer punishment, for anything immaterial is insensible to pain, and the soul, because it is immortal, needs nothing from God."

Then he, smiling slightly, said, "Tell us your opinion of these matters, and what is your idea of God, and what your philosophy."

2. "I will tell you," said I, "how it seems to me. For philosophy is, in fact, a very great possession, and most honorable in the sight of God, to whom it alone leads us and commends us; and those are truly holy men who have given themselves to

---

[5] The Stoics are apparently described here.
[6] The Platonists.

philosophy. What philosophy is, however, and why it was sent down to men, few have understood; otherwise, there would be neither Platonists, nor Stoics, nor Peripatetics,[7] nor Theoretics,[8] nor Pythagoreans, since this knowledge is one.[9]

"But I will tell you how it became many-headed. It happened that those who first handled it, and who were therefore revered as illustrious, were succeeded by others who themselves made no investigations into truth, but only admired the steadfastness and self-discipline of the older men, as well as the novelty of their doctrines; and each one thought that whatever he learned from his teacher was true. Then these later ones handed down their notions to *their* successors, and others similar to them; and their system was called by the name of him who they said was the father of their doctrine.

"I at first was eager to talk with one of these men and surrendered myself to a certain Stoic; but after spending considerable time with him, when I had not acquired any further knowledge of God (for he did not know himself, and said such instruction was unnecessary), I left him and betook myself to another, who was called a Peripatetic, and, in his own opinion, a shrewd fellow. After entertaining me for a few days, he proposed to me to settle on a fee, that our intercourse might not be unprofitable. For this reason I abandoned him too, convinced he was no philosopher at all. But since my soul was still eagerly desirous to learn the peculiar excellence of philosophy, I went to a Pythagorean, very celebrated, a man who thought much of his own wisdom. But when, anxious to become his hearer and disciple, I interviewed him, he said, 'How now? Do you know music, astronomy, and geometry? Do you expect to apprehend any of the principles

---

[7] Aristotelians.

[8] A name, perhaps, for the Skeptics.

[9] Julian, *Oration*, VI, says: "Let no one divide our philosophy into many parts, or cut it into many parts, and especially let him not make many out of *one*: for as truth is one, so also is philosophy."

that conduce to a happy life without first being taught those subjects which wean the soul from objects of sense and render it fit for the intellectual, so that it can contemplate that which is honorable and that which is good in their essence?' He then commended to me these branches of learning, and told me they were necessary, but dismissed me when I confessed my ignorance. This disappointment I took rather to heart, as was to be expected, the more because I thought the man had some knowledge; but reflecting again on the time I would have to spend over those other branches of learning, I could not endure to wait so long. In my desperation it occurred to me to try the Platonists, for their fame stood high. I thereupon spent as much of my time as possible with one who had lately settled in our city, a sagacious man and distinguished among the Platonists, and I progressed and made great improvement daily. I was thrilled by the perception of immaterial things, and the contemplation of ideas lent wings to my mind, so that before long I supposed I had become wise, and in my stupidity, expected forthwith to be seeing God; for this is the aim of Plato's philosophy.

3. "While in this state of mind I wished to steep myself in quietness, and shun the paths of men, and I used to frequent a certain place not far from the sea. But one day when I was near the spot at which I purposed to be alone, an old man of venerable appearance and gentle and serious manner, followed me at a little distance. Then I turned round to him, and halted, fixing my eyes sharply on him.

"And he said, 'Do you know me?'

"I replied that I did not.

"'Why, then, do you look so at me?'

"'I am surprised,' I said, 'that you happen to be with me in this place, for I had not expected to see anyone here.'

"'I am concerned,' he said, 'about some members of my household. They have gone away from me; so I have come to search for them, on the chance of their appearing somewhere. But why are you here?'

" 'I am fond,' I said, 'of walks where my attention is not distracted, and I can converse with myself uninterruptedly. Such places are best suited for rational thought.'

" 'Are you, then, a student of reason,' said he, 'and not a lover of action or of truth? And do you aim at being not a practical man so much as a sophist?'

" 'What greater thing,' said I, 'could one accomplish than disclose the reason which governs all, and having laid hold of it, and being lifted up by it, look down upon the errors and occupations of others? And without philosophy and right reason, no man can possess practical judgment. Wherefore it is necessary for every man to philosophize, and to esteem it the greatest and most honorable occupation, and other things of only second-rate or third-rate importance. If, indeed, they are made to accord with philosophy, they are of some value, and worth our while; but if deprived of it, and unaccompanied by it, they are vulgar and coarsening to those who pursue them.'

" 'Does philosophy, then, give happiness?' said he, 'and what is happiness? Do tell me unless you have some reason for not saying.'

" 'Philosophy,' said I, 'is the knowledge of reality and the perception of truth; and happiness is the reward of such knowledge and wisdom.'

" 'And what do you call God?' said he.

" 'That which is always the same in being and in manner of being, and which is the cause of all other things—that, indeed, is God.' So I answered him; and he listened to me with pleasure, and then asked me another question:

" 'Is not wisdom a name applied alike to different things? For in arts of all kinds, he who has skill in any one of them is called wise—in the art of warfare, or of navigation, or of medicine. But this wisdom does not apply to the divine and the human. Is there a knowledge which brings understanding of the human and the divine, and then acquaintance with God and his righteousness?'

" 'Certainly,' I replied.

" 'What then? Do we know man and God in the same way as we know music, arithmetic, astronomy, or any other science of the sort?'

" 'Not at all,' I replied.

" 'You have not answered me correctly, then,' he said; 'for knowledge of these latter subjects comes to us from instruction or practice, while of the former we get knowledge by sight. If one were to tell you there exists in India an animal of a nature unlike all others, of such and such a species, varied in form and color, you would not know it without seeing it; neither could you give any account of it, unless you had heard from one who had seen it.'

" 'Certainly not,' I said.

" 'How then,' he said, 'can the philosophers think or say anything true of God, when they have no knowledge of him, having neither seen him at any time, nor heard from anyone who has?'

" 'But, father,' said I, 'the Deity cannot be seen merely by the eyes, as other living beings can. He is visible to the mind alone, as Plato says; and I believe him.'

4. " 'Has then,' said he, 'the mind so keen and so great a power? Or could a man perceive him by the senses sooner? And can the mind ever see God, if it is not instructed by the Holy Spirit?'

" 'Plato says,' I replied, 'that the mind's eye is of such a nature, and that it has been given us for the end that by that pure eye we may see the very Being who is the cause of all, discerned by the understanding, but having himself no color, no shape, no size—nothing, indeed, which the bodily eye can see. But this very Being, he goes on to say, that is beyond all essence, ineffable and indescribable and alone honorable and good, comes suddenly into souls ennobled by their kinship with him and longing to see him.'

" 'But what kinship,' replied he, 'have we with God? Is the soul, too, divine and immortal, and a part of that royal mind of which you speak? And even as it sees God, so can we attain to grasp the divine in our minds, and thenceforth become happy?'

" 'Surely,' I said.

" 'And are all the souls of all living things able to comprehend him?' he asked; 'or are the souls of men one kind and the souls of horses and of asses another?'

" 'No; the same souls are in us all,' I answered.

" 'Then,' said he, 'even horses and asses will see God, or have seen him at one time or another?'

" 'No,' I said; 'nor even the majority of mankind, but only such as live justly, purified by righteousness, and every other virtue.'

" 'So it is not,' said he, 'through his kinship that a man sees God, nor because he has mind, but because he is temperate and righteous?'

" 'Yes,' said I; 'and because he has that whereby he can perceive God.'

" 'What then? Do goats or sheep injure anyone?'

" 'No one at all,' I said.

" 'Then by your reasoning these animals will see God,' said he.

" 'No; for the nature of their body is an obstacle to them.'

" 'If these animals could speak,' he retorted, 'you may be sure they would with greater reason ridicule our bodies. But let us now drop this subject, and grant you your point. Yet tell me this. Does the soul see God while it is in the body, or only after it has been liberated from it?'

" 'Even while it is in human form it can,' I said, 'attain that sight through the mind; but above all when it is freed from the body and separate by itself does it possess that for which it has always passionately and wholly longed.'

" 'Does it remember this, its vision of God, when it is again in a man?' [10]

" 'I do not think so,' I said.

" 'Then what advantage have those who have seen God? Or what has one who has seen more than one who has not seen, if he remembers not even the fact that he *has* seen?'

" 'I cannot tell,' I answered.

" 'And what do the souls suffer who are judged unworthy of this vision?' said he.

" 'They are imprisoned in the bodies of certain wild beasts, and this is their punishment.'

" 'Do they know, then, that is why they are in these bodies, and that they have committed some sin?'

" 'I do not think so.'

" 'Then, apparently, they gain no benefit from their punishment. I should even say that they are not punished if they are not conscious of being punished.'

" 'Indeed, no.'

" 'Then such souls neither see God nor migrate into other bodies; else they would know they were being punished thereby, and would be afraid to commit the most trivial sin afterwards. But that even they can perceive that God exists, and that righteousness and piety are good, I too agree,' said he.

" 'You are right,' I replied.

5. " 'These philosophers, then, know nothing about these matters; for they cannot tell what kind of thing the soul is.'

" 'Evidently not.'

" 'Certainly it ought not to be called immortal; for if it is immortal, it is plainly unbegotten.'

---

[10] The old man proceeds to criticize the Platonic doctrine of the transmigration of souls.

" 'It is both unbegotten and immortal, according to some so-called Platonists.'

" 'Do you then say the world too is unbegotten?'

" 'Some say so. I do not myself agree with them.'

" 'You are right. For how can anyone imagine that a body so solid, resistant, composite, changeable, decaying and re-newing itself every day, did not start from some cause? But if the world is begotten, it follows inevitably that souls too had a beginning, and perhaps may some time cease to be. For they were made for the sake of men and other living creatures, if you believe they were framed separately and not as parts of their respective bodies.'

" 'I think you are right.'

" 'They are not then immortal?'

" 'No; as long as we call the world begotten.'

" 'I do not say, however, that all souls die; for that would be truly a piece of good luck for the bad. What then? The souls of the righteous inhabit a better place, while those of the unjust and wicked are in a worse, awaiting the time of judgment. Thus those who have shown themselves worthy of God die no more; but the others are punished just as long as God wills them to continue existing and being punished.'

" 'Is what you say, then,' said I, 'something like what Plato in the *Timaeus* suggests about the world, when he calls it mortal, inasmuch as it was once created, but says that through the will of God it will neither be dissolved nor meet the fate of death? Do you think the very same can be said of the soul, and in general of all things? Or is it that the things which came into being after God, or ever will be, have a nature of decay, and as such may be blotted out and cease to be; for God alone is unbegotten and incorruptible. Therefore he is God, and all other things after him are created and cor-ruptible. Hence it is possible that souls may both die and be punished. But, if they were unbegotten, they would neither sin nor steep themselves in folly, nor be one instant cowardly and the next valorous; nor would they of their own will change into swine, and snakes, and dogs. Nor would it be right to put compulsion on them, if they were unbegotten. For whatever is unbegotten is like to, equal to, and the same with the unbegotten; neither in power nor in dignity should one be preferred to the other. So not many things are unbegotten. And if there were any difference between them, you could not, though you searched for it, discover the cause of the difference; but after sending your mind forever traveling into infinity, you would at length, wearied out, take your stand on the one Unbegotten, and declare it the Cause of all. But was all this unknown to Plato and Pythagoras, those wise men,' I asked, 'who have been as a wall and fortress of philosophy to us?'

6. " 'It is nothing to me,' said he, 'whether Plato or Pythagoras or, in fact, any other man held those opinions. For the Truth says this; and you may learn from it. The soul either is or it has life. If it is life, it would make something else, not itself, live, even as motion moves something else besides itself. Now that the soul lives, no one would deny. But though it lives, it lives not as being itself life, but as a partaker in life; and that which partakes of anything is different from that of which it partakes. Now the soul partakes of life, when God wills it to live. In the same way, it will not partake of life whenever God does not will it to live. For life is not its attribute, as it is God's. A man does not live forever, and as the soul is not forever joined to the body, but when their harmony must be broken, the soul leaves the body and the man is no more; even so, when the soul must cease to be, the spirit of life leaves it, and there is no more soul, but it goes back to the place whence it was taken.'

7. " 'But to whom should one go as a teacher?' I asked, 'or where may one find help, if even in the philosophers there is no truth?'

" 'Long ago,' he replied, 'there lived men more ancient than all the so-called philosophers, men righteous and beloved of God, who spoke by the Divine Spirit and foretold things to come, that even now are taking place. These men were called prophets. They alone both saw the truth and proclaimed it to men, without awe or fear of anyone, moved by no desire for glory, but speaking only those things which they saw and heard when filled with the Holy Spirit. Their writings are still with us, and whoever will may read them and, if he believes them, gain much knowledge of the beginning and end of things, and all else a philosopher ought to know. For they did not employ logic to prove their statements, seeing they were witnesses to the truth, and above all proof by logic, and worthy of trust. The things that took place, and that still are taking place, compel us to believe their words. Because, also, of the miracles they performed they are entitled to our belief. They glorified the Creator of all things, as God and Father, and proclaimed the Christ sent by him as his Son, a thing which false prophets, filled with a lying and unclean spirit, never have done nor do yet. Their aim is to work wonders that will astonish men, and glorify the spirits and demons of error. But pray that, before all else, the gates of light may be opened to you. For not everyone can see or understand these things, but only he to whom God and his Christ have granted wisdom.'

8. "After saying this and much more, which there is not time to repeat at present, he went away, bidding me follow his advice; and I saw him no more. But straightway a flame was kindled in my soul, and a desire came over me to know the prophets, and the men who were friends of Christ. And as I revolved his words in my mind, I decided that this was the only philosophy safe and serviceable. Thus, and for these reasons, I am a philosopher. Furthermore, I wish that everyone would make a resolution like my own, and not keep himself a stranger to the words of the Saviour. For they have

in themselves something of dread majesty, sufficient to inspire with fear those who turn aside from the right way; while the sweetest peace comes to those who diligently observe them. If then you have any care for yourself and are seriously searching for salvation and believe in God, you may—since you are earnest in the matter—learn to know the Christ of God, be initiated,[11] and live a life of happiness." . . .

THE FIRST APOLOGY

1. To the Emperor, Titus Aelius Hadrian Antoninus Pius Augustus Caesar, and to his son Verissimus the philosopher, and to Lucius the philosopher, natural son of a Caesar and adopted son of Pius,[1] lover of learning, and to the sacred Senate, and all the Roman people, I, Justin, son of Priscus and grandson of Baccheius, natives of Flavia Neapolis [2] in Palestine, present this address and petition on behalf of persons of every nation who are unjustly hated and wantonly abused, myself being one of them.

2. Men truly pious and philosophical are led by their reasons to honor and love only what is true, and refuse to follow traditional opinions, when they are false. Nor does sound

---

[11] Literally: become perfect. Some scholars take the words to refer to perfection of character, others to initiation by baptism. The term was used of initiation into the pagan mysteries.

[1] Justin's *First Apology* was addressed to the Emperor Antoninus Pius, whose reign extended from 138 to 161 A.D., and his two adopted sons. The first, called here simply "Verissimus the philosopher," was to succeed Antoninus as the Emperor Marcus Aurelius The young man's family name was Verus, a Latin word meaning "true." The old emperor, Hadrian, seems to have nicknamed him affectionately Verissimus, that is, "most true."

[2] This town is also known as Shechem in Samaria.

reason call on us merely to reject the guidance of those who have done or taught anything wrong, but the lover of truth himself must always, even under threat of death, and regardless of his own life, choose to do and say what is right. I ask you then, who are called pious and philosophers, guardians of justice and lovers of learning, to give good heed and attention to my address. If you are such indeed, it will be made manifest. For we have come, not to flatter you by our words nor to entertain you by our speech, but to beg that after accurate and thorough investigation you pass judgment, refusing to be swayed by prejudice or by desire to please the superstitious, or to be influenced by irrational fears, or the evil rumors that have long been circulated, to give a decision that will prove to be an injury to yourselves. As for us, we are sure no harm can be done us, unless we are proved evil-doers or wicked men. For you can kill us, but you cannot harm us.

3. Now lest anyone think this statement unreasonable and rash, we demand that the charges against the Christians be investigated, and, if they are substantiated, that the Christians be punished as they deserve; or rather, we ourselves will punish them. But if no one can prove anything against us, true reason forbids you for the sake of a malicious rumor to wrong blameless men, and yourselves as well, who are willing to govern not by judgment but by passion. Any right-minded person would pronounce this the only fair and just method, namely, that subjects render an honest account of their lives and doctrine; and that rulers, in their turn, give their decision not with violence tyrannically, but piously, by the dictates of philosophy. For thus both rulers and ruled will prosper. One of the ancients somewhere said, "Unless both rulers and ruled are philosophers, states cannot be happy.[3] It is our duty, accordingly, to allow everyone an opportunity to inspect our

_____
[3] Plato, *Republic*, V. See Classics Club edition, p. 362.

life and teachings, lest, by keeping people ignorant of our ways, we share the penalty due them for mental blindness. It is your duty, when you hear us, to be, as reason demands, just judges. For if, after learning the truth, you fail to do what is just, you will be without excuse before God.

4. By mere use of a name nothing is decided, either good or evil, unless some action is implied in the name. But so far as one may judge from the name applied to us we are most excellent people.[4] But as we think it unfair to ask for acquittal on the ground of our name, if we are proved evil-doers, so, on the other hand, if we are found guiltless of offense in the matter either of the name we bear or of our conduct as citizens, it is for you to take care to preserve yourselves from the punishment justly due to those who unjustly punish innocent men. For a name could not be cause for either praise or punishment, unless it were proof of some excellent or some base act. And among yourselves you do not punish accused persons before they are convicted; but in our case you treat our name alone as proof against us, although, so far as the name goes, you ought rather to punish our accusers. For we are accused of being Christians, yet to hate what is *excellent* [chrestian] is unjust. Further, if any of those you accuse deny the name and say he is not a Christian, you acquit him, as if you had lost your evidence against him as a wrong-doer; but if anyone confess he is a Christian, you punish him for this confession. Justice requires that you inquire into the life both of the man who confesses and of him who denies, that by his deeds it may be clear what kind of man he is. For as some, taught by our Master Christ not to deny Him, give encouragement to others when they face their trial, so in all probability some who lead wicked lives give excuse to those who

---

4 Justin avails himself here of the similarity in sound of the Greek words "Christos" (Christ) and "chrestos" (good, worthy, excellent). The play upon these words is kept up throughout this paragraph and cannot always be represented to the English reader.

accuse all Christians indiscriminately of impiety and wickedness. Yet this is not right. For in philosophy too there are men who assume the name and the garb who are all unworthy of their profession. You are well aware that ancients whose opinions and teachings were quite diverse are still all called by the one name of philosophers. Some of these taught atheism; and poets who are famous among you raised a laugh out of the uncleanness of Jupiter with his own children. Those who now repeat their stories are not restrained by you. On the contrary, you bestow prizes and honors on men who elegantly insult the gods.

5. Why, then, should this be? In our case, who pledge ourselves not to do evil or to hold these godless beliefs, you do not examine the charges against us, but yield to unreasonable passion and the instigation of evil demons [5] and punish us without consideration or judgment. For I shall tell you the truth. Of old time these evil demons, showing themselves in apparitions, defiled women, corrupted boys, and presented such fearful sights to men that all who did not use their reasons to judge those events were struck with terror; and overcome by their fear, not knowing that they were devils, they called them gods, and gave to each one the name he chose for himself. [6] And when Socrates endeavored, by true reason and inquiry, to bring these facts to light and deliver men from the rule of demons, then the demons, through the agency of men who loved iniquity, compassed his death as an atheist and profane person, on the charge that "he was introducing new divinities." In our case they are showing themselves equally active. But both among the Greeks did reason prevail to con-

---

[5] The word *daemon* means in Greek a divinity, but the Christians used the word to signify an evil spirit. Justin uses the same word here for god and demon. The connection which Justin and other Christian writers supposed to exist between evil spirits and the gods of the heathens will be apparent from Justin's own statements.

[6] Milton has a similar idea of the origin of pagan mythology. See *Paradise Lost*, I, 378. Classics Club edition, p. 103.

demn these things through Socrates, and again, among the
barbarians were they condemned by Reason itself, the Word,
who took shape and became man and was called Jesus Christ.
In obedience to Him, we deny that the doers of such evil
things are gods, and pronounce them wicked and impious
demons, whose acts will not bear comparison with those of
virtuous men.

6. Hence we are called atheists. And we confess we are
atheists so far as gods of this sort are concerned, but not with
regard to the most true God, the Father of righteousness and
temperance and the other virtues, who is free of all impurity.
But both Him, and the Son who came forth from Him and
taught these things to us and to the host of good angels who
follow and are made like to Him, and the prophetic Spirit
we worship and adore, knowing them in reason and in truth,
and declaring what we have been taught, without grudging,
to everyone who wishes to learn.

7. But someone will say: "Some Christians have already
been arrested and convicted of wrong-doing." Yet usually
when you are trying a group, you investigate the life of each
of the accused separately; but you do not so treat those of
whom we are speaking. And this is our contention, that even
as among the Greeks the teachers of every sort of theory are
called by the one name "philosopher," though their doctrines
are widely different, so also among the barbarians this name
which is the object of accusation is given both to those who
are and those who only seem to be enlightened. For they are
all called Christians. Wherefore we demand that the deeds of
every one who is accused be judged, so that whoever is convicted of crime may be punished as a criminal, but not as a
Christian; and whoever is clearly blameless may be acquitted,
since by the mere act of being a Christian he does no harm.
We will not ask you to punish our accusers, they being suffi-
ciently punished by their present wickedness and ignorance
of the good.

8. Believe that it is for your sakes we say these things; for it is in our power, when questioned, to deny we are Christians; but we would not live by telling a lie. For impelled by love of the eternal and pure life, we seek the abode that is with God, the Father and Creator of all, and are eager to confess our faith, persuaded and sure as we are that all who prove to God by their works that they follow Him and long to abide with Him, where there is no more sin to trouble them, can obtain it. This, in brief, is what we expect and have learned from Christ and do teach. Plato likewise said that Rhadamanthus and Minos would punish the wicked who came before them.[7] We say that Christ will do the same to the wicked, who will wear the same bodies as now, reunited to their spirits; and that they will then undergo everlasting punishment, not only, as Plato said, for a period of a thousand years. And if anyone call this an incredible or impossible belief, our error is one which concerns ourselves only and no one else, so long as you cannot convict us of any harmful act.

9. We do not honor with sacrifices and garlands of flowers the deities men have framed and set in shrines and called gods, for we see they are soulless and dead, and have not the form of God; and we do not consider God has a form such as they say they imitate in His honor. These have the names and the forms of the wicked demons which in the past appeared to men. Why need we tell you, who know already, in what forms the craftsmen carve and cut, cast and hammer and fashion their materials? They often take vessels of dishonor, and by merely changing the form and making an image of the requisite shape, make out of them what they call a god; which we consider not only senseless, but actually insulting to the God of ineffable glory and form, whose name is thus attached to things corruptible, in need of constant care. The makers of

---

[7] See Plato's *Apology*, and *Republic*, X, Classics Club edition, pp. 59, 488.

these objects are intemperate men, practiced generally in every vice, as you well know; they even corrupt their own girls, who work along with them. What folly, that dissolute men should be set to fashion and make gods for your worship, and that you should appoint such men the guardians of the temples where they are enshrined, not realizing that it is sin to think or say that men are guardians of gods.

10. But we have heard from of old that God does not need the material offerings which men can give, since He Himself is the provider of all things. And we have been taught, and are convinced, and do believe, that He accepts only those who imitate the excellences that reside in Him, His temperance, justice, and loving kindness, and all the virtues that belong to a God who is called by no given name. We have also been taught that He in the beginning did of His goodness, for man's sake, create all things out of formless matter. And if men by their works show themselves worthy of His purpose, He accepts them, we are told, as worthy of reigning with Him, delivered from corruption and pain. For as in the beginning He created us when we were not, so also, we believe, He holds those who choose what is pleasing to Him, on account of their choice, worthy of incorruption and fellowship with Him. Our coming into being at first was not in our own power; and in order that we may follow the things that please Him, He does Himself endow us with rational faculties to choose, and persuades and leads us to faith. We think it to all men's advantage not to be hindered from learning these things, but rather to be urged thereto. And the hindrance which human laws might effect, the Word, who is divine, would have prevented, had not the wicked demons, taking as their ally the lust of wickedness which is in every man and leads him variously to all manner of vice, spread many false and profane and irrelevant accusations against us.

11. When you hear that we look for a kingdom, you assume without further inquiry, that we speak of a human kingdom; whereas we speak of one that is divine. This is shown by the confession of faith made by persons charged with being Christians, when they know death is the punishment inflicted on one who confesses. For if we were looking for a human kingdom, we would deny our Christ, to keep from being slain, and would strive to escape detection, to win what we expect. But our thoughts are not fixed on the present, and therefore it matters not when men put us to death, since death is a debt which we must in any case pay.

12. More than all other men indeed we are your helpers and allies in promoting peace, seeing we hold it impossible for either the wicked or the covetous or the conspirator or the virtuous man to escape the notice of God, and are sure that each man goes to everlasting punishment or to salvation according to the merit of his deeds. And if all men knew this, no one would choose wickedness even in little things, knowing he would go to an everlasting punishment of fire; but he would do his utmost to govern himself and adorn himself with virtue, that he might obtain the good gifts of God and escape punishment. For those persons who, in fear of your laws and punishments, try when they have offended to escape detection, offend in the belief that they can escape detection, since you are but men; but if they had been taught and were convinced that no crime, whether actually committed or only intended, could escape the knowledge of God, they would then live uprightly for fear of his threatened penalties, as you yourselves will admit. But you seem to fear that if all men become righteous, you will no longer have anyone to punish. Such might be the anxiety of public executioners, but not of benevolent princes. As we said before, we are persuaded that our persecution is prompted by evil spirits, who extort sacrifices and service from the unreasoning. But you who strive for piety and philosophy will, we trust, do nothing against reason. However, if, like the foolish, you prefer popular notions to truth, do what you have power to do. But the power of rulers who value common opinion more than truth is like that of robbers in the desert. That you will not really succeed is declared by the Word, who of all rulers after God who begat Him we know is most kingly and just. And even as all men, following their fathers' advice, seek to avoid poverty and suffering and obscurity, so no good man will choose what the Word forbids us. That all these things should come to pass, our teacher, I say, foretold, He who is both Son and messenger of God, the all Father, and our King, Jesus Christ, from whom we take our name of Christians. For this reason too we grow more and more assured of the truth of the things He taught us, since all that He foretold beforehand should come to pass, is actually coming to pass. And this is the work of a god, to tell of a thing before it happens, and to show it happening as it was foretold. We might stop here and add no more, convinced that we are asking of you only what is just and true. But we know it is not easy suddenly to change a mind possessed by ignorance. We propose therefore to continue a little further, in hope of persuading those who love truth, for we believe it possible to dispel ignorance by presenting the truth.

13. What fair-minded man, then, will not admit that we are no atheists, worshiping as we do the Maker of this universe, and declaring, as we have been taught, that He is beyond need of blood and libations and incense. To the utmost of our power we praise Him by services of prayer and thanksgiving for all things wherewith we are supplied. For we are taught that the way to honor Him worthily is not to destroy by fire what He has framed for our sustenance, but to use it for ourselves and those who need, and to offer Him thankful prayers and hymns in gratitude [8] for our creation, and for all the means of health, and for the varied qualities of the dif-

---

[8] The hymns of this period were either psalms of David, or the psalms and songs composed by primitive Christians, which are mentioned by early writers.

ferent species of things, and the changes of the seasons, and to present to Him our petitions for a second and incorruptible life through faith in Him. Our teacher in these matters is Jesus Christ, who was born for this end, and was crucified under Pontius Pilate, procurator of Judaea, in the time of Tiberius Caesar. That we do right to worship Him, accepting Him as the Son of the true God, and holding Him in the second place, and the prophetic Spirit in the third, we will now prove. For our accusers call us mad in that we give to a crucified man a place second to the unchangeable and eternal God, the Creator of all. They fail to perceive the mystery hidden in Him, to which, as we explain it to you, we pray you pay heed.

14. We warn you first to be on your guard, lest the demons whom we have been accusing deceive you and divert you from reading and understanding what we say. For they strive to keep you their slaves and servants; and sometimes by apparitions in dreams, or again by cheating magic, they prevail over those who make no great struggle for their own salvation. So we, since our conversion by the Word, keep away from demons, and follow the only unbegotten God through His Son. We who once enjoyed the pleasures of lust now embrace chastity. We who once resorted to magical arts, now dedicate ourselves to the good and unbegotten God. We who prized above all else the acquisition of wealth and possessions, now bring what we have into the common stock, and share with everyone in need.[9] We who hated and destroyed one another, and, because their manners were strange, would not live with men of a different race, now since Christ has come, live familiarly with them and pray for our enemies. And our endeavor is to persuade those who hate us unjustly to live themselves by the good precepts of Christ, that they too may become partakers with us of the same joyful hope of reward

[9] The church was still practicing the primitive communism of the days of the apostles.

from God, the ruler of us all. But we would not seem to be arguing as the sophists do. We wish, instead, before giving you the promised explanation, to cite a few of the precepts of Christ Himself. It is for you, powerful rulers, to inquire whether we truly are taught and do teach these things. Brief and concise were the utterances of his lips, for He was no sophist; but his word was the power of God.

15, 16. (Justin quotes from Christ's teachings on the duty of chastity, brotherly love, trust in God, patience, honesty.) . . . And let those who are found not living as He taught be recognized as no Christians, even though they profess with their lips the precepts of Christ; for not those who make a profession, but those who do the works, shall be saved, according to His word: "Not everyone who saith to me, Lord, Lord, shall enter into the kingdom of heaven, but he that doeth the will of my Father which is in heaven." [10] . . . .

17. Everywhere we are more ready than anyone else to pay your collectors the taxes both ordinary and extraordinary,[11] as we are taught by him to do. For men once came to him and asked if they ought to pay tribute to Caesar; and he answered, "Tell me, whose image does the coin bear?" And they said, "Caesar's." And He replied, "Render therefore to Caesar the things that are Caesar's, and to God the things that are God's." [12] Wherefore to God alone we render worship, but in other things we gladly serve you, acknowledging you as kings and rulers of men, and praying that with your kingly power you may possess also sound judgment. But if you ignore our prayers and sincere explanations, the loss will not be ours, since we believe (or, rather, are persuaded) that everyone will suffer punishment in eternal fire according as his deeds deserve it, and will render account of the power he once

---

[10] Matthew, vii, 21.

[11] The former is the annual tribute; the latter, any occasional assessment.

[12] Matthew, xxii, 17, 20, 21.

received from God; as Christ implied when He said, "To whom God has given more, of him shall more be required." [13]

18. Reflect on the end of the kings who came before you, how they died the death common to all men. If that meant only a cessation of consciousness, it would be a boon to the wicked. But since consciousness survives in all who have ever lived, and for some an eternal punishment is laid up, see that you refuse not to be convinced, and believe that what we say here is true. Even your necromancy, and the divinations you practice with immaculate children,[14] and your evokings of departed souls,[15] and of those whom the magi call Dream-senders and Familiars,[16] and other performances of experts in such matters show you that after death souls are in a state of sensation. There are men seized and wrenched about by spirits of the dead, whom we call demoniacs or madmen;[17] there are what you consider the oracles of Amphilochus, Dodona, and Pytho, and others. There are the opinions of your authors, Empedocles, Pythagoras, Plato and Socrates, and the pit of Homer,[18] and the descent of Odysseus to inspect the world

---

[13] Luke, xii, 48. Justin quotes his Scripture mostly, apparently, from memory, so that his wording of a passage often differs from that recorded in our Bible text.

[14] In some of the obscurer pagan sects, it was said, boys and girls, and even children prematurely taken from the womb, were slaughtered, and their entrails inspected, in the belief that the souls of the victims, being still conscious, would reveal things hidden and future.

[15] A form of spirit-rapping was familiar to the ancients.

[16] The so-called magi had a kind of familiar spirit who was sent to inspire men with dreams which might give them intimations of the future.

[17] Justin is not the only author in ancient or recent times who classed demoniacs and madmen together; neither does he stand alone among the ancients in the opinion that demoniacs were possessed by the spirits of the departed.

[18] The philosophers Empedocles and Pythagoras had taught the transmigration of souls. For references to Plato's doctrine of the after-life, see above, p. 264, n. 7. Homer's *Odyssey*, Book XI, tells of Odysseus' visit to the house of Hades.

of the dead, and whatever else has been written of the sort. The approval you bestow on these authors, bestow also on us, who believe in God not less but even more firmly than they; for we expect to receive our own bodies again though they be dead and cast into the earth, for we declare that with God nothing is impossible.

19. Would anything appear more incredible to any thoughtful mind than if, before we were ever given bodies, someone were to say that from a small drop of human seed bones and sinews and flesh would be formed into the shapes we now see? Let us now suppose this situation: that you yourselves were not what you now are, born of your parents, and that someone showed you human seed and a picture of a man, and asserted positively that from such a substance such a being could be produced. Would you believe without witnessing the actual production? No one will deny that such a statement would have seemed unbelievable. In the same way, you are now incredulous because you have never seen a dead man rise again. But as in the previous instance, you would not have believed it possible that creatures of such size could be produced from a small drop, yet you now see they are thus produced, so also admit it is not impossible that the bodies of men, after being dissolved and like seeds turned again into earth, should in God's appointed time rise again and put on incorruption. What conception they have of divine power who say that everything returns to its source, and that not even God Himself can do anything differently we cannot imagine. This much we see plainly, that they would not have believed they could become what they are out of the materials from which they now see they and the whole world are derived. And we have learned it is better to believe even what is beyond the power of our natures and of any man than to be unbelieving like the rest of the world. For we know what our Master Jesus Christ said, that "what is impossible with men is possible with God," [19] and "Fear not them that kill you, and after that can do no more; but fear Him who after death is able to cast both soul and body into hell." [20] Hell is the place where those are punished who have lived wickedly, and who do not believe in the certainty of the things which God has taught us by Christ.

20. Both the Sibyl and Hystaspes [21] say there will come a destruction by God of things corruptible. And the philosophers called Stoics teach that even God Himself shall be dissolved in fire. They say too that the world will be remade after this revolution. But we know that God, the Creator of all things, is superior to the things that change. Since, however, on some points we teach the same things as do the poets and philosophers whom you honor, and on other points are fuller and more divine in our teaching, and since we alone can prove our assertions, why are we unjustly hated more than the rest? When we say that all things were formed and arranged in a world by God, we are repeating the doctrine of Plato; and when we say that all will end in fire, we are repeating the doctrine of the Stoics. And when we say that the souls of the wicked after death are punished, and those of the good are delivered from punishment and live in blessedness, we are saying the same things as the poets and philosophers. And when we declare that men should not worship the works of their own hands, we are saying the very things that were said by the comic poet Menander and other writers like him, for they too insisted that the workman was greater than his work.

21. When we say also that the Word, who is the first-born of God, was produced without sexual union, and that He, Jesus Christ, our teacher, was crucified, died, rose again, and

---

[19] Matthew, xix, 26.
[20] Matthew, x, 28.
[21] The so-called Sibylline oracles and the prophecies of Hystaspes were collections of veiled and mysterious predictions of the future that were taken seriously at this time by many Christians as well as pagans.

ascended into heaven, we are propounding nothing different from what you believe regarding those you call sons of Zeus. You know how many sons your esteemed writers ascribe to Zeus: Hermes, the interpreting word and teacher of all; Aesculapius, the great physician, who was struck by a thunderbolt, and so ascended to heaven; Bacchus, who did the same on being torn limb from limb; Hercules, who threw himself into the flames to escape his sufferings; the sons of Leda, the Dioscuri; Perseus, son of Danae; and Bellerophon, who, though sprung from mortals, soared to heaven on the horse Pegasus. What too is to be said of Ariadne and those other mere mortals, who you declare are elevated to the stars? And what of the emperors who die among you, whom you deem worthy of deification, and in whose behalf you produce some fellow who swears he saw the burning Caesar rise to heaven from his funeral pyre? As to what kind of deeds are recorded of these reputed sons of Zeus, it is needless to inform you who already know. This only we shall say, that they are recorded for the corruption and pollution of young scholars, who all reckon it honorable to imitate the gods. Far be it from every decent soul to have such ideas of the gods as to fancy that Zeus, the governor and creator of all things, was himself a parricide and the son of a parricide, and that overcome by love of base and shameful pleasures, he went to Ganymede and the many women whom he violated, and that his sons committed like acts. As we said above, wicked devils perpetrated these things. We know that only those who have lived near to God in holiness and virtue are deified; and we believe that those who live wickedly and do not repent are punished in everlasting fire.

22. Now the Son of God called Jesus, even if only a man of ordinary generation, yet on account of His wisdom is worthy to be called a Son of God; and all writers call God the Father of men and gods. And if we maintain that as Word of God he was born of God in a peculiar manner, different

from ordinary generation, let this, as we said above, seem no strange thing to you, who call Hermes the angelic word of God. And if anyone objects to His crucifixion, in this also He is on a par with your reputed sons of Zeus, who suffered as we have just described. Their sufferings at death were by the records not all alike, but different; so that not by any peculiarity of His sufferings is He inferior to them. On the contrary, we will prove Him superior, as we promised earlier in our discourse. Indeed, we have already proved Him so, for the superior is revealed by His acts. And if we declare Him born of a virgin, accept this along with what you accept of Perseus. And even when we say He healed the lame, the paralytic, and men born blind, we are attributing to Him deeds very similar to those said to have been performed by Aesculapius.

23. So, to make our doctrine all plain to you, we shall now proceed to show, first, that what we tell you has been taught us by Christ and the prophets who preceded Him as the only truth, that it is older than all the writers who ever were, and that we claim your sanction not because we say the things your writers said, but because we say what is true; secondly, that Jesus Christ is the only genuine Son begotten by God, being His Word first-begotten, and His power, and that He became man according to God's will, and taught us these things for the conversion and salvation of the human race; thirdly, that before He became a man among men, there were persons taught by the demons before mentioned, who described in forms of poetry the events of His coming as if they had already happened. And having fictitiously devised them, they narrated them in the same style in which they are now fabricating the scandalous reports against us of infamous and sacrilegious deeds of which they have neither witness nor proof.

24. In the first place, then, observe that although we say things like what the Greeks say, we alone are hated for the

name of Christ, and though we do no wrong, we are put to death as sinners. But other men in other places worship trees and rivers, mice, cats and crocodiles, and other irrational animals. Nor are the same animals reverenced everywhere, but in one place one is worshiped, and in another another, so that all are profane in someone's judgment, because they do not worship the same creatures. Yet this is the sole accusation you bring against us, that we do not reverence the same gods as you do, nor offer libations and the odor of fat to the dead, and crowns for their statues, and sacrifices. But you very well know that the same animals that are treated as gods by some are treated by others as wild beasts and by others as sacrificial victims.

25. But we, who, gathered as we are out of every race of men, used once to worship Bacchus, son of Semele, and Apollo, son of Latona (who in their loves with men did things shameful even to mention), and Proserpine and Aphrodite (who went mad with love of Adonis, and whose mysteries also you celebrate), and Aesculapius, and many another of those you call gods—have now, through Jesus Christ, learned to despise them, even though threatened with death for it, and have dedicated ourselves to the unbegotten and untouchable God. Of Him we knew that never was He goaded by lust for Antiope and other women like her, or for Ganymede, nor was He ever rescued by that hundred-handed giant whose aid was obtained through Thetis, nor did He on that account consent that her son Achilles should destroy a host of Greeks for the sake of his concubine Briseis.[22] We pity all who believe such things, and those who invented them we know to be devils.

26. Lately, since Christ's ascension into heaven, the devils have put forward certain men who said they were gods; and

---

[22] For the story of Zeus' debt to Thetis and his approval of Achilles' anger against the Greeks, see Homer, *Iliad*, I. Classics Club edition, pp. 18-19.

they were not only not persecuted by you, but even re-
warded with honors. There was a Samaritan, Simon, a native
of the village called Gitto, who in the reign of Claudius
Caesar, and in your royal city of Rome, did mighty acts of
magic, by virtue of the art of the devils working in him. He
was accepted as a god, and as a god honored by you with a
statue erected on the river Tiber, between the two bridges.
It bears this inscription in the Roman tongue:

> Simoni Deo Sancto [23]
> (To Simon, the holy god)

Almost all the Samaritans and a few even of other nations
worship and revere him as first god; and a woman, Helena,
who went about with him at that time and had formerly been
a prostitute, they say was the first idea generated by him. A
man, Meander, also a Samaritan, of the town Capparetaea, a
disciple of Simon and inspired by the devils, deceived many,
we know, in Antioch by his magical art. He persuaded his
disciples that they would never die; even now there are some
living who believe this. There is Marcion,[24] too, a man of
Pontus, who is still alive, and teaching his disciples to believe
in some other god greater than the Creator. With the devils'
aid he has caused many from every nation to speak blas-
phemies, and to deny that God is the maker of this universe,
and to assert that some other being, greater than He, has done
more marvelous works. All who take their beliefs from these

---

[23] In the year 1574 a marble fragment was dug up on the island of the
Tiber, bearing the inscription "Semoni Sanco Deo." It was probably
part of the base of a statue erected to an ancient Sabine deity, Semo
Sancus. Justin seems to have taken this dedication to an old, provincial
Latin god for one to a certain notorious Simon of Samaria who had appeared in Rome in the previous century. Later Christians identified Justin's Simon with the sorcerer Simon whom the apostles encountered in
Samaria, as related in Acts, viii, 9-24. Thus grew up the famous legend
of Simon Magus at Rome.

[24] Marcion was a leader of a so-called heretical sect that attracted a
good many followers in the second century.

men, are, as we said earlier, called Christians; just as those who teach doctrines different from those of the philosophers are yet called like them by the name of philosophers. Whether they do indeed perpetrate those rumored, shameless deeds— the upsetting of the lamp, promiscuous intercourse, eating human flesh—we know not; but we do know that they are neither persecuted nor put to death by you, not, at least, for their opinions. I have written a treatise [25] against all the heresies that have so far arisen, which if you wish to read, I will give it you.

27. As for us, we are taught that even to expose newly-born children is a wicked act.[26] We are taught this because we must do no one an injury, and also because we must not sin against God, for we see that almost all so exposed, not only the girls, but also the boys, are brought up to prostitution. And as the ancients are said to have reared herds of oxen, or goats, or sheep, or grazing horses, so now we see you rear children for this shameful use. A multitude of women and hermaphrodites and unmentionable perverts exists for this vile purpose in every nation. And you receive the price of their hire and dues and taxes from them, whom you ought to exterminate from your realm. . . .

28. But among us the prince of the wicked spirits is called the serpent, Satan, and the Devil, as you may learn by looking into our writings. And Christ has foretold that he will be sent into the fire with his host and the men who follow him, and they will all be punished forever. The reason why God has delayed to do this is His regard for the human race. For He foreknows that some will yet be saved by repentance, even some perhaps not yet born. He made the human race in

---

[25] This treatise has been lost.

[26] By ancient Roman law any father had the right to order the exposure of any child of his born sickly or weak or whom he did not wish to bring up. Children so exposed might be left to die or be picked up and raised by anyone who happened to come across them.

the beginning with the power of thought and of choosing truth and doing right, so that men are all without excuse before God; for they are born rational and capable of seeing. Whoever doubts that God cares for such things does thereby imply either that God does not exist, or that though He exists He is pleased with vice, or else is as unfeeling as a stone, and that neither virtue nor vice are anything in themselves, but only in the opinions of men are reckoned as good or evil. But this is the greatest blasphemy and wickedness.

29. (*Justin says more of the continence of Christians.*)

30. Someone may now raise the question: Why is not He whom we call Christ a man born of men, who performed what we call His mighty works by magical art, and thus made Himself the Son of God? Accordingly, we will now present our proofs; for we rely not on mere assertions, but are ourselves compelled to believe by the prophecies of those who foretold these things before they came to pass. And with our own eyes we behold the things that have happened and are now happening just as they were predicted. This will, we think, appear even to you as strong and convincing evidence.

31. There were then among the Jews certain men who were prophets of God, through whom the prophetic Spirit announced beforehand things that would come to pass, ere ever they happened. Their prophecies, as they were spoken and at the time they were uttered, were carefully preserved and kept by the kings who happened then to be reigning among the Jews, after the prophets themselves had arranged them in books in their own Hebrew language. Then when Ptolemy, king of Egypt, was collecting his library and endeavoring to include every man's writings in it, he heard of these prophets and sent to Herod, who was at that time king of the Jews,[27] requesting that the books of the prophets be

---

[27] This is a bad blunder in chronology. The translation of the Old Testament books into Greek, commonly known as the Septuagint, was made, according to the commonly accepted story, at the request of

sent him. And Herod the king sent them, written as they were in the aforesaid Hebrew language. And when their contents proved to be unintelligible to the Egyptians, Ptolemy sent again and requested that men be commissioned to translate them into the Greek language. When this was done, the books remained with the Egyptians, where they are to this day. All the Jews also throughout the world have them; but they, though they read, do not understand what is said, but count us their foes and enemies. Like yourselves, they kill and torment us whenever they have the power, as you can well believe. In the late Jewish war Bar Hochba, the leader of the Jewish rebels, gave orders that Christians should be singled out and cruelly punished, unless they would deny and blaspheme Jesus Christ. But in the books of their prophets we find Jesus our Christ foretold as coming, born of a virgin, growing up to man's estate, healing every disease and every sickness, raising the dead, being hated, unrecognized, crucified, dying, rising again, and ascending into heaven, being and being called the Son of God. We find it also predicted that apostles would be sent by Him into every nation to proclaim these tidings, and that among the Gentiles more than among the Jews men would believe on Him. He was predicted first 5,000 years before He appeared and again 3,000 years before, then 2,000, then 1,000, and again 800; for as the generations succeeded one another, prophet after prophet arose.

32-38. (Justin quotes at length passages from the Psalms and the prophets of the Old Testament that seem to predict Christ's coming, his birth, and his sufferings.)

39. When the Spirit of prophecy speaks predicting things that are to come to pass, He speaks in this way: "For out of Zion shall go forth the law, and the word of the Lord from

Ptolemy Philadelphus, king of Egypt from 284 to 247 B.C. Herod was king of Judea at the time of Christ's birth. It was Eleazar, the Jewish high priest, to whom Ptolemy applied.

Jerusalem. And He shall judge among the nations, and shall rebuke many people; and they shall beat their swords into plowshares, and their spears into pruning-hooks; nation shall not lift up sword against nation, neither shall they learn war any more." [28] And we can show you that it did so come to pass. For from Jerusalem there went out into the world men, twelve in number, without education, of no ability in speaking; but in the power of God they proclaimed to every race of men that they were sent by Christ to teach them all God's word. So now we who formerly used to murder one another refrain from war even against our enemies, and, to avoid lying or deceiving our examiners, are willing to die confessing Christ. For we too might quote the saying, "The tongue has sworn, but the mind is unsworn." [29] But if the soldiers enrolled by you, who have taken the military oath, prefer faithfulness to their oath to life, parents, country, and all their kindred, even though you can offer them nothing incorruptible, it would be truly absurd if we, who long earnestly for incorruption, should not endure all things to obtain our desire from Him who is able to grant it.

40-42. (*Prophecies in the Psalms of Christ's coming, death, and ultimate triumph.*)

43. But some may infer from what we say that we teach that whatever happens, happens by fixed necessity, because it is known beforehand and foretold. This too then we must explain. We have learned from the prophets and hold it true, that punishments, chastisements, and rewards, are rendered to each man according to the merit of his acts. But if this is wrong, and all things happen by fate, then nothing at all lies in our own power. For if it is fated that this man, for instance, will be good, and this other evil, neither is the former meritorious nor the latter blameworthy. Hence, unless mankind has the power of avoiding evil and choosing good by free choice,

---

[28] Isaiah, ii, 3, 4.
[29] Euripides, *Hippolytus*, 608.

it is not accountable for its acts, of whatever sort they be. But we can show that it is by their free choice that men both walk uprightly and stumble. We see the same man changing from one course of life to its opposite. Now, if it had been fated that he would be either good or bad, he could never have been capable of both opposites nor of his various transitions. There would not even be good men and bad men, since we would be making fate the cause of evil, and have her too acting in opposition to herself. Or else what we said before would be true, that neither virtue nor vice is really anything, but things are only reckoned good or evil by our opinions; which, as the true Word shows, is the worst blasphemy and wickedness. But this we do say is inevitable fate, that those who choose goodness receive a worthy reward, and those who choose the opposite get what they deserve. For God did not make man like other things, such as trees and four-footed beasts, which cannot act by choice; nor would man be worthy of reward or praise, if he did not of himself choose the good but were forced to do it. Nor, if he were evil, would he deserve punishment, if he were not evil of his own will but only able to do what he was made to do.

44. The holy Spirit of prophecy taught us this, telling us by Moses that God spoke thus to the man first created: "Behold, before thy face are good and evil: choose the good." [30] . . . So Plato, when he says, "The blame is his who chooses, and God is blameless," [31] took this from the prophet Moses and uttered it. For Moses is older than all the Greek writers. And whenever their philosophers and poets spoke of the immortality of the soul, or punishment after death, or contemplation of things heavenly, or other doctrines of the kind, they had taken suggestions from the prophets to enable them to understand and interpret these things. Thus the seeds of truth are found among all men; but they are blameable for

[30] Deuteronomy, xxx, 19.
[31] Plato, *Republic*, X.

misrepresentation of the truth when they assert contradictories. When too we say that future events are foretold, we do not mean that they came about by fatal necessity. But God, who foreknows all that everyone will do, and by whose decree the future actions of men will be recompensed according to their deserts, foretells by the Spirit of prophecy that He will bestow these meet rewards according to the merit of the act done, always urging mankind to effort and remembrance, and showing that He cares and provides for men. . . .

45. (Other prophecies from the Psalms of Christ's final triumph.)

46. Now some, without reason and for the perversion of what we teach, may repeat what we say, that Christ was born one hundred and fifty years ago under Cyrenius, and subsequently, in the time of Pontius Pilate, taught what He taught. They then may accuse us of imagining that all persons born before Him must have been irresponsible. Let us therefore anticipate and solve the difficulty. We are taught that Christ is the first-born of God, and we have told you already that He is the Word of whom every race of men partakes; and that those who lived by their reasons were Christians, even though they might be called atheists. Such men among the Greeks were Socrates and Heraclitus, and others like them; and among the barbarians, Abraham, Ananias, Azarius, Misael, Elias,[32] and many others whose actions and names we refuse to recount, because we know it would be tedious. In the same way, those who lived before Christ without reason were wicked and hostile to Christ, and they slew those who lived by reason. Then who He was, who through the power of

---

[32] These five last are all heroes of the Old Testament. The first, Abraham, left his father's house for a strange land where he could worship the true God. Genesis, xii. The next three were the companions of the young prophet Daniel, who for refusing to worship the God of the king of Babylon were cast into a fiery furnace. Daniel, i, 6, 7; iii. The great deeds of the prophet Elias or Elijah, are told in I Kings, xvii-xxi and II Kings, i, ii.

the Word, by the will of God the Father and Lord of all, was born as a man of a virgin, was named Jesus, was crucified, died and rose again, and ascended into heaven, any person of intelligence will understand from what we have already said at length. And since more proof of this point is not needed now, we will pass for the present to the proof of other things urgent.

47-51. (Justin cites passages from the prophets Isaiah and Daniel that foretell the work and death of Christ, his rejection by the Jews, and the desolation of their land by the Romans.)

52. Since then we can show that all that has already happened was predicted by the prophets before it occurred, we must believe too that the other things they predicted, that have not yet come to pass, will certainly happen. And as the things already past took place as foretold without anyone realizing it, so shall future things, even though unrecognized and disbelieved, still come to pass. Now the prophets have proclaimed two advents of His; the first, which is already past, when He came as a dishonored and suffering man; the second, when, according to their prophecy, He shall come from heaven with glory, accompanied by His angelic host, when also He shall raise the bodies of all who have ever lived, and clothe those of the worthy with immortality, and send those of the wicked, endued with eternal consciousness, into everlasting fire with the wicked devils. . . .

53. We could cite many other prophecies, but we forbear, judging these sufficient for the persuasion of those who have ears to hear and understand; considering also that they can now see we do not make assertions for which we cannot offer proof, like the fables that are told of the so-called sons of Zeus. For why should we believe that a crucified man is the first-born of the unbegotten God and that He will pass judgment on the whole human race, unless we had testimonies concerning Him, published before He came and was born as a man, and unless we saw other things happening as predicted—the land of the Jews laid waste, and men of every race persuaded by His teaching through the apostles, and casting off their old habits, in which they had lived in blindness? Yea, we see ourselves as well, and know that Christians from the Gentiles are both more numerous and more faithful than those from the Jews and Samaritans. All other races of men are called Gentiles by the Spirit of prophecy; but the Jewish and Samaritan races are called the tribe of Israel, and the house of Jacob. And we can quote the prophecy in which it was predicted that there should be more believers from the Gentiles than from the Jews and Samaritans. It runs thus: "Rejoice, O barren, thou that does not bear; break forth and shout, thou that dost not travail, because many more are the children of the desolate than of her that hath an husband." [33] And the Gentiles were "desolate" of the true God and served the works of their hands; but the Jews and Samaritans, who had the word of God delivered to them by the prophets and were always expecting the Christ, did not recognize Him when He came, except for a few, of whom the Spirit of prophecy by Isaiah had predicted that they should be saved. . . .

54. (The devils tried to delude the Gentiles by ascribing wonderful deeds to the sons of Zeus.)

55. But never, not with any of the so-called sons of Zeus, did they imitate the crucifixion; for it was not understood by them, all the prophetic references to it having been made symbolically. But the cross, as the prophet foretold, is the greatest symbol of His power and rule; as is proved even by things within our own observation. For consider everything in the world, whether without this shape they could be utilized or even hold together. Men do not cross the sea until that which they call a sail is supported secure in the ship; the earth is not plowed without it, and laborers and mechanics cannot

---

[33] Isaiah, liv, 1.

work, except with tools that have this shape. The human form differs from that of irrational animals only in standing erect, with outstretched hands. It has also on the face, extending from the forehead, what we call the nose, through which breath comes to the living creature; and the form it makes is that of a cross. So the prophet said, "The breath before our face is the Lord Christ." [34] The power of this form you show by the symbols on your banners and trophies, with which all your state possessions are marked. You use these as the insignia of power and government, even though you do so unwittingly. And with this form you consecrate the images of your emperors when they die and you name them gods by inscriptions. Since then we have tried to convince you to the utmost of our ability, both by our reasoning and by the evidence of a form, we know we are blameless, even though you disbelieve; our part is done and accomplished.

56-58. (*Justine refers again to the heresies instigated by the devils*). . . . For they who are called devils labor continually to entice men away from the God who made them, and from Christ His first-begotten. They have riveted those who cannot raise themselves above the earth, and do still rivet them to the things of earth and the works of their own hands; and they secretly pull back those who are striving earnestly to contemplate things divine. If these men are wise and soberminded, and pure and passionless in life, they drive them into godlessness.

59. That you may know it was from our teachers—we mean the prophets—that Plato borrowed his statement that God took formless matter to make the world, hear the words spoken through Moses, who, as we said above, was the first prophet, and older than any Greek writers. Through him the Spirit of Prophecy, revealing how and from what materials God first formed the world, spake thus: "In the beginning

---

[34] Lamentations, iv, 20.

God created the heaven and the earth. And the earth was invisible and empty, and darkness was upon the face of the deep; and the Spirit of God moved over the waters. And God said, Let there be light; and it was so." [35] From this both Plato and those who follow him and we ourselves have learned, and you also can be assured, that by the word of God the world was made out of the substance named by Moses. The place too which the poets call Erebus, we know was mentioned by Moses. [36]

60. . . . Among us these things can be heard and learned from persons who do not know their letters and are un-educated and barbarous in speech, though wise and believing in mind; from some even who are maimed and blind. Hence you may understand that such knowledge comes not from human wisdom, but is given us through the power of God.

61. I will next describe the manner in which we who have been made new through Christ dedicate ourselves to God; lest, by omitting it, I seem to be giving you an imperfect account of us. As many as are persuaded and believe that what we teach and say is true and undertake to live accordingly are instructed to pray and entreat with fasting God's forgiveness of their past sins, while we pray and fast with them. Then they are brought by us where there is water, and are born again in the same manner in which we ourselves were reborn. In the name of God, the Father and Lord of all, and of our Saviour Jesus Christ, and of the Holy Spirit, they then receive the washing with water. For Christ said, "Except ye be born again, ye shall not enter into the kingdom of heaven." [37] Now, it is obviously impossible for those who have once been born to reenter their mother's wombs. But Isaiah the prophet, as I said once before, tells how those who have sinned and repent may escape their sins when he

---

[35] Genesis, i, 1-3.
[36] See Deuteronomy, xxxii, 22.
[37] John, iii, 5.

says: "Wash you, make you clean; put away the evil of your doings from your souls; learn to do well; judge the fatherless, and plead for the widow: and come and let us reason together, saith the Lord. And though your sins be as scarlet, I will make them white like wool; and though they be as crimson, I will make them white as snow. But if ye refuse and rebel, the sword shall devour you: for the mouth of the Lord hath spoken it." [38]

The reason for this our rite we have learned from the apostles. At our birth we were born without our knowledge or consent, through the union of our parents, and were brought up in bad habits with wrong training. So in order that we may not remain the children of necessity and ignorance, but may become the children of free choice and knowledge, and may obtain in the water forgiveness for the sins we have already committed, the name of God the Father and Lord of all is pronounced over those who desire to be born again, and have repented of their sins. He who brings to the font a person to be washed names God, but in this way only. For no one can speak the true name of the ineffable God; and whoever dares even to say there is such a name is utterly crazed and astray. Our washing is called "enlightenment," because those who learn these things have their understandings enlightened. In the name of Jesus Christ also, who was crucified under Pontius Pilate, and in the name of the Holy Spirit, who by the prophets foretold all things of Jesus, the enlightened one receives his washing.

62-64. (*Justin describes other efforts of the devils to imitate Christian truth and to blind the Jews to the meaning of their own Scriptures.*) . . . And so much is written to prove that Jesus Christ is the Son of God and his messenger. Of old He was the Word that appeared sometimes in the form of fire and sometimes in the likeness of angels. But now, by the will

---

[38] Isaiah, i, 16-20.

of God, He has become man for the human race and endured
all the sufferings which the devils induced the foolish Jews
to inflict on Him. Though the Jews have it plainly stated in
the writings of Moses, "And the angel of God spake to Moses
in a flame of fire in a bush, and said, 'I am that I am, the God
of Abraham, and the God of Isaac, and the God of Jacob,' [39]
they still maintain that He who said this was Himself the
Father and Creator of the universe. Wherefore the Spirit of
prophecy rebukes them, saying: "Israel doth not know me,
my people have not understood me." [40] Also Jesus, as we have
already told you, while he was with them, said: "No one
knoweth the Father but the Son; nor the Son but the Father,
and those to whom the Son will reveal Him." [41] So the Jews,
who throughout insist that it was the Father of the universe
who spoke to Moses, though the speaker was indeed the Son
of God, who is called both angel and messenger, are justly
accused by the Spirit of prophecy and by Christ Himself of
knowing neither the Father nor the Son.

For those who declare that the Son is the Father prove
thereby that they have no knowledge of the Father and are
unaware that the Father of the universe has a Son, who, being
the first-begotten Word of God, is also God. Of old He appeared in the shape of fire and in the likeness of an angel to
Moses and the other prophets. But now, in the times of your
empire, He has, as we said before, become man by a virgin,
according to the Father's design, for the salvation of those
who believe on Him. And He endured both to be set at
naught and to suffer, that by dying and rising again He might
conquer death. And the words He spake out of the bush to
Moses, "I am that I am, the God of Abraham, and the God
of Isaac, and the God of Jacob, and the God of your fathers,"
these signify that those men, though dead, are still living and

---

[39] Exodus, iii, 6.
[40] Isaiah, i, 3.
[41] Matthew, xi, 27.

belong to Christ Himself. For they were the first of mankind to labor in the search after God. Abraham was the father of Isaac, and Isaac of Jacob, as Moses wrote. . . .

65. Then after we have washed the one who has been converted and has accepted our teaching, we bring him to the place where those whom we call the brethren are assembled, to offer our earnest prayers together for ourselves and for the enlightened one and for all men everywhere, that we, who have learned the truth, may be counted worthy by our works also to be found well-doers and keepers of the commandments, that we may be saved with an everlasting salvation. On ending our prayers, we salute one another with a kiss.[42] Then to the president of the brethren are brought bread and a cup of wine mixed with water. He takes them and offers praise and glory to the Father of all in the name of the Son and of the Holy Spirit, and gives thanks at length that we are counted worthy to receive these things at His hands. And when he has concluded the prayers and the thanksgivings, the whole people present assent, saying Amen. The word Amen in the Hebrew language means "So be it." Then after the president has given thanks and all the people have assented, the men we call deacons give to each of those present a portion of the bread and wine mixed with water over which the thanksgiving was pronounced, and carry away a portion to those who are absent.

66. This food is called among us the Eucharist. No one is allowed to eat of it but he who believes that the things we teach are true, and who has been washed with the washing which is for the remission of sins and unto a new birth, and who is living as Christ commanded. For not as common bread

---

[42] The kiss of charity or the kiss of peace was enjoined by the Apostle Paul in his Epistles to the Corinthians, Thessalonians, and Romans, and thence passed into common Christian usage. It was continued in the Western Church, under regulations to prevent its abuse, until the thirteenth century.

and common drink do we receive them; but even as Jesus Christ our Saviour, being made flesh by the word of God, took on flesh and blood for our salvation, so likewise we are taught that the food which is blessed by the prayer of His word, and from which by transmutation our blood and flesh are nourished, is the flesh and blood of that Jesus who was made flesh. For the apostles, in the memoirs composed by them, which are called Gospels, have delivered unto us what was imparted unto them; that Jesus took bread, and when He had given thanks said: "This do in remembrance of Me, this is My Body"; [43] and that after the same manner He took the cup, and giving thanks He said: "This is My blood"; and that He gave it to them alone. This rite the wicked devils have imitated in the mysteries of Mithras, commanding the same thing to be done. For they set forth bread and a cup of water with certain incantations in their ceremonies of initiation, as you either know or can learn.[44]

67. Afterwards we continually remind one another of these things. The wealthy among us help the needy; and we stay always together. And for all the things with which we are supplied, we bless the Maker of all through His Son Jesus Christ and through the Holy Spirit. On the day called the Day of the Sun, all of us who live either in cities or in the country gather in one place, and the memoirs of the apostles or the writings of the prophets are read, as long as time permits. Then, when the reader has finished, the president by word of mouth instructs and exhorts us to imitate these excellent things. Afterwards we all rise together and offer prayers and, as I said before, when our prayer is ended, the bread and wine and water are brought. Then the president likewise offers his prayers and thanksgivings, as he has ability,

---

[43] Luke, xxii, 19.

[44] The Persian cult of the sun-god Mithras had as one of its rites a sacred meal not unlike the Christian Eucharist. Its greatest festival was held on December 25.

and the people assent, saying "Amen." Then comes the distribution and partaking of that for which thanks was given, and a portion is sent to the absent by the hands of the deacons. Those who are prosperous and willing, give each one what he thinks fit; and what is collected is deposited with the president, who relieves orphans and widows and whoever through sickness or any other cause is in want, and prisoners and strangers sojourning among us. In short, he takes care of all who are in need. We hold our common assembly on the Day of the Sun, because it is the first day on which God, having transformed darkness and matter, created the world; and on the same day, Jesus Christ our Saviour rose from the dead. For He was crucified on the day before Saturn's; and on the day after Saturn's, which is the Day of the Sun, he appeared to His apostles and disciples and taught them the things which we have submitted to you for your consideration.

68. If these things seem to you reasonable and true, honor them, and if they seem foolish, despise them as folly; but do not condemn to death, as you would your enemies, those who have done no wrong. For we warn you, that if you persist in your injustice, you will not escape the coming judgment of God. By the rescript of the great and illustrious Emperor Hadrian, your father, we have a right to demand that you order judgment to be given as we desire. Yet we make our appeal and explanation, not on the ground of Hadrian's order, but because we know that we ask only what is just. We append a copy of Hadrian's rescript, that you may see we are speaking the truth. The following is a copy.

"Rescript of Hadrian with regard to the Christians: [45]

"I have received the letter addressed to me by your predecessor, the most illustrious Serenius Granianus, and will not leave the communication unanswered; for innocent per-

---

[45] Addressed to Minucius Fundanus, proconsul of Asia.

sons must not be disturbed, nor opportunity given to false in-
formers to practice villainy. If the inhabitants of your province will so far sustain this petition of theirs as to accuse the
Christians regularly in some court of law, I do not forbid
their doing so. But I will not permit resort to mere clamor
and excitement. If anyone desires to bring a formal charge,
it is right for you to give judgment upon it. If, then, anyone
brings a charge and furnishes proof that the said men are
violating the laws, you shall fix the punishment in proportion to the offense. Above all, by Hercules, you shall see to
it that if any man, through mere spite, brings an accusation
against any of these persons, you punish him as severely as
his malice deserves."

THE MARTYRDOM OF
THE HOLY MARTYRS

Justin, Chariton, Charito, Paeon, and
Liberanus, who suffered at Rome

1. In the time of the lawless followers of idolatry, wicked decrees were passed against the godly Christians in town and country, to force them to offer libations to vain idols. Accordingly these holy men were arrested and brought before the prefect of Rome, Rusticus by name. And when they had been led before his judgment-seat, the prefect Rusticus said to Justin, "Obey the gods at once, and submit to the emperors." Justin said, "To obey the commandments of our Saviour Jesus Christ deserves neither blame nor condemnation." Rusticus said, "What kind of doctrine do you profess?" Justin said, "I have studied to learn all doctrines, but have accepted at last the true doctrines of the Christians, even though they offend the believers in falsehood." Rusticus said, "Are those the doctrines that satisfy you, poor wretch?" Justin said, "Yes, for I support them with the right creed." Rusticus said, "What is your creed?" Justin said, "That we worship the God of the Christians, whom we hold to be one from the beginning, the Maker and Fashioner of all creation, visible and invisible; also the Lord Jesus Christ, the Son of God, who was promised beforehand by the prophets as coming to the race of men, the herald of salvation and teacher of good disciples. I, being but a man, think that what I can say is insignificant in comparison with His boundless divinity. But I believe in the power of prophecy, since there were prophecies of Him whom now I call the Son of God. And I know that of old the prophets foretold His appearance among men."

2. Rusticus the prefect said, "Where do you meet?" Justin said, "Wherever anyone chooses and can. Do you imagine we all meet in the same place? No; the God of the Christians is not fixed in any set place, but being invisible He fills heaven and earth, and is worshiped and glorified everywhere by the faithful." The prefect said, "Tell me where you hold your meetings, in what place you collect your followers?" Justin said, "I live over the Bath of one Martin, son of Timiotinus. In the whole time of my residence in Rome (and I am now living here for the second time) I know of no other meeting than his. But whoever has chosen to come to me, I have imparted to him the doctrines of truth." Rusticus said, "Are you, then, a Christian?" Justin said, "Yes, I am a Christian."

3. Then Rusticus said to Chariton, "Come on then, Chariton, are you too a Christian?" Chariton said, "I am a Christian by command of God." Rusticus asked the woman Charito, "What do you say, Charito?" Charito said, "I am a Christian by the grace of God." Rusticus said to Euelpistus, "And what are you?" Euelpistus, a servant of Caesar, said, "I too am a Christian, freed by Christ; and by the grace of Christ I share in the same hope." Rusticus said to Hierax, "And you, are you a Christian?" Hierax said, "Yes, I am a Christian, for I revere and worship the same God." Rusticus said, "Did Justin make you Christians?" Hierax said, "I was a Christian and will always be a Christian." And Paeon stood up and said, "I too am a Christian." Rusticus said, "Who taught you?" Paeon said, "From our parents we received this good confession." Euelpistus said, "I listened gladly to the words of Justin; but from my parents also I learned to be a Christian." Rusticus said, "Where are your parents?" Euelpistus said, "In Cappadocia." Rusticus asked Hierax, "Where

are your parents?" And he answered and said, "Christ is our true father, and faith in Him is our mother. My earthly parents are dead. I was expelled from Iconium in Phrygia, and so came here." Rusticus said to Liberianus, "And what do you say? Are you too a Christian, refusing to worship the gods?" Liberianus said, "I too am a Christian, and worship and reverence the only true God."

4. The prefect said to Justin, "Listen, you who are called learned, and think you know true doctrines; if you are scourged and beheaded, do you believe you will ascend into heaven?" Justin said, "I hope that if I endure these things I shall receive His gifts. For I know that for all who have lived by this faith there abides God's mercy unto the end of the world." The prefect said, "Do you imagine, then, you will rise up to heaven and receive a reward?" Justin said, "I do not imagine it, but I know and am fully convinced of it." The prefect said, "Let us come to the business in hand; time presses. Before this assembly, offer a sacrifice together to the gods." Justin said, "No honest person gives up a true religion for a false." Rusticus said, "Unless you obey, you will be mercilessly punished." Justin said, "By prayer we can be saved through our Lord Jesus Christ even after punishment, for that will become to us salvation and confidence at the more terrible and universal judgment-seat of our Lord and Saviour." The other martyrs said also, "Do what you will; we are Christians and do not sacrifice to idols."

5. The prefect then pronounced sentence, saying, "These persons who have refused to sacrifice to the gods and to comply with the command of the Emperor shall be scourged,[1] and then taken out to punishment by decapitation, as the law prescribes." The holy martyrs having thus glorified God, and gone forth to the regular place, were beheaded and com-

---

[1] This wholesale sentence implies a great indifference to the probable Roman citizenship of some of the condemned, if not of Justin himself.

pleted their witness in confession of the Saviour. And some
of the faithful secretly removed their bodies and laid them
in a suitable spot, the grace of our Lord Jesus Christ having
wrought along with them. To Him be glory for ever and
ever. Amen.

MARIUS THE
EPICUREAN[1]

XXIII

Divine Service

"Wisdom hath builded herself a house: she hath mingled her wine: she hath also prepared for herself a table."

THE more highly favored ages of imaginative art present instances of the summing up of an entire world of complex associations under some single form, like the *Zeus* of Olympia, or the series of frescoes which commemorate *The Acts of Saint Francis*, at Assisi, or like the play of Hamlet or Faust. It was not in an image, or series of images, yet still in a sort of dramatic action, and with the unity of a single appeal to eye and ear, that Marius about this time found all his new impressions set forth, regarding what he had already recognized, intellectually, as for him at least the most beautiful thing in the world.

To understand the influence upon him of what follows the reader must remember that it was an experience which came amid a deep sense of vacuity in life. The fairest products of the earth seemed to be dropping to pieces, as if in men's very hands, around him. How real was their sorrow, and his! "His observation of life" had come to be like the constant telling

---

[1] This chapter from Walter Pater's novel, *Marius the Epicurean*, presents an account of a second-century Christian service.

of a sorrowful rosary, day after day; till, as if taking infection
from the cloudy sorrow of the mind, the eye also, the very
senses, were grown faint and sick. And now it happened as
with the actual morning on which he found himself a spectator of this new thing. The long winter had been a season of
unvarying sullenness. At last, on this day he awoke with a
sharp flash of lightning in the earliest twilight: in a little
while the heavy rain had filtered the air: the clear light was
abroad; and, as though the spring had set in with a sudden
leap in the heart of things, the whole scene around him lay
like some untarnished picture beneath a sky of delicate blue.
Under the spell of his late depression, Marius had suddenly
determined to leave Rome for a while. But desiring first to
advertise Cornelius [1] of his movements, and failing to find him
in his lodgings, he had ventured, still early in the day, to seek
him in the Cecilian villa. Passing through its silent and empty
courtyard he loitered for a moment, to admire. Under the
clear but immature light of winter morning after a storm, all
the details of form and color in the old marbles were distinctly
visible, and with a kind of severity or sadness—so it struck him
—amid their beauty: in them, and in all other details of the
scene—the cypresses, the bunches of pale daffodils in
the grass, the curves of the purple hills of Tusculum, with the
drifts of virgin snow still lying in their hollows.

The little open door, through which he passed from the
courtyard, admitted him into what was plainly the vast
Lararium, or domestic sanctuary, of the Cecilian family, transformed in many particulars, but still richly decorated, and
retaining much of its ancient furniture in metal-work and
costly stone. The peculiar half-light of dawn seemed to be
lingering beyond its hour upon the solemn marble walls; and

---

[1] Cornelius was an officer in the emperor's service and a Christian,
with whom Marius had made friends.

here, though at that moment in absolute silence, a great company of people was assembled. In that brief period of peace,
during which the church emerged for awhile from her
jealously-guarded subterranean life, the rigor of an earlier
rule of exclusion had been relaxed. And so it came to pass
that on this morning Marius saw for the first time the wonderful spectacle—wonderful, especially, in its evidential power
over himself, over his own thoughts—of those who believe.

There were noticeable, among these present, great varieties of rank, of age, of personal type. The Roman *ingenuus*,
with the white toga and gold ring, stood side by side with his
slave; and the air of the whole company was, above all, a
grave one, an air of recollection. Coming thus unexpectedly
upon this large assembly, so entirely united, in a silence so
profound, for purposes unknown to him, Marius felt for a
moment as if he had stumbled by chance upon some great
conspiracy. Yet that could scarcely be, for the people here
collected might have figured as the earliest handsel, or pattern,
of a new world, from the very face of which discontent had
passed away. Corresponding to the variety of human type
there present, was the various expression of every form of
human sorrow assuaged. What desire, what fulfillment of desire, had wrought so pathetically on the features of these ranks
of aged men and women of humble condition? Those young
men, bent down so discreetly on the details of their sacred
service, had faced life and were glad, by some science, or light
of knowledge they had, to which there had certainly been
no parallel in the older world. Was some credible message
from beyond "the flaming rampart of the world"—a message of hope, regarding the place of men's souls and their
interest in the sum of things—already molding anew their very
bodies, and looks, and voices, now and here? At least, there
was a cleansing and kindling flame at work in them, which
seemed to make everything else Marius had ever known look

comparatively vulgar and mean. There were the children, above all—troops of children—reminding him of those pathetic children's graves, like cradles or garden-beds, he had noticed in his first visit to these places; and they more than satisfied the odd curiosity he had then conceived about them, wondering in what quaintly expressive forms they might come forth into the daylight, if awakened from sleep. Children of the Catacombs, some but "a span long," with features not so much beautiful as heroic (that world of new, refining sentiment having set its seal even on childhood), they retained certainly no stain or trace of anything subterranean this morning, in the alacrity of their worship—as ready as if they had been at play—stretching forth their hands, crying, chanting in a resonant voice, and with boldly upturned faces, *Christe Eleison!*

For the silence—silence, amid those lights of early morning to which Marius had always been constitutionally impressible, as having in them a certain reproachful austerity—was broken suddenly by resounding cries of *Kyrie Eleison! Christe Eleison!* repeated alternately, again and again, until the bishop, rising from his chair, made sign that this prayer should cease. But the voices burst out once more presently, in richer and more varied melody, though still of an antiphonal character; the men, the women and children, the deacons, the people, answering one another, somewhat after the manner of a Greek chorus. But again with what a novelty of poetic accent; what a genuine expansion of heart; what profound intimations for the intellect, as the meaning of the words grew upon him! *Cum grandi affectu et compunctione dicatur*—says an ancient eucharistic order; and certainly, the mystic tone of this praying and singing was one with the expression of deliverance, of grateful assurance and sincerity, upon the faces of those assembled. As if some searching correction, a regeneration of the body by the spirit, had begun, and was already gone a great way, the countenances of men, women, and children alike had a brightness on them which he could fancy reflected upon himself—an amenity, a mystic amiability and unction, which found its way most readily of all to the hearts of children themselves. The religious poetry of those Hebrew psalms—*Benedixisti Domine terram tuam: Dixit Dominus Domino meo, sede a dextris meis*—was certainly in marvelous accord with the lyrical instinct of his own character. Those august hymns, he thought, must thereafter ever remain by him as among the well-tested powers in things to soothe and fortify the soul. One could never grow tired of them!

In the old pagan worship there had been little to call the understanding into play. Here, on the other hand, the utterance, the eloquence, the music of worship conveyed, as Marius readily understood, a fact or series of facts, for intellectual reception. That became evident, more especially, in those lessons, or sacred readings, which, like the singing, in broken vernacular Latin, occurred at certain intervals, amid the silence of the assembly. There were readings, again with bursts of chanted invocation between for fuller light on a difficult path, in which many a vagrant voice of human philosophy, haunting men's minds from of old, recurred with clearer accent than had ever belonged to it before, as if lifted, above its first intention, into the harmonies of some supreme system of knowledge or doctrine, at length complete. And last of all came a narrative which, with a thousand tender memories, everyone appeared to know by heart, displaying, in all the vividness of a picture for the eye, the mournful figure of him towards whom this whole act of worship still consistently turned—a figure which seemed to have absorbed, like some rich tincture in his garment, all that was deep-felt and impassioned in the experiences of the past.

It was the anniversary of his birth as a little child they celebrated today. *Astiterunt reges terrae:* so the Gradual, the

"Song of Degrees," proceeded, the young men on the steps
of the altar responding in deep, clear, antiphon or chorus—

> Astiterunt reges terrae—
> Adversus sanctum puerum tuum, Jesum:
> Nunc, Domine, da servis tuis loqui verbum tuum—
> Et signia fieri, per nomen sancti pueri Jesu.

And the proper action of the rite itself, like a half-opened
book to be read by the duly initiated mind took up those
suggestions, and carried them forward into the present, as
having reference to a power still efficacious, still after some
mystic sense even now in action among the people there assembled. The entire office, indeed, with its interchange of
lessons, hymns, prayer, silence, was itself like a single piece
of highly composite, dramatic music; a "song of degrees,"
rising steadily to a climax. Notwithstanding the absence of
any central image visible to the eye, the entire ceremonial
process, like the place in which it was enacted, was weighty
with symbolic significance, seemed to express a single leading
motive. The mystery, if such in fact it was, centered indeed
in the actions of one visible person, distinguished among the
assistants, who stood ranged in semicircle around him, by the
extreme fineness of his white vestments, and the pointed cap
with the golden ornaments upon his head.

Nor had Marius ever seen the pontifical character, as he
conceived it—*sicut unguentum in capite, descendens in oram
vestimenti*—so fully realized, as in the expression, the manner
and voice, of this novel pontiff, as he took his seat on the
white chair placed for him by the young men, and received
his long staff into his hand, or moved his hands—hands which
seemed endowed in very deed with some mysterious power—
at the *Lavabo*, or at the various benedictions, or to bless certain objects on the table before him, chanting in cadence of
a grave sweetness the leading parts of the rite. What profound
unction and mysticity! The solemn character of the singing

was at its height when he opened his lips. Like some new sort of *rhapsôdos*, it was for the moment as if he alone possessed the words of the office, and they flowed anew from some permanent source of inspiration within him. The table or altar at which he presided, below a canopy on delicate spiral columns, was in fact the tomb of a youthful "witness," of the family of the Cecilii, who had shed his blood not many years before, and whose relics were still in this place. It was for his sake the bishop put his lips so often to the surface before him; the regretful memory of that death entwining itself, though not without certain notes of triumph, as a matter of special inward significance, throughout a service, which was, before all else, from first to last, a commemoration of the dead.

A sacrifice also—a sacrifice, it might seem, like the most primitive, the most natural and enduringly significant of old pagan sacrifices, of the simplest fruits of the earth. And in connection with this circumstance again, as in the actual stones of the building so in the rite itself, what Marius observed was not so much new matter as a new spirit, molding, informing, with a new intention, many observances not witnessed for the first time today. Men and women came to the altar successively, in perfect order, and deposited below the lattice-work of pierced white marble, their baskets of wheat and grapes, incense, oil for the sanctuary lamps; bread and wine especially—pure wheaten bread, the pure white wine of the Tusculan vineyards. There was here a veritable consecration, hopeful and animating, of the earth's gifts, of old dead and dark matter itself, now in some way redeemed at last, of all that we can touch or see, in the midst of a jaded world that had lost the true sense of such things, and in strong contrast to the wise emperor's renunciant and impassive attitude towards them. Certain portions of that bread and wine were taken into the bishop's hands; and thereafter, with an increasing mysticity and effusion the rite proceeded. Still in a strain of inspired supplication, the antiphonal

singing developed, from this point, into a kind of dialogue
between the chief minister and the whole assisting company—

SURSUM CORDA!

HABEMUS AD DOMINUM.

GRATIAS AGAMUS DOMINO DEO NOSTRO!—

It might have been thought the business, the duty or service
of young men more particularly, as they stood there in long
ranks, and in severe and simple vesture of the purest white—
a service in which they would seem to be flying for refuge,
as with their precious, their treacherous and critical youth in
their hands, to one—Yes! one like themselves, who yet claimed
their worship, a worship, above all, in the way of Aurelius,
in the way of imitation. *Adoramus te Christe, quia per crucem
tuam redemisti mundum!*—they cry together. So deep is the
emotion that at moments it seems to Marius as if some there
present apprehend that prayer prevails, that the very object
of this pathetic crying himself draws near. From the first
there had been the sense, an increasing assurance, of one
coming: actually with them now, according to the oft-re-
peated affirmation or petition, *Dominus vobiscum!* Some at
least were quite sure of it; and the confidence of this rem-
nant fired the hearts, and gave meaning to the bold, ecstatic
worship, of all the rest about them.

Prompted especially by the suggestion of that mysterious
old Jewish psalmody, so new to him—lesson and hymn—and
catching therewith a portion of the enthusiasm of those beside him, Marius could discern dimly, behind the solemn reci-
tation which now followed, at once a narrative and a prayer,
the most touching image truly that had ever come within the
scope of his mental or physical gaze. It was the image of a
young man giving up voluntarily, one by one, for the greatest
of ends, the greatest gifts; actually parting with himself,
above all, with the serenity, the divine serenity, of his own
soul; yet from the midst of his desolation crying out upon the

greatness of his success, as if foreseeing this very worship.[2] As center of the supposed facts which for these people were become so constraining a motive of hopefulness, of activity, that image seemed to display itself with an overwhelming claim on human gratitude. What Saint Louis of France discerned, and found so irresistibly touching, across the dimness of many centuries, as a painful thing done for love of him by one he had never seen, was to them almost as a thing of yesterday; and their hearts were whole with it. It had the force, among their interests, of an almost recent event in the career of one whom their fathers' fathers might have known. From memories so sublime, yet so close at hand, had the narrative descended in which these acts of worship centered; though again the names of some more recently dead were mingled in it. And it seemed as if the very dead were aware; to be stirring beneath the slabs of the sepulchers which lay so near, that they might associate themselves to this enthusiasm—to this exalted worship of Jesus.

One by one, at last, the faithful approach to receive from the chief minister morsels of the great, white, wheaten cake, he had taken into his hands—*Perducat vos ad vitam aeternam!* he prays, half-silently, as they depart again, after discreet embraces. The Eucharist of those early days was, even more entirely than at any later or happier time, an act of thanksgiving; and while the remnants of the feast are borne away for the reception of the sick, the sustained gladness of the rite reaches its highest point in the singing of a hymn: a hymn like the spontaneous product of two opposed militant companies, contending accordantly together, heightening, accumulating, their witness, provoking one another's worship, in a kind of sacred rivalry.

Ite! Missa est!—cried the young deacons: and Marius departed from that strange scene along with the rest. What was

---

2 Psalm xxii. 22-31.

it? Was it this made the way of Cornelius so pleasant through the world? As for Marius himself, the natural soul of worship in him had at last been satisfied as never before. He felt, as he left that place, that he must hereafter experience often a longing memory, a kind of thirst, for all this, over again. And it seemed moreover to define what he must require of the powers, whatsoever they might be, that had brought him into the world at all, to make him not unhappy in it.

THE END